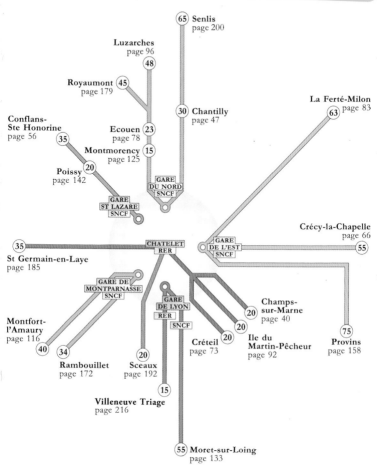

Senlis (65)
page 200

Luzarches (48)
page 96

Royaumont (45)
page 179

Chantilly (30)
page 47

La Ferté-Milon (63)
page 83

Conflans-Ste Honorine (35)
page 56

Ecouen (23)
page 78

Montmorency (15)
page 125

Poissy (20)
page 142

GARE DU NORD SNCF

GARE ST LAZARE SNCF

Crécy-la-Chapelle (55)
page 66

St Germain-en-Laye (35)
page 185

CHATELET RER

GARE DE L'EST SNCF

GARE DE MONTPARNASSE SNCF

GARE DE LYON RER SNCF

Champs-sur-Marne (20)
page 40

Montfort-l'Amaury (40)
page 116

Rambouillet (34)
page 172

Sceaux (20)
page 192

Créteil (20)
page 73

Ile du Martin-Pêcheur (20)
page 92

Provins (75)
page 158

Villeneuve Triage (15)
page 216

Moret-sur-Loing (55)
page 133

Showing journey time in minutes by train from Paris.

Minutes from Paris

Annabel Simms

An Hour from
Paris

PALLAS ATHENE

OISE

Chanti

Giverny

VEXIN
FRANÇAIS

VAL D'OISE

Auvers-sur-Oise

Royaumont
Viarmes
Seugy
Luzarches
Belloy-
en-France

Ecouen

PARISIS

Montmorency

FRAN

Conflans-
Ste Honorine
Andrésy

Herblay

Médan

Villennes

Poissy

St Germain-
en-Laye

Malmaison

Seine

HAUTS DE SEINE

S

ST-

PARIS

MANTOIS

YVELINES

Versailles

Choisy-
le-Roi

Crête

Montfort-
l'Amaury

Sceaux

VAL DE

Villeneuve-Triage

FORET
DE
RAMBOUILLET

EURE

Yvette

Rambouillet

HUREPOIX

Orge

ESSONNE

Essonne

KEY TO LAND USE

Urban development

Parks and Forests

Agriculture

DEPARTEMENT

Department boundary ———

HUREPOIX Pays

EURE-
ET-LOIRE

Juine

LOIRET

Ile de France

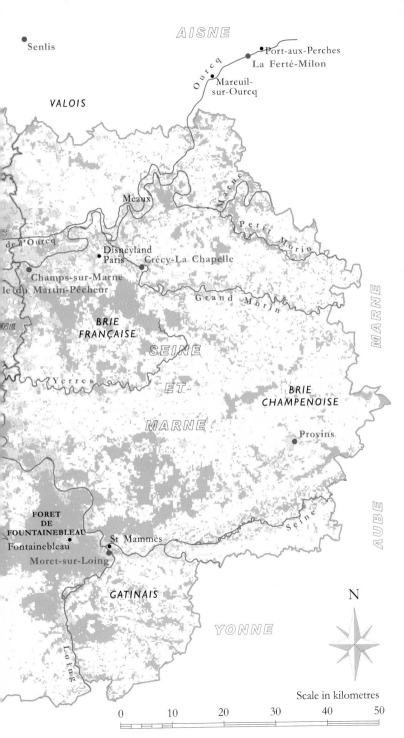

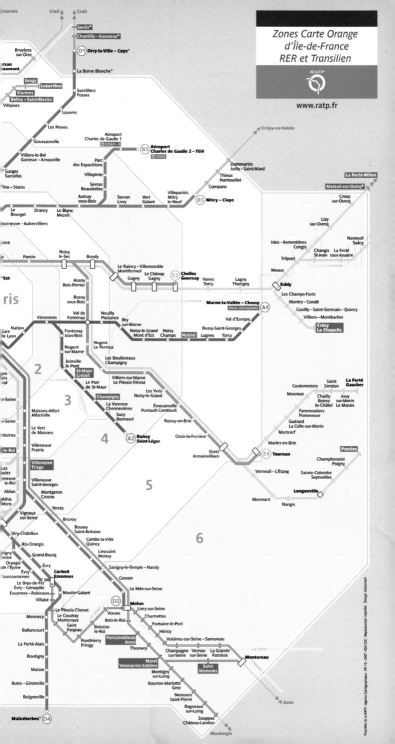

Contents

Emile Zola's study at Médan (Poissy)

Route du Pré Curé, Forest of Ecouen

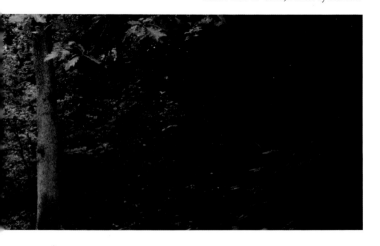

Preface

Several years ago I found myself in the middle of a wood, as completely lost as if I were in Africa, rather than 19 kilometres from Paris. Three paths lay in front of me with no indication of where they might lead and there was not a soul in sight. It suddenly occurred to me that no one knew where I was and that I would never dream of venturing out alone like this near London.

On impulse I took the left path, which soon brought me to houses at the edge of the wood, and knocked on the door of the nearest one. Five minutes later, following the owner's directions through the same wood, I saw the rooftops of an elegant château emerging through the trees and came out onto a sweeping lawn leading straight up to it. Feeling as if I had stepped into a fairytale, I skirted the château, which looked as if it might vanish as unexpectedly as it had appeared, and peeked over a stone balustrade to the left.

Sunny rolling countryside lay below me, stretching into the distance as far as I could see, crossed by the moving shadows of the clouds overhead. A few planes purred in the distance and I realised I was under the flight path to Charles de Gaulle airport. Otherwise, I could have believed myself back in the 16th century, when the château behind me had been built.

This particular château houses the Museum of the Renaissance at Ecouen, 23 minutes from Paris by train. I had rung the Museum and been told that it was 'about five kilometres' on foot from the station. In fact it is just over one kilometre, and the woodland paths are now signposted. But it was this early experience that first made me aware of just how interesting and accessible the countryside around Paris is, and how little-known to the French themselves, as well as to foreigners.

Abbaye de Royaumont

Château d'Ecouen

As I began to explore further afield the phrase 'Ile de France' gradually began to take on colour and meaning. The rolling countryside I had seen from the château at Ecouen is part of the old *Pays de France*, the fertile plain surrounded by rivers to the north of Paris that first made the city prosperous. Its rulers slowly extended their dominion over the rest of the country, which became known simply as 'France'. The Ile de France contains the key to the history of the whole country. Paradoxically, it is also one of the least-visited parts of France, overlooked by foreign visitors with their sights set on Paris, while modern transport now whisks Parisians themselves off to ever more remote and exotic destinations.

As a result, large parts of the Ile de France, although easily accessible from Paris, have escaped the effects of mass tourism. I began to appreciate the incongruity of using efficient commuter trains, uncrowded at weekends, to arrive less than an hour later at some quiet, unassuming place so remote from Paris as to feel like another world. I would be charmed by the back streets of a tiny medieval town, by the French families spending hours over Sunday lunch in a country restaurant or by the discovery of a riverside footpath leading to another village and railway station. Arriving by train makes a difference. If you are in a car, your perception of a place is unconsciously coloured by where you have come from and where you can get to next, and your time-scale is the one you carry with you, not the one imposed by the place itself. You are also less likely to notice the fascinating details that would strike someone arriving on foot.

I had spent some years discovering the region in this way, using the hit or miss approach of combining the green Michelin guide with the railway map, before I realised that I had the makings of a book which could offer something unique to its readers: a guide entirely conceived with the needs of the foreign visitor arriving by train in mind. Not only would it have clear, detailed instructions and usable local maps which showed the station, it would, where possible, give interesting routes which led from one station to another, rather than the circular route imposed by having to return to a car.

Ile Ste Catherine, Créteil

As the book took shape, so did my picture of the kind of reader I had in mind. It was no longer simply someone who did not have a car. More importantly, it was someone who was essentially curious about everything, rather than with a specialist interest in walking, architecture, gastronomy or whatever, someone who was interested in the present as well as the past, who loved the countryside and enjoyed walking, but who also liked stopping at cafés and appreciated the humbler type of restaurant where they would probably be the only foreigner. Above all, it was someone who avoided crowds and pre-packaged experience wherever possible and was happiest when exploring off the beaten track.

This kind of reader would probably not want to use a guide at all, but I felt that it would be worth their while to buy my book for two reasons. They could easily adapt the techniques I had spent years perfecting to find authentic places for themselves, and they could use my book to visit some of the little places I describe. Not only would they be the very people most likely to appreciate these, their presence in greater numbers might also help to halt the process of decline and creeping standardisation which is gradually taking hold. After all, Giverny now has a local bus service from the station because a few Americans first started the fashion of going there.

With this rather unusual reader in mind, my criteria for selecting places to visit were interest, accessibility, lack of crowds and added value, in that order. The interest is usually historical, literary or artistic, but not exclusively so. A boat trip through the countryside or a visit to a *guinguette* (a riverside restaurant where people dance in the open air) also qualify as offering experiences not usually available to visitors staying in Paris.

Accessibility means that the places described are all within an 80-kilometre radius of Paris and generally an hour or less away by train. I have taken particular care to check that any walking is by the pleasantest route, avoiding hills and main roads as far as possible, an approach which has sometimes required

Eglise de St Ayoul, Provins

Fromager, St Germain-en-Laye

several return visits to test out all the options for myself. I have learned to distrust official directions.

My personal preference is for places that do not attract crowds, but I have tried to strike a balance by including some better-known places which do. In these cases I have given alternative routes or times so that the visit can be enjoyed in the company of rather fewer other visitors than you would normally expect.

By added value I mean that a visit should justify the journey, whether by train or car, in more than one respect. A starting point might be a château or museum, but all of the visits offer at least one other attraction, such as a good local restaurant, a concert or an interesting walk. Several, such as Moret-sur-Loing or Poissy, offer far more than this, but the focus is always on what can be pleasurably accomplished on foot. Again, I have tried to strike a balance by giving alternatives, so that if a five-kilometre walk seems excessive it can be skipped without missing the point of the visit.

Whether you are a first-time visitor, an old hand or, like me, another expatriate living in Paris, I hope that you will enjoy discovering Paris's best-kept secret: the unspoilt countryside rich in historical associations which lies just a stone's throw from the capital.

This book is dedicated to David, my cheerful and tireless fellow-traveller.

Jardin Anglais, château de Rambouillet

Preface to the second edition

For this second edition I re-visited every one of the twenty destinations described in *An Hour From Paris* and re-walked each step of the way. I discovered that not only were a lot of details out of date – that was only to be expected after five years – but that some of the maps and the directions were not as easy to follow as I had imagined. I would particularly like to thank the following people who patiently accompanied me on these revision trips, giving me invaluable help in correcting the omissions, providing new insights, and helping to test the new material: David Lowrey; Leigh Mount; Rayanne Dupuis; Juelle Daley; Joan Fleming Le Bras; Una and Richard Daher; Bronwen and Jean Nicolas; Françoise Cle'ach. My grateful thanks also to readers who wrote to me with comments and suggestions.

The other thing that struck me more and more as the revision progressed was how much the Ile de France itself had changed. It is a tidier, more managed place than it was, but also blander, reflecting the changes that are taking place everywhere else. There are more supermarkets and video outlets, but fewer traditional cafés, restaurants and markets. The raft to the Ile du Martin-Pêcheur has been replaced by a bridge and the ferry at Médan has been discontinued, because of new health and safety regulations. There is an increasing reliance on machines rather than on people to supply the public with information. In theory, the Internet has made some information, such as maps and train timetables, more accessible – if you know where and how to look, as some of it is available only in French. I have taken great pleasure in discovering useful short-cuts through official websites and 'interactive' voice messaging systems and putting them into the revised 'Practical details' section at the back of the book, sometimes with the generous

Rousseau's house, Montmorency

La Goèlette, Andrésy (Conflans-Ste-Honorine)

connivance of the staff employed by these organisations.

Fortunately, some of the changes are for the better. There are new or improved bus services to Montmorency, Châtenay-Malabry and the Ile du Martin-Pêcheur, a footbridge has been built to the Menier buildings on the formerly inaccessible island at Champs and admission to the Musée de l'Ile de France at Sceaux is now free. There are free concerts of Renaissance music every Saturday at Ecouen.

Better still, some changes provoked heartening new discoveries. The closure of a riverside restaurant at Conflans-Sainte Honorine led to an investigation of the riverside walk in the other direction to Andrésy, where there is another ferry, two good riverside restaurants and an unsuspected riverside walk to Poissy. For the Poissy chapter itself, the closure of the riverside restaurant at Médan led to the discovery of an excellent new restaurant at Villennes-sur-Seine, which is reassuringly popular.

The surprising continued existence of places like this is what makes France the most popular holiday destination in the world, even though most visitors never actually find them. The success of *An Hour From Paris* shows that this is indeed what some visitors are looking for, and several places I re-visited for the revised edition have expressed their appreciation of the adventurous foreigners who arrived clutching a copy of the book. The fact that I have not needed to change the original twenty destinations is confirmation of the continuity of a way of life that is changing, but not as fast as in most other countries.

Some places just go on quietly being French, like the Café de l'Est mentioned on p. 82, where the head waiter's reply when I complimented him on the *choucroute* (pickled cabbage) was, 'Ce n'est pas mauvais' – the exact words recorded by Elizabeth David when she made a similar remark to a French restaurateur in the 1950s. The more such places are patronised by appreciative visitors, the less likely they are to be engulfed by the tide of blandness, which is what most visitors come to France to get away from.

I hope that you will find a great deal of pleasure in using this book.

Paris, Spring 2008

Chateaubriand's house,
Châtenay-Malabry
(Sceaux)

The Ile de France: past and present

*Place-names in **bold** appear in the main guide.*

A *foreigner's first impressions*

When I first came to live in Paris I was puzzled by the phrase 'Ile de France' (the island of France). I gradually realised that it referred to the area around Paris for a radius of about 80 kilometres (I was vague about this) and that *les Franciliens* meant the inhabitants of this region, rather like Greater London, except that no one talks about Greater Londoners.

Beyond noticing that it seemed to contain a lot of famous places, which I felt slightly guilty about not wanting to visit (Versailles, Fontainebleau, Barbizon) I had no clear idea of it as a region, nor did I feel the need for one. When I thought of the French countryside, I thought of the south of France, the Auvergne, the Loire, Burgundy, Brittany or, at a pinch, Normandy, which really seemed too close to England to count.

I also began to think of the area around Paris as the *banlieue* (a much more negative word than 'suburb') with an authentically Parisian shudder of fear, pity or contempt. My Paris, *real* Paris, did not extend beyond Zone One of the *Carte Orange*, the monthly Métro and bus pass which covers up to six zones around Paris. The limits of zone one are those of the old city boundary, traceable by the circle of Métro stations beginning with the word *Porte*, indicating that the entrance to the city was once guarded by gates. I assumed that these gates had disappeared in the Middle Ages and was amused to hear Parisians referring to a place as being *intra muros*, 'within the walls'. Clearly, these walls still existed in people's imaginations,

Tour du Bourreau, Provins

confirming my view that Paris was essentially a charmed circle enclosing all that was civilised and that the *banlieue*, a desert of concrete containing dreary new industries and inhabited by philistines, began just outside the gates. In fact, the fortifications surrounding the city were only demolished in 1919 and have been effectively replaced by the *boulevard péripherique* (ring road), which explains the pervasiveness of this mind-set and the rapidity with which I picked it up.

Like most visitors, I was really only familiar with the fifth *arrondissement*, the Latin Quarter. I had to gradually extend my mental map of the city to include the other 19 *arrondissements*, all beginning with the postcode 75 and therefore *intra muros*. Meanwhile, my job as a teacher of business English was forcing me to make forays outside these walls into what Parisians call *la proche banlieue* (inner suburbs) where many businesses and business schools are located. I travelled to La Défense and Cergy to the west, Noisy le Grand and Bussy St Georges to the east and Evry to the south. I found the modern architecture of these places dismayingly soulless, pitied the people who actually lived there and cursed the excellence of the public transport system which made them all too accessible from Paris, depriving me of an excuse not to go there.

At the same time, I was learning to adapt to the endless succession of public holidays the French enjoy – among the highest number in Europe. Almost every month is punctuated by at least one and suddenly Paris empties as people decide to *faire le pont*: 'bridge' the official holiday to the weekend by taking the days in between as additional holiday. They go skiing or mushroom-picking, redecorate the house or head for their relatives or *résidences secondaires* in the country. As a newly arrived, underpaid expatriate, none of these options seemed to be available to me (I didn't even know where to look for the mushrooms) but there was no work for me in Paris and the urge to get into the countryside, *any* countryside, if only for a day, would become irresistibly strong at these times.

So, armed with my *Carte Orange* and the green Michelin guide to the Ile de France, I found myself getting on the suburban trains outside working hours, determined to make the

Château de Rambouillet

most of what was, after all, on my doorstep. I soon discovered that the efficiency of the commuter network surrounding Paris had its positive side – the 17th-century parks of **Sceaux**, Meudon and St Cloud were easily accessible and a world away from the shopping centres, flats and offices of places like Noisy le Grand and Evry. Encouraged, I began to go further afield, to *la grande banlieue* (outer suburbs): **Versailles, St Germain-en-Laye**, Chevreuse, **Rambouillet, Chantilly** and **Senlis** and became gradually aware of a whole rich hinterland of old towns and villages, châteaux, parks and forests surrounding Paris, extending for up to 80 kilometres to the south and east, 32 kilometres to the north and 56 kilometres to the west, the limits of the Ile de France railway network.

The two faces of the Ile de France: the old and the new

In fact, there seemed to be two Ile de Frances: the pastoral region evoked by the names of the old *pays* mentioned in Michelin, accessible to car-drivers, and the modern *banlieue* served by the SNCF and divided into new and meaningless *départements* with unfamiliar postcodes. Not possessing a car, I was forced to superimpose one map on the other and gradually discovered that the modern administrative region had grown out of the historic, pastoral one and that in many places they exist side by side. I began to look at the horrible places where I had to work with new eyes. For example, Bussy St Georges, close to Disneyland, is a new business, educational and residential complex, tastefully planned and quite lifeless. The little village of Bussy St Georges, a long walk from the new RER (express suburban train) station, pre-dates it by several centuries, perhaps a millennium, and belongs to a different world. It is inseparable from the surrounding countryside, the old Brie region where the famous cheese is made, just as the modern complex of the same name spiritually belongs to the new town of Marne-la-Vallée and the RER station, without which it could not exist.

Yet both are typical of the complicated historical relationship between Paris and the Ile de France, which has been variously neglected, feared, nourished or exploited by the capital. At this stage, however, my mental map of the Ile de France was still largely formed by the Michelin guide and I had only the dimmest notions of the places it *doesn't* mention and of the context in which I was living and working. I had just about heard of working-class suburbs like St Denis and Sarcelles to the north and of the new towns of Cergy-Pontoise, St Quentin-en-Yvelines, Evry, Melun-Sénart and Marne-la-Vallée encircling Paris. Indeed, I had worked in Evry and never wanted to go there again.

But I was becoming more adventurous as I became more knowledgeable about the train network. I discovered that St Denis, the 'red' immigrant suburb eight minutes from Paris by train, reminded me nostalgically of London's Brixton, and had acutally developed from the 12th-century *Basilique* where the

Former raft to island and guinguette, *Ile du Martin-Pêcheur*

kings and queens of France are buried – and that it was possible to walk there from Paris along the Canal St Denis. I began to go to places to the north and east of Paris which hardly rated a mention in Michelin, attracted by the **Canal de l'Ourcq** and the **River Marne**. Their historical importance, if any, was over a long time ago and they are less elegant than the prosperous suburbs to the west of Paris, but I sensed the continuity of a popular culture there, which I found unexpected and attractive. Their 1950s atmosphere, which reminded me of all the old black and white French films I had seen in London, was in fact older than I thought, and not limited to the east of Paris. Old river ports like **Conflans-Ste Honorine** and **St Mammès** had it, as did Joinville and **Créteil**, which are just outside Paris. What they had in common was a working river or canal and the tradition of eating, drinking, dancing and generally having a good time by the water. In fact, by taking the train on a Sunday to places like the *guinguette* on the **Ile du Martin-Pêcheur** on the Marne, I was unconsciously following an old Parisian tradition: using the transport routes which follow the network of rivers surrounding the city as an escape from the pressures of living in it.

A weekend escape for Parisians, past and present

Gradually I became aware of the persistence of other traditions, national as well as local, bourgeois as well as popular. But the most obvious one, shared by all social classes, is the Parisian habit of using the Ile de France as a kind of weekend playground, a countryside refuge from the stress and pollution of the city. Picturesque places easily accessible from Paris, like **Conflans-Ste Honorine** and **Herblay** or **Montfort-l'Amaury** contain almost as many weekend residents as permanent ones and there is nothing new about this. The dense scattering of châteaux around Paris, the richest concentration in France outside the Loire valley, is simply the older, aristocratic version of the same impulse. No one with any ambition, then or now, could afford to be too far away from Paris, which has always been the cultural and economic as well as the administrative and political capital of the country.

Eglise St Martin at Herblay (Conflans-Ste Honorine)

The 20th-century decline of the traditional industries of the North and of St Etienne has been followed by the emergence of new high-tech industries, concentrated – where else? – in the area closest to Paris. So, despite recent efforts to relieve the pressure on the capital by building new towns around it, it is still the most densely populated city in Europe and the urge to escape from it into the surrounding countryside has remained as strong as ever.

Although the pollution in Paris has increased dramatically since the 1990s, there is also nothing new about Parisian awareness of it. For example, the town of **St Germain-en-Laye**, on the heights 20 kilometres west of Paris, the first royal *résidence secondaire*, was renamed 'Montagne Bon Air' during the Revolution. Significantly, it was chosen as the destination for the first suburban railway line to be built in France, which linked it to Paris in 1837. The line has now been replaced by the first RER, line A, which was completed in 1977, confirming the town's status as an exclusive suburb of Paris.

On a humbler level, the same impulse to breathe fresh air and renew contact with rural roots can be seen in the weekend invasion of the Forest of Fontainebleau by amateur rock-climbers, by the number of ramblers' associations affiliated to the FFRP (Féderation Française de la Randonnée Pedestre) and by the existence of countless other groups who go cycling, riding or bird-watching in the forests of the Ile de France. There is even a group which specialises in mushroom excursions in the autumn, when the more accessible forests are regularly denuded by enthusiastic amateurs.

The triumphant survival of the countryside: some surprising statistics

In spite of all this urban invasion, the Ile de France remains remarkably untamed, by English Home Counties standards. I saw my first snake (harmless, I was assured by my shrugging French companions) on a bird-watching excursion less than 60 kilometres north of Paris and was horrified when they

Provins

identified the droppings of a wild boar nearby. I had to take their word for it that boars leave you alone if you leave them alone and, judging by the speedy disappearance of the snake and the invisibility of the boar, the wildlife does seem to be more frightened of us than we are of it. I have also noticed that wild flowers and birds that are rare in England are commonplace here, not to mention the carpets of wild strawberries that no one bothers to pick.

The reason for the survival of an authentic countryside around Paris is that, although the Ile de France is the most heavily and densely populated region in the country with just under 11 million inhabitants, almost a fifth of the total population of France, this population is very unevenly distributed. Only 15 per cent of the total surface area of 12,000 square kilometres is completely urbanised, concentrated in a radius of about 30 kilometres around Paris, while 23 per cent is still forest. So although the population density of Paris is twice that of central London, the situation is reversed for the surrounding countryside, the density in Greater London being four times higher than that in the Ile de France. Beyond *la proche banlieue*, huge tracts of land are given over to intensive agriculture and it is possible to walk for miles without seeing more than a handful of people. Villages such as **Seugy** or **Belloy-en-France** seem completely untouched by the twenty-first century and the nearby presence of Paris, apart, of course, from the fact that you can reach them relatively easily, even without a car. The medieval town of **Crécy-la-Chapelle**, nine kilometres from Disneyland, but centuries away in spirit, is another example.

A rural retreat for artists ...

A favourite haunt of painters, notably Corot, Crécy is also a good example of why so many famous artists are associated with obscure villages in the Ile de France. Concentrated as they were in Paris, the artistic capital of Europe, what more natural than that struggling painters should take their easels into the nearby countryside, easily accessible by train? So the rivers, forests and the shifting skies of the region around Paris are captured in the canvases painted by Corot, Monet, Millet, Renoir, Seurat and Sisley, around the Forest of Fontainebleau in particular, while the landscape at Auvers-

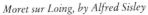

Moret sur Loing, by Alfred Sisley

Rousseau's study at Montmorency

sur-Oise is dramatically evoked in the paintings of Vincent van Gogh. Various schools of painting – the Impressionists at Barbizon, the Fauves at Chatou, the Nabis at **St Germain-en-Laye** – originated in the Ile de France. The region has always attracted painters, musicians and writers in search of pastoral surroundings not too far from the capital: Sisley at **Moret-sur-Loing**, Corot at **La Ferté-Milon**, Satie at **Luzarches**, Ravel at **Montfort-l'Amaury**, Hugo at **Créteil**, Zola at **Médan** (Poissy), Chateaubriand at **Châtenay-Malabry** (Sceaux) and Rousseau at **Montmorency**, to mention only the ones included in this book.

... and for royalty

Not surprisingly, the kings of France were the first to use the Ile de France as a countryside retreat from Paris, preserving some of the surrounding forest for the pleasures of the hunt. The royal palace of Fontainebleau began as a hunting lodge in the 12th century, as did Versailles five centuries later, while the attractions of the forest surrounding the château at **St Germain-en-Laye** had already made it a favourite royal residence by the 12th century. The nobles followed suit, the fortified castles of the Middle Ages dotted around Paris being superseded by the *châteaux de plaisance* of a less warlike age, notable for the artistic design of their parks and gardens, those of **Chantilly**, **Rambouillet** and **Sceaux** among them. The supreme example of the garden as a countryside retreat from the pressures of court life is, of course, Le Petit Trianon at Versailles, where Marie Antoinette played at being a shepherdess, while the creation of the garden Maurice Denis named 'Le Prieuré' at **St Germain-en-Laye** is an artist's response to the same impulse.

Why the Kingdom of France began in the Ile de France

However, the French kings had political as well as frivolous reasons for building châteaux in the Ile de France. The name of the region itself provides the clue. Why is it called an island when it is nearly 160 kilometres from the sea, and why 'France' when it covers less than three per cent of the surface area of modern France? The region takes its name from the rich grain-producing plateau around St Denis to the north of Paris, the old *Pays de France*, sometimes referred to as the *Plaine de France*. It is an 'island' in the sense that it is surrounded by three rivers – the Seine, the Marne, and the Oise. However, the term 'Ile de France' has always referred to the area around Paris rather than to a geographically or culturally distinct region, such as Brittany, for example. Its administrative boundaries have been shifting since the Middle Ages, shrinking to a radius of 30 kilometres around Paris or expanding for up to 100 kilometres from the centre. As an official term, 'Ile de France' is not

Porte de Jouy, Provins

recorded before 1519, although it was probably in use earlier. By that date the rulers of this once tiny but prosperous region had consolidated their power to such an extent that their kingdom of 'France' included almost the whole of the country.

The reasons for the gradual emergence of the rulers of Paris as the dominant political power in the country are ultimately geographical. The city, first mentioned by Caesar in 53 BC, was established on the Ile de la Cité, where the passage across the Seine was easiest. It is at the heart of a low-lying region surrounded by rivers. A natural crossroads, it allowed navigable access to the sea and to northern Europe as well as to central and south-eastern France. The importance of river transport in a region of uncleared forest was crucial; a boat has always featured in the heraldry of the city and now forms the official logo of the City of Paris. The rich, silty soil of the region and its mixed continental and oceanic climate also favoured the early development of agriculture, and 50 per cent of the area is still agricultural. The growth of its capital stimulated demand for its produce, attracting migrants from poorer parts of the country. The symbiosis between Paris and its setting, the growth of the city depending on the prosperity and accessibility of the region and vice versa, can be seen by glancing at any map of modern transport routes, which follow the old routes formed by the river valleys, all converging on Paris.

However, the political importance of the region and its capital fluctuated considerably following the collapse of Roman rule. Lyon had been the capital of Gaul under the Romans, but in 508 Paris became the official capital of Clovis the Frank. It was the election of Hugues Capet, Count of Paris and Duke of France, as leader by his fellow-nobles at **Senlis** in 987 that really marked the beginning of the political power of Paris and its region, and of the history of modern France.

How fragile and uncertain this power was can be seen by a glance at the political map of France for six centuries after 987. The ninth-century Viking invasions from Normandy were followed by invasions by their descendants, the kings of England, in alliance with the dukes of Burgundy, not to mention the threat of invasion by the Holy Roman Emperors in Germany.

The king of France, ringed by powerful neighbours in England, Germany, Italy and Spain, was only the nominal leader of vassals whose territories were much bigger than his: Normandy, Brittany, Burgundy, Aquitaine, Toulouse, Anjou and Provence. The English were only driven out in the 15th century and the country did not become fully unified under the kings of France until the late 16th century, with the ending of the Wars of Religion.

La Tour aux Saints, Crécy-la-Chapelle

Physical reminders of the fragility of royal power still exist in the border towns of the Ile de France. Almost every old town mentioned in this guide – **Conflans, Crécy, La Ferté-Milon, Luzarches, Montfort, Montmorency, Moret, Provins, St Germain** and **Senlis** – has its medieval ramparts or ruined keep, originally built to defend the approach to Paris and protect the inhabitants from attack, whether by the English or by unruly vassals. Churches, monasteries, towns and farms were systematically fortified and equally systematically pillaged, destroyed and rebuilt, the town of **Montfort** and the château of **St Germain** among them.

The ambiguous relationship between Paris and its province in the past...

That the rebuilding took place at all was largely due to the agricultural prosperity and stability of the region and its correspondingly high population, relative to its size, stimulated by the growth of Paris. This enabled its rulers to gradually impose their power on the neighbouring provinces but their relationship with their own province was, and remains, ambiguous.

For example, the protection of the supply routes to Paris, the seat of government, was the original impulse behind the construction of the medieval fortresses dotted around the Ile de France. But Paris itself could become a threat to royal power, and then the fortresses provided a refuge for the king. It is said that Louis XIV never forgot the trauma of the night of 5 January, 1649 when, aged 14, he fled with his mother to **St Germain-en-Laye** from the Fronde uprising in Paris. His decision to move the court to Versailles concentrated the nobles under the eye of the king and away from Paris, where they could do less harm, although the attempt to deprive the city of its predominance did not last.

In fact, the fame and prestige of Paris has effectively eclipsed the region from which it grew. It is not surprising that I had never heard of the Ile de France before I came to Paris: the current area referred to by that name has only been in existence since 1976.

... and in the present

The 1976 reorganisation of the region was a belated attempt to come to terms with a century of unplanned suburban development, in the course of which the rapidly expanding population of Paris had overflowed into *la triste banlieue*. The five new towns, conceived of as centres in their own right, rather than as dormitories of Paris, date from this period, as does the building of the RER express train network, going deep into the countryside, the linking of six motorways to the *boulevard périphérique*, the construction of the Charles de Gaulle airport at Roissy and the relocation of research and higher educational establishments from Paris to the Ile de France.

But despite these more or less successful attempts to rationalise the growth of Paris and to develop a coherent policy for the whole region, the persistence of the traditional 'Paris-province' split, so typical of the rest of France, is still striking,

RER station at Sceaux

at any rate to a Londoner. Although it accounts for less than one per cent of the surface area of the Ile de France, the City of Paris is a *département* in its own right, and its former Mayor, Jacques Chirac, was President of France for 12 years. Provincial distrust of the power and arrogance of Paris seems to be shared by some of the inhabitants of its own region. The old *curé* in **Belloy-en-France** who felt that the archaeological interest of his church was best kept from 'them' in Paris (see p. 1132) may not be typical. But the general criticism of the new Métro line 14 in central Paris, which opened in 1998, as being an unjustified luxury while the suburbs were still waiting for the much-needed RER line E to be finished, shows that the city does still seem to exercise a disproportionate weight in the region, given that four times more people live in the *banlieue* than in Paris itself.

The 21st century: the 'green' city and the countryside?

However, the fact that these criticisms have been voiced so loudly may be a sign that the balance is shifting towards a new relationship between Paris and its region. Since the 1960s various factors – the falling national birth rate, a slowdown in foreign immigration, improved educational opportunities in the provinces – have affected population growth in the Ile de

France. The population of Paris is now around 2 million, compared to 2.7 million 40 years ago, partly as a result of the success of the new towns and the transport infrastructures created after 1976. The population of the Ile de France, Paris included, is 11 million rather than the 14 million anticipated in the 1960s and is expected to reach around 12 million by 2015. This slowing down has allowed greater emphasis to be given to the preservation of the environment, 'Le Plan Vert Régional'.

Although a surprising 80 per cent of the region still consists of agricultural land, forest or open spaces, the policy has been to make these more accessible to the public. One consequence has been the gradual acquisition of islands and towpaths by the *Conseil Régional* and the creation of more forest and riverside walks and cycle paths. However, little was actually done to encourage people to leave their cars at home before setting out for a day in the countryside. For example, until very recently, the official map of the *parc naturel régional* created by the 'Plan Vert' in the Valley of the Chevreuse, south-west of Paris, only showed access by road. The latest map shows the RER stations from Paris, a significant change of emphasis. I first had the idea for this book because none of the existing guides, official or otherwise, gave clear, detailed directions on how to get to the less well-known places in the Ile de France by public transport, places that were well worth getting to. The reaction at the time from a well-known publication (English) based in Paris was, 'Oh, no one would want to travel on those *banlieue* trains for pleasure.'

But now pollution in Paris has reached such unacceptable levels that the number of cars has been restricted on certain days. People are beginning to wonder if *les écolos* (environment fanatics) were right, after all. The strikes which paralysed all transport in Paris in November 1995 gave Parisians a taste of life in a city without cars and they discovered to their surprise that walking to work through car-less streets could be a pleasure. The spontaneous take-over of the streets of central Paris by roller-bladers on Friday evening and Sunday afternoon in the summer of 1998 has now become a weekly event and the two clubs which organise it have seen their membership shoot

Roller-bladers in Paris

up. They are escorted by the first roller-blading national police division in the world and have won a legal battle, enabling them to continue to choose their own routes through Paris, subject to police agreement. Their website on www.pari-roller.com posts the route every week. It shows that there is a new current of popular feeling in favour of that elusive commodity, the quality of life – and that it is attracting more and more official support.

The current mayor of Paris, Bertrand Delanoë, has encouraged the development of even better public transport and inaugurated the highly successful *Paris Plage*: the annual banning of cars from the quays of the Seine in central Paris from

mid-July to mid-August so that the riverside can be transformed into a public beach. In 2007 the City of Paris launched
the even more ambitious and successful Vélib *(vélo-liberté)*
bicycle rental scheme, putting 20,000 bicycles at the disposal of
the public, who can jump on a bike and then leave it at any of
the bike stations dotted around Paris at 300-metre intervals
for a modest fee. Official support for greater environmental
awareness was already apparent in 1998, when the glossy free
booklet published by the Mairie de Paris, *Les Canaux de Paris*
(see p. 241) first appeared. Subtitled 'Un réseau fluvial à décou-
vrir', it shows Parisians how to make the most of the
130-kilometre canal network around the city, which is also
part of their own history. The excellent free cycling map of the
Ile de France (see p. 239) was published by the usually low-
profile government agency, IAURIF (Institut d'aménagement
et d'urbanisme de la région Ile-de-France) in 2005.

But along with these signs that, at long last, the city is
beginning to wake up to the enormously rich resource on its
own doorstep, the traditionally negative Parisian attitude to the
banlieue was dramatically endorsed in October and November
2005, when the poorer parts of *la proche banlieue* were swept
by riots, which quickly spread to similar suburbs in other
parts of France. The size of these suburbs and the crime rate is
one tenth of that in American cities and the *banlieues* are no
longer in the news, but the unrest has acted as a wake-up call
to the authorities. One positive result has been the acceleration
of the demolition programme for the 1960s concrete tower
blocks and the adoption of a more imaginative public housing
policy, based on human needs rather than on planners' visions.

My own experience of exploring such suburbs is of those
which are picturesque as well as poor, such as Corbeil-Essonnes
or Savigny-sur-Orge, where a Portuguese café-owner gave me
a portion of his own lunch when I asked if they were serving
food. People in these places do not often hear an English accent
and they are intrigued and pleased when they realise that you
have come for the pleasure of visiting their town, on foot.

At the beginning of the 20th century, the fear was that
the explosive growth of Paris would engulf the Ile de France,

turning the entire region into a megalopolis. This has not happened. Instead, two contradictory trends are emerging. On the one hand there is the apparently irresistible tide of consumer-based uniformity, with its accompanying social division of the region into pretty but sterile villages and equally sterile concrete housing estates. On the other hand, there is a growing awareness of the human costs of environmental exploitation and a willingness to spend public money on making the countryside a better place to live in, as well as more accessible to visit. Both these trends are accelerating and it is impossible to predict the outcome. But the traditional *joie de vivre* which continues to flourish in parts of the Ile de France is rooted deep in the French psyche. It looks increasingly possible that the city of the 21st century will evolve in partnership with, rather than at the expense of, the surrounding countryside. With the help of this book, which only scratches the surface, I hope that you will enjoy discovering it for yourself.

Le Pavillon d'Aurore, Parc de Sceaux

Using this guide: quick reference

All visits begin at the local railway station, where it is suggested that you park if you are arriving by car.

If you are going by train, the only essential **map** is the RATP *Grand Plan de l'Ile de France*, no. 3 (see p. 240). You should also read the section on trains on pp. 235–238. For drivers, the most useful map to take is Michelin no. 106, *Environs de Paris* (see p. 240).

Each of the 20 visits ends with a boxed summary of essential information to help you decide at a glance if the visit is practical. The summary is followed by details of how to get there, when to go, other useful information such as admission times and prices, and brief details, sometimes recommendations, of local restaurants and cafés.

The **Carte Orange Zone** in the inset box refers to the zones covered by the weekly or monthly Navigo travel pass, which are shown on the railway map on pp. 6–7.

The frequency of trains depends on when you are travelling. Generally, there are more trains during weekday rush hours and fewer at weekends, and the Saturday timetable may be different from Sunday. However, for some destinations there are more trains on Sunday than on weekdays. Train timetables also change slightly every summer and winter, usually by a few minutes, but not all trains are affected. For these reasons, the information on trains under the heading **Getting there** gives the frequency of trains, which hardly ever changes, rather than the timetables, which might. If weekends are not mentioned, this means that there is no change in frequency from the weekday service. For detailed information on train times you should check with the SNCF (see pp. 236-7).

The times of the last train back in the **Getting there** section

Alley near Porte St Côme, Luzarches

and the opening times in the **When to go** section may affect your plans. Check the table on p. 232, Best days to visit, for a summary of which places are open on which days. Opening hours, and other things too, change all the time, so the details given under **Useful information** may be out of date. If you have chosen a visit because of a particular attraction, **always phone first** to make sure it is still available and open on the day and at the time you plan to go.

Journey time in the inset box refers to the time spent in the train. To work out the time you should allow for a visit, check the inset box for the distances between two places and also look at the scale of the local map. If an **alternative return** station is given, you have the choice of returning to Paris from the station you arrived at or of walking to the alternative station. It takes about an hour to walk three to five kilometres (two to three miles), depending on whether you are a slow or a brisk walker. The half or full day suggested in **length of visit** is a rough guide. Generally, a half day is the minimum you should allow, which would become a full day if you included certain options, such as a walk to an alternative station.

In general

French words likely to be unfamiliar to an English reader are followed by a translation in brackets. There is also a glossary of the French words most frequently used in the text on p. 244 and a train traveller's glossary on p. 246. However, I have not translated the basic words which you would find in a general phrase-book or dictionary, to avoid irritating readers who speak French.

All **distances** in the inset box are given in kilometres first, as this is how the information will be presented on road signs, and then in miles. One mile = 1.6 km, one km = 0.6 miles.

Teachers and journalists from all countries are entitled to **free or reduced admission** to national museums or monuments, including the Louvre and Versailles, but this generous French quirk is rarely publicised. Where it is mentioned in the text, take proof of your professional status with you and ask 'Est-ce qu'il y a un tarif réduit pour les professeurs/la presse?' There is usually a reduction for children, students and people aged under 26 or over 60. Again, take a student card or passport with you.

Any **ticket reductions** which may apply are specified in the text and are also described in more detail on p. 235 in the 'Getting around' chapter. It is cheaper to buy your train tickets at the Métro station, as a Métro journey is always included in the price. See p. 234.

It is not essential to have read the rest of the 'Getting around' chapter, nor the chapter on the Ile de France before going on any of these trips, although you might find them interesting to browse through in the train. They are intended as helpful background information, likely to be of special interest to those readers who have developed a taste for exploring and want to branch out on their own.

Ottoman 16th-century plate
Musée de la Renaissance,
château d'Ecouen

1. Champs-sur-Marne

A brief journey through three centuries, from the
new town of Noisiel to the Victorian Menier
chocolate factory on the River Marne,
then across a woodland park to
Madame de Pompadour's 18th-century château

The great attraction of a visit to Champs is the fact that, as it
is now part of the new town of Marne la Vallée, few people actually stop off there on their way home from Paris or to
Disneyland. If they did, they would be astonished to discover
a village and its 18th-century château set in parkland by the
river, a mile away from the busy RER station ferrying
commuters from Noisiel to Paris.

The tree-lined walk to the château from the station, itself
an example of successful modern urban planning, takes you to
the former Menier factory overlooking the Marne. Built
between 1871 and 1905, it was conceived as a model of its
kind, designed to be both functional and aesthetic. A listed
monument and something of a curiosity (it has been called 'an
industrial Chenonceau', a reference to one of the Loire châteaux,
at one time also owned by the Menier family), it is now the
headquarters of Nestlé France.

A walk along the Marne and through the woodland park,
which has been deliberately preserved as part of a green belt for
the inhabitants of Marne la Vallée, brings you to the state-
owned château. Entrance to the château park is free and there
are usually a few local people enjoying the panoramic view, with
its formal flowerbeds and sweeping perspective, laid out in
strict accordance with French classical taste. It was used as the
film set for *Marie Antoinette* in 2006.

From the château an efficient bus service will whisk you
back to Noisiel and the 25-minute train ride to Paris.

La Cathédrale *(former Menier chocolate factory)*

Suggested visit to Champs

From **Noisiel station** take the exit marked 'Cours des Roches' to the 220 bus stop on the other side of the road. There is a café, the Cours des Roches, to the right of the bus stop if you have to wait (the timetable is displayed at the stop) but I would recommend walking downhill to the château via the Menier factory and the Parc de Noisiel and taking the bus back from the château. The quickest route to the Menier factory (or to the model village at Noisiel one stop further) is bus 211 from the same stop, but the service is less frequent than the 220.

If you decide to walk, take the first left from the bus stop into a tree-lined pedestrian and cycle path sloping slightly downhill. This is the Allée des Bois which leads straight to the Parc de Noisiel, crossing a bridge over the A199 motorway. You will see a pedestrian sign for the château en route and also the red and yellow GRP signs (see p. 239). This walk, past new houses, community buildings and a children's playground, comes out on to the Cours du Château with the château to the

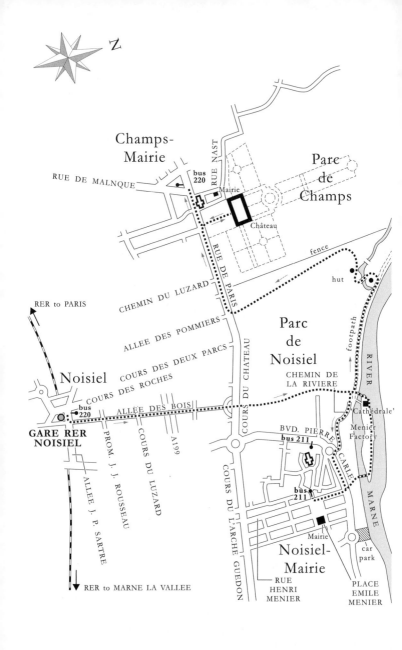

Champs-sur-Marne

0   500 metres

left and a water tower to the right, an ugly but useful landmark. A pedestrian crossing leads to the main entrance to the Parc de Noisiel, a vast expanse of grass sloping downhill to the River Marne. The imposing building surrounded by trees in the distance is known as the *Cathédrale*, and is part of the former Menier factory.

From the pedestrian crossing, the Cours du Château leads directly to the château, but you may prefer to make a detour through the park to see the Menier factory.

2 km walk through the park via the Menier factory to the château

Cross the grass straight towards the Cathédrale until you are stopped by a fence encircling more 19th-century Menier buildings. Bear left, joining a path that skirts the fence enclosing the Salle Pierre Carle, follow it round the building to the right and you will find yourself on a path leading to the river, with the **Cathédrale** to your right. You can now see that it is actually built on an island, with an elegant bridge, the Pont Hardi, linking it to the mainland, originally designed to carry wagonloads of warm cocoa paste by rail to the other buildings for processing into the legendary chocolate bars. It was constructed in 1905 by Stephen Sauvestre, a former colleague of Gustave Eiffel, who pioneered the use of reinforced concrete to create a modern temple to the Menier chocolate empire.

The spectacular pink brick building behind the Pont Hardi is the Moulin Saulnier, dating from 1871, and the other Menier buildings, attractively decorated with coloured tiles featuring the cocoa flower, extend for about half a kilometre, the full length of the island. Although the Menier factory is not open to the public, there is a wonderful view of it from the newly-built wooden footbridge to the island. The footbridge leads to a path right round the island and back to the mainland via another footbridge leading to the *cité ouvrière* (workers' village) of Noisiel.

You could continue along the river instead of crossing the main road at this point, but although the walk is quiet and very

Moulin Saulnier and the Pont Hardi (former Menier chocolate factory)

pretty (I saw yellow irises growing by the water and a friend reports seeing a green woodpecker there) the gate through to the car park further on is sometimes locked and you have to continue for another half-kilometre before you can cross the road.

If you are interested in seeing 19th-century model workers' houses, cross the Boulevard Pierre Carle into Place Gaston Menier, which leads via the Rue Henri Menier into the quiet, tree-lined Place Emile Menier. It contains the *Mairie*, two cafés (closed on Sundays) and a bust of Emile Menier (1826–1881). It belongs to an earlier industrial age and now exudes a village-like sleepiness, far removed from the new Noisiel near the RER. The old and new parts of Noisiel represent different stages of development, the progressive ideas of the Victorian entrepreneur, whose workers' village was inspired by English prototypes, being succeeded by those of the state planners who created the new town of Marne la Vallée in the 1970s. Emile Menier had Noisiel constructed in 1874 as a model village to ensure decent housing for his workers. Each house had a little garden and a bathroom and was let for a peppercorn rent of one franc. This benevolent paternalism extended to the provision of pensions, and the grateful workers consistently voted for a member of the Menier family as mayor of Noisiel until 1959, when the family sold the company. Chocolate production finally ceased at Noisiel in 1992.

Returning via the Chemin de la Rivière, re-enter the **Parc de Noisiel** and follow the Marne until you come to a little round hut on your left. Turn left over a little bridge across a stream and keep following the stream on your right, past another little hut and a second little bridge. When the path eventually forks, turn left, away from the stream and continue uphill, until you come to a ruined lodge next to a gateway. This is the exit from the park nearest to the château, the grounds of which are part of the same park, but are fenced off. Although entrance to both is free, the park is run by the local authority and the château is owned by the state, which apparently explains this curious state of affairs.

Follow the road to your right, the Rue de Paris, until you come to the main gates. The entrance to the **park** is to the right, leading to the back of the château and a spectacular **view** stretching down to the Marne, invisible in the distance. Two rectangular flowerbeds, so elaborately designed that they look like an enormous embroidered tablecloth, fill the foreground, converging on a fountain in the middle distance, with another rectangular flowerbed prolonging the perspective beyond.

The **château** itself is gratifyingly easy to visit, as despite its imposing appearance it is quite small and you need not follow a guided tour. Ask for the folder containing detailed notes in English or French, given to you at the entrance, and returned when you leave. It was essentially a rich man's house, built by a financier from 1703–08 and tastefully restored in 1895 by another wealthy individual, Louis Cahen d'Anvers, the father of the two little girls in a famous Renoir portrait of 1881, *Alice et Elisabeth Cahen d'Anvers*. The building incorporated several features designed to ensure comfort and privacy which were new at the time, such as a closet and boudoir for each bedroom and corridors to separate them from other rooms, as well as one of the first dining rooms to be built in France. The château's most famous inhabitant was Madame de Pompadour, who rented it from 1757 to 1760. The **Chambre d'Honneur** on the first floor was her bedroom and the corner salon next to it contains an interesting portrait of her by Drouais, showing a face sparkling with intelligence.

The most remarkable rooms on the ground floor are the **Salon Chinois** and the blue boudoir next to it. The walls of the Salon, even the window-shutters, are covered with delicate paintings of flowers and birds and playful animals in the fashionable 'Chinese' style, reminiscent of the Grande Singerie (Monkey Room) at Chantilly, by the same artist, Christophe Huet, *c.* 1735. He also painted the **Boudoir** with pastoral scenes in shades of blue, featuring dreamy Chinese shepherdesses.

The **Salon de Musique** on the first floor has the best **view** of the park, with its flowerbeds, statues and fountain descending in an unbroken perspective towards the Marne. If you turn around you will see a continuation of the same perspective to the south, extending from the *cour d'honneur* in front of the château and across the main road, but almost invisible at ground level. Designed by Claude Degots, a nephew of Le Nôtre, the château park is a model of the French grand classical style in gardens. It also marks the beginning of the taste for the romantic English landscape garden, which can be seen east of the park, blending into the woodland of the Parc de Noisiel.

The 220 bus stop is a few yards to the right of the château entrance, next to the Café de la Poste. You can use a Paris métro ticket if you happen to have bought a carnet, and will find yourself back at **Noisiel RER station** in less than ten minutes.

Distance from Paris: 30 km (18 miles)
Depart: Châtelet-les-Halles
Arrive: Noisiel
Journey time: 25 minutes
Length of visit: half day
Carte Orange Zone: 5
Single ticket: 4.10€
Distance from station to château: 1.5 km (1 mile)
Distance from Parc de Noisiel to château via Menier factory: 2 km (1¼ miles)
Pop. (Champs): 24,858

Getting there

RER A4 trains to Marne la Vallée, stopping at Noisiel, leave from Châtelet-les-Halles and other stations in central Paris every 10 minutes. The last train back is at around 12.30 am.

From Noisiel station **bus** 220 to Bry sur Marne goes past the château (*Mairie de Champs* stop). Buses run approximately every 15 minutes on weekdays and every half hour at weekends, returning up to midnight.

Bus 211 to Chelles goes from Noisiel station to Noisiel Mairie, passing the Menier factory (*Chocolaterie* stop). It runs every half hour on weekdays, every hour on Saturday. No Sunday service.

Car: Autoroute A4, exit Champs or Noisiel.

When to go

Summer would be the best season to appreciate the château's elaborate flowerbeds and to enjoy a picnic in the Parc de Noisiel, but the park is also particularly attractive in the spring when it is full of wild flowers. You may want to time your visit for the first Sunday of the month between October and May, when entrance to the château is free. The château is closed on Tuesdays.

NB: While this book was going to press, the ceiling of the Salon Chinois collapsed and the château has been closed for repairs, although the park is open. It is hoped to re-open the château to the public in summer 2008, but do ring first to check.

Useful information

Château de Champs-sur-Marne, 31 Rue de Paris, 77420 Champs-sur-Marne, tel 01 60 05 24 43. Open 10–12 am and 1.30–5.30 pm (6 pm at weekends and on public holidays) from April to September. Closes at 4.30 pm from October to March. Closed on Tuesdays, and on 1 January, 1 May, 1 and 11 November, and 25 December. Admission 6.50€, students under 26 and teachers on proof of status 4.10€. Free to visitors under 18. The château park is open from 9.45 am to 5.30 pm. Admission free.

Café and restaurants

Le Café des Sports, 19 Rue de Paris, Champs-sur-Marne, tel 01 64 68 22 98. Open from Tuesday to Sunday. A few yards from the château, next to the church, it has a sloping *terrasse* where you can sit outside away from the road.

Le Clos du Château, 36 rue de Paris, tel 01 64 68 66 00. Open from Tuesday to Sunday afternoon. Opposite and slightly to the left of the château, with a garden, it offers traditional French cooking: weekday *formules* at 15€ and 17€, evening/weekend menus at 21€ and 27€. The cheapest wine is 13€ a bottle. I haven't yet tried this restaurant, but any new gastronomic initiative in Champs is to be welcomed.

2. Chantilly

A château, two museums, a park, a forest and a racecourse – Chantilly has something for everybody, including Chantilly cream

The château of Chantilly makes an undeniable impression, with its fairytale turrets rising above an ornamental lake and the imposing equestrian statue of its Renaissance builder, Constable Anne de Montmorency, silhouetted alongside. It is almost as well-known as Versailles or Fontainebleau and contains some remarkable works of art, the most precious being the 15th-century Book of Hours, *Les Très Riches Heures du Duc de Berry*, as well as paintings by Raphael, Botticelli, Ingres and Delacroix.

You can ramble in the park designed by Le Nôtre – France's most famous landscape gardener – see the original play-village which inspired the Trianon at Versailles, take a boat ride along the ornamental canals and watch a dressage demonstration at the nearby Musée Vivant du Cheval (Living Museum of the Horse). Avoid the crowds by taking a little-used path through the forest from the station direct to the château and by following a canal on the way back before turning into the town of Chantilly for the station.

The château is actually two châteaux in one, known as the Petit and the Grand Château. They were built around 1560 on the foundations of a 14th-century fortress by Constable Anne, 'le Grand Connétable', formidable head of the Montmorency family (see the chapters on Ecouen, p. 88, and Montmorency, p. 127). The square Petit Château was originally separated from the triangular Grand Château by a moat, today filled in. The main entrance is to the Grand Château, which is a 19th-century reconstruction of the original destroyed in the Revolution.

Chantilly stayed in the Montmorency family until the

Chantilly

execution of Henri de Montmorency in 1632 and then passed by marriage to the Princes of Condé, the younger Bourbon branch of the royal family. In 1662 Louis II, the 'Grand Condé', commissioned Le Nôtre to transform the park and forest along lines that Louis XIV was later to outclass at Versailles, in terms of size and extravagance. However, Chantilly's canals, waterfall and fountains continued to be visited by everyone who was anyone in the 17th century, from the king himself to artists, philosophers and gossips – Molière, La Bruyère, Racine, La Fontaine, Madame de Sévigné among them. It is thanks to a letter of Madame de Sévigné's that the tragic story of François Vatel, the Grand Condé's master chef, has survived the centuries. In despair at being expected to feed more than 600 courtiers accompanying the *Roi Soleil* on his visit to Chantilly, he was told at the last minute that certain dishes could not be procured in time. Unable to survive the disgrace to his reputation, he fell on his sword during the night of 23–24 April 1671. Regret was expressed, but the festivities went ahead all the same. In the 18th century the nobles, influenced by Rousseau, played at being peasants in the Hameau (hamlet) at Chantilly, a fashion later imitated at Versailles and Rambouillet.

The destruction of the Grand Château in the Revolution did not put an end to Chantilly's ability to attract an elegant crowd.

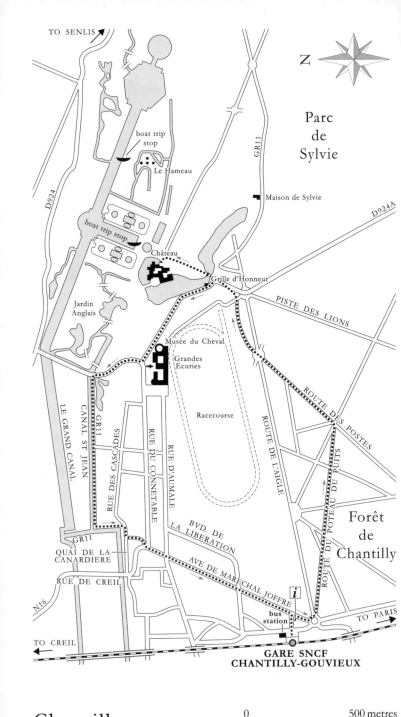

Chantilly

0   500 metres

The first horse races were held there in the 1830s, encouraging the creation of the excellent railway service to Chantilly, which is the racing capital of France. Its last owner, the Duc d'Aumale, rebuilt the Grand Château between 1875 and 1881 and left the estate, together with his art collection, to the nation. It is this collection which forms the Musée Condé, housed on the first floor and part of the ground floor of the château.

Suggested visit to Chantilly

From the **station** cross the Place de la Gare into the Rue des Otages, past the Hotel de la Gare on your left. The **Office de Tourisme** is on the corner at the end of this road, just past the *boulangerie*. Turn right, past the tourist office and cross the main road at a little roundabout a few metres away, into the woods on the other side.

A few metres along this path you will see a pedestrian sign-post on the left marked 'Château 2.1 km'. Ignore the footpath it points to (too close to a forest road) and take the dead straight unmarked footpath just right of the signpost. Within minutes you will be far from the sound of traffic and you are unlikely to meet more than an occasional stroller, although there are thoughtfully-placed benches along the way. I saw bullfinches, wild violets and wood anemones when I was there in spring, and harebells in August.

The path crosses a small road (unmarked). Keep straight on until you come to a kind of walker's crossroads, with pedestrian signs pointing in every possible direction. Take the third left, marked 'R.F. des Postes vers le Château'. This wider path leads to a small road, with a car park and an ice-cream stand. (All the ice-cream stands near the château sell ices topped with Chantilly cream, well worth a try.)

Cross the road diagonally to your right and continue along the same footpath. There is an excellent **view** of the race-course and the 18th-century stables to the left, which can easily be mistaken for the château itself until you see it rising into view on your right.

Turn right, past the coach car park, and cross the grass down to the *Grille d'Honneur*, the gates leading to the **château** and the ticket office. The main entrance to the Musée Condé is in the Grand Château, through the *Cour d'Honneur*. A useful free map of the château collections in French and English is available at this entrance. The ticket includes entrance to the Picture Galleries in the Grand Château and a guided tour of the Petit Château, both on the first floor. Guided tours start from the main entrance. It would be a pity to miss one as this is the only way you can get to see some of Chantilly's treasures, so if while you are wandering through the Picture Galleries you see a guide rushing through, yelling something in French, drop everything and follow him or her back to the entrance.

One of the stipulations of the Duc d'Aumale's bequest to the nation was that the paintings should be left in their original places. This explains the curious logic of the display, in which paintings from different periods, by artists of wildly differing ability, are arranged side by side. It has its charm, as you can come across a masterpiece like Piero di Cosimo's painting of **Simonetta Vespucci**, the model for Botticelli's *Venus*, next to work by a completely obscure artist of another school. Chantilly lends itself to the game of 'Spot the Botticelli' in a way that no other gallery containing work by world-famous artists does. The collections include Greek and Roman antiquities, Chantilly porcelain and lace, paintings by Filippino Lippi, Holbein, Van Dyck, Watteau and Corot, as well as forty illuminated miniatures by Jean Fouquet from a 15th-century Book of Hours.

You must join the guided tour of approximately 45 minutes to see the main apartments on the first floor of the Petit Château, the Renaissance part of the building. It is well worth it for a glimpse of the miniatures from *Les Très Riches Heures du Duc de Berry*. What you see are facsimiles, not the originals, but far superior to the reproductions familiar to most people. The guided visit includes **La Grande Singerie** (Large Monkey Room), the walls of which are coverd by bizarre and beautiful paintings of monkeys serving men and men serving monkeys. These are by the same 18th-century artist, Christophe Huet, who decorated the 'Chinese' rooms at Champs (see p. 54).

You can buy tickets in the museum shop for a supplementary guided tour of the Petits Appartements on the ground floor of the Petit Château, which includes 'La Petite Singerie', another boudoir decorated with monkey paintings.

It is possible to spend hours rambling in the **park**, visiting the **Maison de Sylvie** (a hunting lodge built for Henri IV in 1604), the **Hameau** and the **Jardin Anglais**. The walk to the Maison de Sylvie along the lake is pretty and often deserted, although the house itself cannot be visited. However, it is very easy to get lost on the wilder, un-signposted paths between the Maison de Sylvie and the Hameau, although you might see a deer bounding past, as I did. If you have gone as far as the Jardin Anglais you will find that there is only one way out of the park, the same way that you came in, necessitating a tiresome detour around the ornamental lakes back to the main entrance to the château. For this reason I would recommend taking the **boat ride** from the château to the Hameau and walking back. This is the easiest way to appreciate Le Nôtre's design and also the most authentic, as the Prince of Condé's guests were boated along the Grand Canal with music playing, on their way to supper in the Hameau.

On leaving the château at the *Grille d'Honneur* turn right along the road, skirting the park and lake, to the stables housing the **Musée Vivant du Cheval**. The road turns right just past the Museum (D924, Route de Senlis), opposite a convenient café, L'Etrier (The Stirrup) with tables outside. Follow the Route de Senlis for a few minutes and then turn left to follow the GR11 (see p. 239) along the Canal St Jean, a haven of peace and quiet. You might pass the occasional fisherman, and a few local families out for a stroll or feeding the ducks. It is the kind of walk on which people say 'Bonjour' to each other. All too soon, the GR turns right, at which point you turn left towards the town of Chantilly, passing a little lock on your right. This is the River Nonette, part of which Le Nôtre diverted to form the Grand Canal for the park.

Turn right into the Rue des Cascades which becomes Quai de la Canardière, and then left into Rue de la Machine, which joins the Rue de Paris to become the Avenue du Maréchal Joffre. This is Chantilly's High Street, lined with shops, cafés, restaurants and cinemas. You will soon recognise it as the road you started from when you see the forest stretching away to the left, with the tourist office and the **station** on the right.

Distance from Paris: 41 km (25 miles)
Depart: Gare du Nord SNCF
Arrive: Chantilly-Gouvieux
Journey time: 26 minutes or less via fast trains, up to 45 minutes via stopping trains
Length of visit: Half or full day
Carte Orange Zone: Not applicable, outside Ile de France (Oise)
Single ticket: 6.90€
Distance from Chantilly station to château: 2½ km (1½ miles)
Pop.: 10,916

Getting there

SNCF fast trains *(Grandes Lignes)* to Creil leave Gare du Nord around once an hour, stopping only at Orry-la-Ville-Coye before Chantilly-Gouvieux. The last train back is at around midnight. You may be eligible for a 25% reduction on this ticket (see p. 235 in the 'Getting Around' chapter)

Local stopping trains (*SNCF Ile de France/RER D*) from Gare du Nord to Creil run at variable intervals, with long gaps between trains on Sundays, returning up to around midnight.

Local buses from the station to the château are free, although relatively infrequent. Check the bus station next to the railway station for a blue bus labelled 'DUC' or the bus to Senlis which stops near the Musée Vivant du Cheval.

Taxi from the station to the château: tel 06 80 02 15 90 or 06 07 45 37 55, about 6€.

Car: Autoroute A1, exit no. 7 Survilliers/St Witz or via the N16 or N17.

NB: IGN map 2412 OT is recommended if you want to walk through the forest to the next station, Orry-la-Ville. It is about 12 km from the château via the GR11 and GR12. I have not tried the GR routes, preferring to halve the distance by taking more direct paths to the station. I discovered that they are not suitable for walkers, being either soft sand for horses or roads for cars.

When to go

It is possible to avoid the crowds at Chantilly by going on a Monday or a Wednesday. It is closed on Tuesday and Thursday is a favourite day for school groups, especially in May and June. It attracts a lot of visitors at weekends, especially if the weather is sunny. Guided tours can start at any time, whenever there are enough people waiting for one.

NB: You could combine a visit to Chantilly in the morning with a visit to Senlis in the afternoon. See p. 214 for details.

Useful information

Office de tourisme, 60 Avenue du Maréchal Joffre, B.P. 233, 60631 Chantilly, tel 03 44 67 37 37. www.chantilly-tourisme. com. Open 9.30 am–12.30 pm and 1.30–5.30 pm Monday to Friday all year round, and on Sunday from 10 am to noon and 1.30–4 pm in May and June, 10 am–1.30 pm from July to September.

Musée Condé, Château de Chantilly, B.P. 70243, 60631 Chantilly, tel 03 44 62 62 62. www.chateaudechantilly.com. Open 10 am–6 pm every day except Tuesday from April to October, and 10.30 am–12.45 pm and 2–5 pm on weekdays, 10.30 am–5 pm at weekends, from November to March. The **park** is open to 8 pm daily in summer, closing at 6 pm and on Tuesdays in winter: adults 4€, children under 12, 2.50€. Admission to the château includes the park and a guided visit to the Grands Appartements. Adults 8€, adolescents under 18, students and teachers on proof of status, 7€, children under 12, 3.50€. Supplementary guided visit to the Petits Appartements 7€.

Musée Vivant du Cheval, Grandes Ecuries (opposite the race-course), Chantilly, tel 03 44 57 40 40. www.museevivantducheval. fr. Housed in the grandest stables ever built, fit for humans rather than horses, the Museum possesses 30 horses of different breeds and gives daily half-hour dressage demonstrations. Open 10.30 am–5.30 pm every day except Tuesday from April to October and 10.30 am–6.30 pm at weekends, 2–5.30 pm on weekdays, from November to March. Admission 8.50€, teenagers under 18, 7.50€, children aged 4–12, 6.50€.

Boat trip around the château park. In summer only. From the château to the Hameau (approximately 20 minutes) adults 5€, children 3€. Return trip 10€.

Petit train (30-minute train ride around the château park). Summer only, adults 5€, children 3€.

Restaurants

La Capitainerie, tel 03 44 57 15 89. Serves lunch and tea in the 16th-century kitchens of the château, once the domain of Vatel. Lunch *formules* 22 and 28€.

Terroirs et Châteaux, Le Hameau, in the château park, tel 03 44 57 46 21. Serves lunch and tea with Chantilly cream cakes in La Grande Chaumière du Hameau, the 18th-century summer dining room where the Prince of Condé fed his guests on the famous Chantilly whipped cream in fashionably rustic surroundings. Lunch 17.50–37.50€.

3. Conflans-Ste Honorine

**Perched above the Seine and the Oise,
the little town of Conflans is a major river port
which still feels like a riverside village**

Anyone who likes boats will feel at home in Conflans-Ste Honorine. Built on the cliffs overlooking the Seine at its confluence (*conflans*) with the Oise, it prospered in the Middle Ages on the toll paid by boats supplying Paris. Technical improvements in river transport had made it a port of European importance by the 19th century and the coming of the railways turned it into a favourite place for Parisians to spend their Sundays bathing and fishing. Although road transport has diminished its importance, Conflans is still very much a working port, with enormous barges from Belgium and the North of France moored five abreast along its quays and a population which includes retired bargees as well as weekend visitors.

Some of these visitors (still mainly French) head for the

*Conflans-Ste
Honorine*

Musée de la Batellerie, a national centre for the history of inland waterways transport. But this need not be your only reason for choosing a trip to Conflans. Very quick and easy to reach by train from Paris, it offers maximum *dépaysement* (change of scene) for minimum effort. A visit to the town can easily be combined with a towpath walk along the the Seine to the old village of Andrésy, lunch at an island restaurant reached by private speedboat, and the option of returning to Paris from the station at Andrésy or continuing the towpath walk to Poissy. Or you could prolong the riverside walk in the other direction, returning from Herblay, which is even closer to Paris. There is an interesting old church at both Andrésy and Herblay, as well as a free public ferry at weekends to parks on the other side of the river, a little-known service which only local people seem to use. Both walks offer pretty views of the river; Herblay attracts fewer people, but the shorter walk to Andrésy is more rewarding in terms of food and historical interest.

Suggested visit to Conflans

From the **SNCF station at Conflans-Ste Honorine**, take the exit marked 'Sortie Place Colonel Coutisson' and turn right downhill into the Avenue Jean Jaurès. Turn left at the traffic lights into the Avenue Carnot and then take the second right into the Rue Maurice Berteaux. (The stone steps on your left lead up to the Parc Gévelot and are a useful short cut to the Musée de la Batellerie). Rue Maurice Berteaux leads to the Place Fouillère, the liveliest part of the town, facing the Seine. The **tourist office** is a few steps from here, on your left.

There is a rich choice of places to explore in the little maze of streets and houses rising above the Seine in the heart of the oldest part of the town. There are steps everywhere, winding between the houses and leading to sudden glimpses of the river between their descending roofs. From the Place Fouillère it is tempting just to walk along the river, looking at the huge barges moored along the quay of what is still a working port,

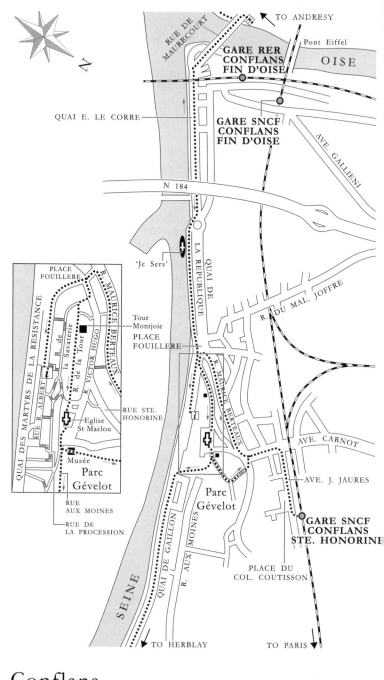

Conflans-Ste Honorine

0   500 metres

and deciding which café looks the most attractive.

However, the best **view** of the port and of the little back streets is from the Rue de la Tour, 20 metres above the Seine, which is reached via the Rue Victor-Hugo behind the Place Fouillère. Climb the steps on your right which are called Rue de la Savaterie and take the left turn which leads straight to the **Tour Montjoie**. This square tower is actually a shell, 15 metres high and with walls 1.65 metres thick, the surviving keep of a castle built to protect Conflans after the border wars of the 11th century. Follow the Rue de la Tour to the Place de l'Eglise, where the **Eglise de St Maclou** is the only other survivor of this period. It houses the relics of a third-century martyr, Sainte Honorine, originally carried to Conflans by monks fleeing the Viking invasions of Normandy in 876. It contains two early 14th-century tombstones of the Montmorency family, rulers of Conflans from 1270 to 1642 (see the chapter on Montmorency) and it also has a distinctly medieval atmosphere. Restoration work is currently being carried out on the church, so it may occasionally be locked.

Opposite the church, in the Place Jules Gévelot, is what appears to be a Renaissance château. In fact, it was built in the 19th century on the ruins of the old Priory founded in 1080 to guard the relics of Sainte Honorine and now houses the **Musée de la Batellerie**. The grounds of the former priory are now a pretty public **park** behind the Museum, the **Parc Gévelot**. From the terrace of the Place Gévelot there is another sweeping **view** (*Les Terrasses*) of the port and the river below, winding into the distance.

The museum itself is a great place for people who are fascinated by the details of barge construction and the history of river transport. For a rapid visit, start with an overview on the first floor before studying the models on the ground floor. If your taste for technical detail does not match that of your companions, you can always leave them to it while you explore the church and the park a few steps away.

Behind the museum there is a path through the park which eventually forks left and leads to steps down to the Avenue Carnot and the **SNCF station**.

4 km walk to Andrésy

Andrésy is now a prosperous residential suburb, but still retains some of the atmosphere of its medieval village past. It was once the Roman port of Anderitum, the base from which Julius Caesar's fleet controlled access to Lutetia (Paris), although no traces of the Roman occupation remain.

From the **Musée de la Batellerie**, take any of the small streets with steps leading down to the river and turn right, past the Place Fouillère. You will eventually pass a 70-metre barge, *Je Sers* (I Serve), permanently moored alongside the Promenade François Mitterrand. Built just after the First World War, it has served as a floating parish church and social centre for bargees since 1936. Mass is said every day at 6.30 pm and it is a rather moving experience to join the local congregation for a few minutes in the boat-shaped chapel.

Further along the Quai Eugène Le Corre you will come to the windswept headland at the confluence of the Oise and the Seine, dominated by a war memorial to bargees, with the 19th-century Pont Eiffel railway bridge spanning the Oise to your right. Take the busy Rue de Maurecourt which is actually a bridge across the Oise, and leave by steps on the right-hand side to continue along the Seine to Andrésy.

The landing stage for the **public ferry** across to the nature reserve on the Ile Nancy is just past the rather impressive Hotel de Ville. It is always fun to take a ferry, especially when it is free, but I must confess that I found the **'parc naturel'** a trifle disappointing. It extends for about a kilometre from the northern tip of the island but the only way out is the way you came in. There is not much scope for exploring off the carefully delineated paths, and the only wildlife I saw was a cormorant which has its nest on an islet at the very tip of the island. However, the spacious **view** of the river from this further-most point, opening out on either side as if you were at the prow of a boat, is deeply satisfying.

Continuing along the river, you will pass the 13th-century **Eglise St Germain**, dedicated to the fifth-century bishop who is buried in the better-known church of St Germain-des-Prés

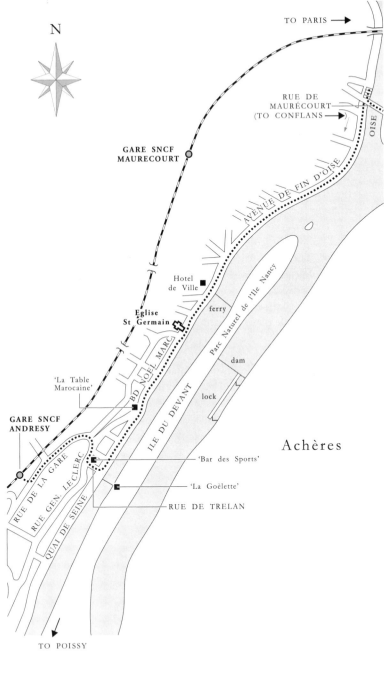

N

TO PARIS →

RUE DE
MAURÉCOURT
(TO CONFLANS →

OISE

GARE SNCF
MAURECOURT

AVENUE DE FIN D'OISE

Hotel
de Ville

ferry

Parc Naturel de l'Ile Nancy

Eglise
St Germain

dam

BD NOEL MARC

'La Table
Marocaine'

lock

ILE DU DEVANT

GARE SNCF
ANDRESY

Achères

'Bar des Sports'

'La Goëlette'

RUE DE TRELAN

RUE DE LA GARE

RUE GEN. LECLERC

QUAI DE SEINE

TO POISSY

Andrésy

0   500 metres

in Paris. It is open on Saturday and Sunday mornings and is worth visiting, if only for the curious sculpted figures holding up the top of the columns. The covered walkway along the river from this point is known as Les Halles and has been the site of a **market** since the Middle Ages.

Just past the market there is a good Moroccan restaurant, **La Table Marocaine**, facing the weeping willows by the river. It is a friendly place, a favourite with local families. However, the island restaurant, **La Goèlette** a little further on is well worth its higher prices for the charm of the setting and the exceptional quality of the cooking.

To reach it, continue along the river as far as the Rue de Trelan. There is a little jetty with an electric bell to the right, which you press to summon the small speedboat opposite. You are whisked across to the restaurant, which used to be an inn and has scarcely changed its appearance since the 1950s. There is a little riverside garden in which you can eat outside in the summer (where I saw a red squirrel) and the tiled floor, lace curtains framing the river and the old-fashioned oak furniture make a cosy retreat inside. You are served toast with salty home-made anchovy and tapenade paste while waiting for your order. I had a *ris de veau aux morilles* (calf's sweetbreads

Public ferry, Andrésy

with morel mushrooms) cooked in cream and accompanied by crisp sauté potatoes, one of the best versions of this dish I have ever eaten. The cheapest wine on the list, a bottle of Médoc at 19€, proved an excellent choice. The restaurant is family-run, catering for an unpretentious but discerning local clientele.

It is not possible to explore the rest of the island from here, so once back on the mainland you have the choice of returning to Paris via **Andrésy station** or of continuing the walk along the Seine to Poissy. To reach the station, follow the Rue de Trelan and turn right into the Rue Général Leclerc, then left uphill into the Rue de la Gare.

4½ km walk from Andrésy to Poissy

This riverside walk is popular with local families on Sundays, when the Andrésy section is closed to traffic. Continue along the towpath, past the Ile de la Dérivation. This residential island is accessible by a single bridge leading to the central Avenue de la Gaule, but the river views on either side are on private land, so it is not really worth a detour. The towpath after the lock at this point is too narrow for cars, so it is a peaceful pretty walk to Poissy. You will see the Peugeot Talbot factory on the other side of the river, just before the modern Pont de Poissy. Take the steps up to this bridge from the towpath, cross the river into Poissy and continue along the main road for the **station** on the right (see map of Poissy on p. 144).

5 km walk from Conflans to Herblay

From the **Musée de la Batellerie** take Rue aux Moines, between *Les Terrasses* and the Museum, and take the unmarked right-hand lane leading to steps down to the river, which come out at Quai des Martyrs de la Résistance. Weeping willows frame the towpath and the barges with washing outside, which appear to be permanently moored here. As you follow the river along the Quai de Gaillon, the houses along the waterfront gradually thin out until you are surrounded by grass and trees and meet only the occasional stroller or cyclist. Keep following the river and after about 20 minutes you will come to **Les Gourmand'Ises**, a restaurant with tables in a roadside garden next to the towpath. I have not tried this restaurant, which may be more interesting than it looks.

Continue to stroll along the Seine for another mile. The road beside the river is closed to cars a little further on, so this is the quietest and most countrified part of the walk, with only a few strollers or moorhens breaking the silence. You will know you are approaching civilisation again when you can see the church at Herblay coming into view. Eventually you will pass an incongruous pink pagoda facing the river, which appears to have been lifted straight out of an illustration from *The Arabian Nights*. Known as the 'Maison Mauresque', it once belonged to a painter and is only the most exotic example of the architectural fantasies indulged in by Parisian escapees, who have been building second homes in Herblay since the 19th century.

It is a useful landmark to help you locate the jetty opposite on the Quai du Génie. From here a little **ferry** (*bac*) plies to and from the Pépinière de la Ville de Paris on the other side of the Seine. This is where the plants for the public gardens of Paris are cultivated and the *bac* is still in service because it is the quickest way for the gardeners to reach the other side of the river. It can be used by the general public at weekends, an odd survival of a medieval right of passage, and makes the crossing whenever there are passengers waiting at the jetty.

Some of these, armed with suncream, picnic lunches and bicycles, are clearly in the habit of spending the day in the **park** opposite, where there is a little stream and children's rides dotted around the grass. Further away from the river, the park gives way to rows of plants and a rather flat road leading to Achères, although it is probably possible to cycle from here to the nearby Forest of St Germain. Do not cross at lunchtime unless you plan to picnic in the park, as there is no service between 11.30 am and 2.30 pm and no café on the other side.

The Rue du Val opposite the ferry is the shortest way to the church. Take this uphill street, past the Impasse du Val on your right and then climb the steps of a very steep winding GR footpath (see p. 239) on your right, opposite the Sente de la Martinière. It will bring you out on to the grassy terrace bordering the cemetery outside the **Eglise St Martin**. From here there is a superb **view** of the valley of the Seine looping to the left, with the Forest of St Germain-en-Laye stretching into the distance. The church itself is 12th century, with additions and alterations dating from the 14th to the 16th centuries. If it is locked, you can ask for the key at the presbytery on the left. There is a very graphic 17th-century wooden relief of St Martin dividing his cloak and a 16th-century stained glass window representing the Tree of Jesse.

From the church, take the Rue Jean XXIII which leads back to the Rue du Val. Turn left at the top of the Rue du Val into the Boulevard Oscar Thévenin. The **station at Herblay** is a little further on, on the left.

Distance from Paris: 25 km (15 miles)
Depart: Gare St Lazare or Châtelet-les-Halles
Arrive: Conflans-Ste Honorine or Conflans Fin D'Oise
Journey time: 35 minutes or less
Length of visit: Half or full day
Alternative return from: Andrésy, Poissy or Herblay
Carte Orange Zone: 5
Single ticket: 4.10€
Distance from Conflans to Andrésy: 4 km (2½ miles)
Distance from Andrésy to Poissy: 4½ km (2¾ miles)
Distance from Conflans to Herblay: 5 km (3 miles)
Pop.: 31,857

Getting there

SNCF trains stopping at Herblay and Conflans-Ste Honorine leave from Gare St Lazare *(Ile de France)* every half hour. Look for trains going to Gisors or to Mantes-La-Jolie/ Pontoise via Argenteuil.

For Conflans Fin D'Oise and Andrésy take trains going to Mantes-La-Jolie via Argenteuil. Trains on this line run roughly every half hour on weekdays, hourly at weekends, returning up to 11.30 pm.

RER A3 trains to Cergy, stopping at Conflans Fin D'Oise, leave Châtelet-les-Halles twice an hour.

Both SNCF and RER trains

back to Paris run up to approximately midnight, at half hourly intervals, hourly from Andrésy at weekends.

Car: Autoroute A15, exit Conflans-Ste Honorine. Free parking at the Musée de la Batellerie.

When to go

The market at Andrésy is on Saturday and Wednesday mornings and the public ferry there operates on Wednesdays and at weekends between mid-April and mid-October. You could visit the market and have lunch in Andrésy and then walk to Conflans to visit the museum, which is only open in the afternoon at weekends.

Useful information

Conflans-Ste Honorine
Office du Tourisme, 1 rue René Albert, 78700 Conflans-Ste Honorine, tel 01 34 90 99 09. Open 10.30 am–12.30 pm and 2.30–5.30 pm from Tuesday to Saturday and on Sunday in summer.

Musée de la Batellerie, Château du Prieuré, 3 Place Gévelot, tel 01 34 90 39 50. Open 9 am–12 noon and 1.30–6 pm on weekdays except Tuesday mornings, and 3–6 pm at weekends and public holidays in summer, 2–5 pm in winter. Closed on 1 January, 1 May and 25 December. Admission 4.10€, 1.50€ if under 18, 3€ for students and teachers on proof of status.

Boat trips

Les croisières-promenades du dimanche One-hour cruise of the Seine and the Oise, leaving from the jetty (*embarcadère*) opposite the Place Fouillère at 3.30 pm and 5 pm on Sundays from May to September. Adults 8€, children under 12, 4€. Tickets are sold at the jetty.

Ask at the tourist office for details of other cruises which may be operating, such as the 'Croisière-Déjeuner du Dimanche' (two hours, 57€ adults, 29€ children, including lunch).

Public Ferries

Andrésy
The ferry to the Ile Nancy leaves from the jetty facing the Hotel de Ville every half hour from 11.30 am to 6 pm on Wednesdays, weekends and public holidays from mid-April to mid October. Maximum 12 passengers, free. Information from the *Mairie* on 01 39 74 66 04.

Herblay
The ferry to the agricultural park leaves from Quai du Génie, opposite the Rue du Val. Operates at weekends and public holidays from 9 am–12 noon and 2–7.30 pm, April to September. Free passage, 11 passengers maximum. If necessary, check with the *Mairie* on 01 34 50 55 55.

Restaurants

Les Gourman'Dises, 38 Quai de Gaillon, Conflans-Ste Honorine, tel 01 39 72 65 03. Closed on Sunday evenings and on Monday. Menus 10.50€ weekday lunchtime, 19.50€ evenings and weekends.

Auberge la Goèlette, Ile du Devant, BP 7, 78570 Andrésy, tel 01 39 74 70 35. Telephone first, in case it has been booked for a private reception. Closed on Mondays, on Tuesday eve-nings, and on Sunday evenings in winter. Menu 27€, *plats du jour* 20-32€,

bottle of wine 19-84€. Exceptional cooking in an exceptional setting.

La Table Marocaine, 64 Boulevard Noël Marc, 78570 Andrésy, tel 01 39 70 90 66. Closed on Wednesdays. Couscous and *tajine* dishes at around 15€, 75 cl *pichet* of house wine 10€. Honest family cooking, friendly atmosphere.

Bar des Sports, 24 Rue du Général Leclerc, 78570 Andrésy. Closed on Mondays, otherwise open 7 am–8 pm. Lunchtime *plats du jour* 11€ Tuesday-Saturday. Not particularly friendly but one of the rare cafés open on Sunday.

4. Crécy-la-Chapelle

**A moated medieval town, nine kilometres and
a world away from Disneyland**

Crécy-la-Chapelle counts some Disneyland executives among
its residents, but you will be pleasantly surprised by how
remote from Disney and Paris it feels, in spite of being so
close to both. The nearby Eglise de la Chapelle is supposed to
be one of the finest examples of Gothic architecture in the
region (true) but the real justification for the visit is Crécy
itself, which in its own way is as remarkable as the church.

Crécy is in the heart of the Brie region, home of the
famous cheese, surrounded by rolling fields, little streams
and watermills. A medieval market town, it is encircled by the
Grand Morin, a tributary of the River Marne. A series of
three moats fortified by towers and walls once allowed goods
to be transported by river and unloaded at its various quays,
and has turned it into a small-scale medieval version of Venice
– without the crowds. At every turn there are old houses
overlooking the water, some with their own miniature
drawbridges, and the little town exudes an air of quiet self-
sufficiency, where the past blends harmoniously into the
present. The code of manners is endearingly provincial.
Remember to reply 'Bonjour, m'sieur/madame' if you are
greeted by perfect strangers strolling along the canals. They
assume you are visiting relatives or friends.

The local tourist office map of the region shows the
surrounding villages, including Serbonne, three kilometres
from the Eglise de la Chapelle along the Grand Morin, which
makes a pleasant walk. Or you could simply cross the footbridge
to the east of Crécy and join the locals for a stroll along the river
to enjoy the lovely view of the Eglise St Georges from just
outside the town. Although the journey from Paris is perfectly

straightforward and Disneyland is a stone's throw away, Crécy is refreshingly under-visited, at any rate by foreign tourists. It has remained a picturesque backwater.

Suggested visit to Crécy

Turn left to leave the **station** and then right into the Rue de Bouleurs. Cross the road and go past a little bridge and the clock tower on your left into the Rue du Marché. Continue into the Place du Marché, where you can buy local cheese direct from the producers on market days. I recommend the *coeur à la crème*, a beautiful soft white cheese taken dripping from a heart-shaped china mould, lifted into a plastic container and then smothered with cream, sold by the lady who makes it. The Bar du Commerce, with tables outside, is the best place to stop for an aperitif.

The tourist office facing the Place du Marché is good for expensive but pretty postcards of Crécy, a local map of the region (*Carte d'orientation*, price 1€) and a leaflet describing the main places of interest in Crécy. The French version (*Visite guidée*) is considerably more detailed than the English 'Visit of Crécy-Town'.

Follow the Rue du Marché which becomes Rue Serret and crosses the middle moat. Stop at the bridge to admire the old houses and footbridges on either side, then turn down the

Eglise de la Chapelle

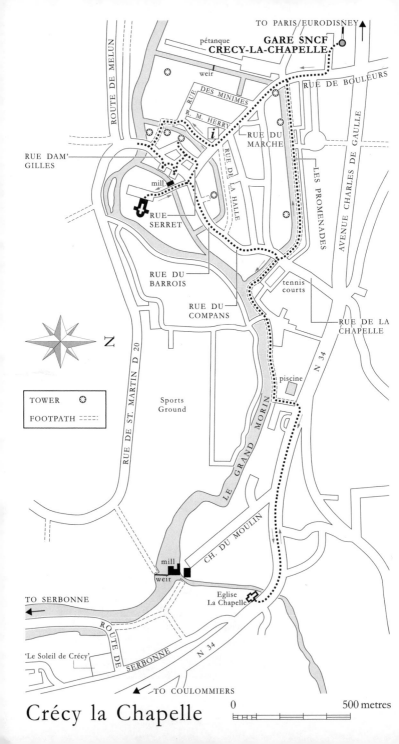

TO PARIS/EURODISNEY

**GARE SNCF
CRECY-LA-CHAPELLE**

pétanque

weir

ROUTE DE MELUN

RUE DES MINIMES

R. M. HERRY

RUE DE BOULEURS

RUE DU MARCHE

i

RUE DAM'
GILLES

RUE DE LA HALLE

mill

RUE
SERRET

LES PROMENADES

AVENUE CHARLES DE GAULLE

RUE DU
BARROIS

RUE DU
COMPANS

tennis
courts

RUE DE LA
CHAPELLE

RUE DE ST. MARTIN D 20

Sports
Ground

LE GRAND MORIN

N 34

piscine

TOWER ⊛

FOOTPATH ┄┄┄

N

mill

weir

CH. DU MOULIN

TO SERBONNE

Eglise
La Chapelle

ROUTE DE SERBONNE

N 34

'Le Soleil de Crécy'

TO COULOMMIERS

Crécy la Chapelle

0   500 metres

Quai des Tanneries on the right, past a medieval *lavoir* (wash house), one of many in Crécy, to a quiet bench at the end. The tallest of the round towers visible on the other side of the water is La Tour aux Saints, the best-preserved of the defensive medieval towers that still dot the town. Cross the moat to follow a winding 12th-century shortcut, Le Chemin de Ronde, which will bring you out into the Rue Dam' Gilles.

Turn right for the bridge across the outer moat, which is actually the Grand Morin river at this point. Weeping willows frame the **views** of the river on either side and you can see why the artist Corot stayed in Crécy in 1873, using one of the medieval towers next to the Tour aux Saints as his studio.

Cross back into the Rue Dam' Gilles and turn right. You will pass two little alleyways leading to the inner moat, a favourite paddling place for children, with an unexpected view of a little **mill-wheel** under a bridge on the left.

Cross the Rue Dam' Gilles again and take the tiny Rue des Anges opposite. Turn left into the Rue de la Tour aux Saints, leading to the **tower** itself, set in a minute public garden. Restored in the 18th century, the tower now houses a local archaeological association. Crécy is full of little surprises like this: the ruins of another tower, accessible through a housing estate on the Rue du Barrois, shelter someone's washing-line and one of the *lavoirs* along the middle moat, reached by the medieval Rue de la Halle, was actually for sale on one of my visits. The little footbridges across the moats lead to mysterious back gardens. Everywhere you can sense the secret presence of water. The best way to explore is to follow the moats and let your curiosity get the better of you.

But if you only have time for a brief visit, follow the route on the map to the 18th-century **Eglise St Georges** with its 13th-century bell-tower, stopping to lean over the bridge on your right to see the other side of the little **mill-wheel**. There is no access to the Grand Morin from here, so retrace your steps and turn right along the Rue du Barrois. This street leads to the Rue de la Chapelle across the outer moat. If you want to return to the **station**, turn left along the moat at this point and follow **Les Promenades**.

1½ km walk to the Eglise de la Chapelle

Turn right along the moat, past the tennis courts and a set of steps from where you can hire **rowing boats** in summer. Continue past the footbridge (*passerelle*) on your right until you come to the open-air swimming pool (*piscine*) which marks the end of the footpath along the river. The entrance is on the N34 to Coulommiers.

Turn right and follow the road for a short distance. The church will soon come into view on your right, incongruously facing the main road. A 13th-century masterpiece, the **Eglise de la Chapelle** is next to a little stream which has caused considerable damage to its foundations over the centuries. The English caused even more destruction during the Hundred Years' War and parts of it had to be rebuilt in the 15th century. However, the overall impression is upliftingly Gothic and the interior is unforgettable for its elegance and simplicity. It is usually locked but if you go round to the ancient low doorway on the right you can see the lovely windows of the apse through a grille which has been placed in front of the open door while restoration work is being carried out inside. The stone figures carved above the doorway represent the Virgin, the Assumption, St Martin, the Gifts of the Magi and the Baptism of Christ. The best **view** is from the bench facing the back of the church across an expanse of grass.

Depending on time, you could take the little Route de Serbonne which follows the Grand Morin to the village, returning across the fields to Crécy (a five-kilometre detour – see the tourist office map). Serbonne is old and picturesque but has no café and seems to be mainly inhabited by the wealthy. The road starts to the right of the church and goes past **Le Soleil de Crécy**, a campsite popular with Dutch visitors to Disneyland. It has a little snack bar and of course, *les toilettes*.

If time presses, return to Crécy, following the outer moat around past the tennis courts and along a shady avenue, aptly named **Les Promenades**. The gardens of houses with footbridges overlook the moat on your left, guarded by the ruins of two of the medieval towers; the trees and benches on your right will have attracted a few strollers and leisurely cyclists. This delightful walk, popular with local people, will take you past ducks waddling on the grass to the Rue de Bouleurs and the **station**.

If you have to wait for a train you could follow the outer moat right round to the end, past the Rue de Bouleurs, a five-minute walk. There is a little weir, a favourite with fishermen, and a *pétanque* (bowling) area beside the moat. It ends in the steps of a little landing stage, a good place to sit with your feet dangling in the water, watching the ducks and the changing light over the Grand Morin before returning to Paris.

However, if you fancy ending the day in a restaurant and don't want to rush dinner to catch the last train back at 9.30 pm, you could do worse than take an earlier train back and head for the **Café de l'Est**, a traditional Paris brasserie with 1930s decor facing the Gare de l'Est. It specialises in the *choucroute* (pork and pickled cabbage) dishes of Alsace, the region served by the station. The quietly cosmopolitan atmosphere makes it a fascinating contrast to a day in Crécy.

Distance from Paris: 43 km (27 miles)
Depart: Gare de l'Est
Changing at: Esbly
Arrive: Crécy-en-Brie-la-Chapelle
Journey time: 55 minutes
Length of visit: Half or full day
Carte Orange Zone: 6
Single ticket: 6.70€
Distance from Crécy to La Chapelle: 1½ km (1 mile)
Distance from La Chapelle to Serbonne: 3.2 km (2 miles)
Distance from Serbonne to Crécy: 1½ km (1 mile)
Distance from Crécy to Disneyland: 9 km (5½ miles)
Pop.: 3,909

Getting there

SNCF trains to Meaux leave from Gare de l'Est (*Ile de France*) approximately once an hour, stopping at Esbly 35 minutes later.

At Esbly change platforms for the tiny connecting train to Crécy, approximately 10 minutes later. On Sundays a local bus service (*car*) replaces the train from Esbly to Crécy. The timetable can be consulted in the station at Esbly and is displayed outside the station at Crécy or you can pick up a *fiche horaire* at Esbly. The last bus or train from Crécy leaves at around 9.30pm.

RER A4 trains from Châtelet-les-Halles to Marne-la-Vallée stop at Chessy, the station for Disneyland, 40 minutes later. From Chessy there is a connecting, hourly bus service, line 59, to Crécy, taking about half an hour. It does not operate on Sundays. For details, ring Cars Marne et Morin on 01 64 63 59 59 or visit www.marne-et-morin.fr.

Car: Autoroute A4, exit Crécy.

Taxi: From Disneyland to Crécy, approximately 18€, tel 01 60 25 60 00 or 06 07 84 36 79

IGN maps: 25140 or 2414ET to include Disneyland.

When to go

There is a market on Sunday and Thursday mornings, the former being smaller. You could buy the materials for a picnic lunch there, as Sunday is not a good day to eat out in Crécy. If possible, choose a warm sunny day when the light is reflected in all the moats and you can picnic by the river.

Useful information

Office de Tourisme, 1 Place du Marché, 77680 Crécy-la-Chapelle, tel 01 64 63 70 19. Open 9.30 am–12.30 pm and 3–6.30 pm from Wednesday to Sunday. Closed on Sunday mornings in winter. For information outside these times, ring the *Mairie* on 01 64 63 94 36.

Promenades en barque sur le Morin (rowing boats for hire) Landing stage opposite the tennis courts. Every weekend from June to September from 3 to 7 pm. 8€ an hour, 5€ half an hour.

Le Soleil de Crécy (campsite) Route de Serbonne, 77580 Crécy-la-Chapelle, tel 01 60 43 57 00. www.campinglesoleil.com.

Restaurants

Chez Nous, 3 rue du Marché, tel 01 64 63 84 05. Open for lunch every day except Sunday and for dinner on Friday and Saturday evening. *Formule* 17€ or à la carte. Recommended by locals, although I have never actually eaten out in Crécy.

Café de l'Est, 78 boulevard de Strasbourg, 75010 Paris, tel 01 46 07 00 94, www.cafedelest.com. Open every day until 2 am. Well-made *choucroute* and seafood dishes from around 14€ (the *choucroute* is enough for two), 25 cl *pichet* of good Riesling 6.10€.

5. The islands of Créteil
Ile Ste Catherine, Ile de Brise Pain,
Ile des Ravageurs, Ile de la Guyère

**Weeping willows frame a hidden pocket of countryside
at the edge of Paris, home to swans, ducks
and the beaver-like coypu, as well as
the lucky human residents**

If you are looking for a day out in the country you can find it, astonishingly enough, at the end of the Métro line to Créteil.

Créteil, characterised by charmless 1960s architecture, is the last place on earth where you would expect to discover four small islands, linked to each other by footbridges, containing only old houses and country villas hidden by trees and encircled by riverside walks and weeping willows. Apart from a swimming pool, a small park and a farmhouse converted into a restaurant, the islands are exclusively residential. The roads feel like footpaths, with scarcely a car in sight.

In the Middle Ages the islands were owned by the canons of Notre Dame in Paris, who leased the land to the local villagers to ensure the maintenance of the weeping willows, necessary to protect the fertile soil from the incursions of the River Marne. The neglected state of the land after the Second World War made it a cheap and attractive proposition to some of the disaffected 1968 generation who were looking for a rural alternative to the new town created by the planners in Créteil. In 1978 these new residents formed an association to preserve the islands from urban development and succeeded in getting the site listed in 1982. Today it is an unexpected survival of the country at the edge of the city, a favourite place for the residents of Créteil to take their Sunday walks, but still relatively unknown to Parisians.

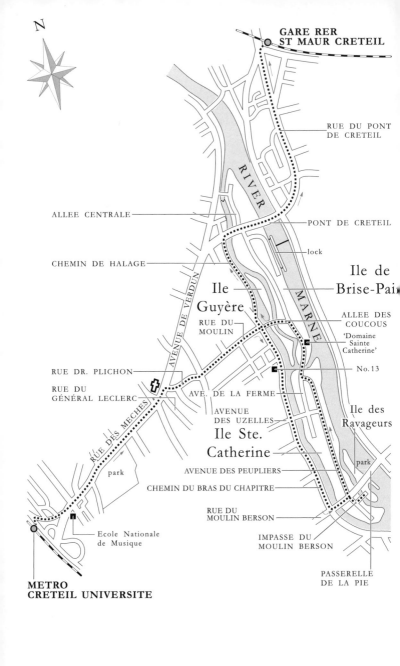

N

GARE RER
ST MAUR CRETEIL

RUE DU PONT
DE CRETEIL

ALLEE CENTRALE

PONT DE CRETEIL

lock

CHEMIN DE HALAGE

Ile de
Brise-Pai

Ile
Guyère

ALLEE DES
COUCOUS

RUE DU
MOULIN

'Domaine
Sainte
Catherine'

RUE DR. PLICHON

No. 13

RUE DU
GÉNÉRAL LECLERC

AVE. DE LA FERME

AVENUE
DES UZELLES

Ile des
Ravageurs

Ile Ste.
Catherine

park

AVENUE DES PEUPLIERS

CHEMIN DU BRAS DU CHAPITRE

park

RUE DU
MOULIN BERSON

Ecole Nationale
de Musique

IMPASSE DU
MOULIN BERSON

METRO
CRETEIL UNIVERSITE

PASSERELLE
DE LA PIE

RIVER

MARNE

RUE DES MECHES

AVENUE DE VERDUN

The islands
of Créteil

0   500 metres

Suggested visit to the islands

From the **Métro station** at Créteil-Université take the left exit for the Rue des Mèches, then the right-hand path marked by a red and white GR sign (see p. 239) and a sign for the Ecole Nationale de Musique. Cross the road at the church, the Eglise St Christophe. The crossing leads to the pedestrianised Rue du Général Leclerc, where a **market** is held on Thursday and Sunday mornings. This is the old part of Créteil, and as you go past the little playground on the right you will see that it is in the Jardin des Mérovingiens, the site of an 8th-century necropolis. Take the Rue Dr Plichon on the right, which becomes Rue du Moulin. It leads down to the river and the main footbridge to the islands. Turn right into the Chemin du Bras du Chapitre and follow the riverside path until you come to **no. 13** just past the corner of the Rue Robert Legeay.

Victor Hugo lived upstairs here in the days when it was an inn and wrote about it in *La Lavandière* (*The Washerwoman*), a poem published in 1865. The inn was owned by a M. Bellier, whose *bateau lessive* (laundry boat) operated on the Bras du Chapitre for fifty years. Between 1943 and 1944 it was the headquarters of the local Resistance group, and its chicken-run concealed a radio receiver used to communicate clandestinely with London. Until quite recently, it was a restaurant, the Cochon de Lait. The owners had been there since the 1950s and I suppose they must have retired, ending the history of an establishment largely unchanged since Victor Hugo's day.

Continue along the quiet Bras du Chapitre, past the occasional fisherman, until you reach a stone bridge. Turn right onto the bridge, the Rue du Moulin Berson, and cross it to the Ile Ste Catherine, across the Avenue des Peupliers, to the Passerelle de la Pie, a footbridge which links the Ile Ste Catherine to the *commune* of St Maur on the other side of the Marne. Ignore this bridge and continue along the Impasse du Moulin Berson past a house with ducks, hens and rabbits outside, which seems to be in the depths of the country. The gate on the left leads to a small footbridge to the **park** on the Ile des Ravageurs, which in itself is not particularly remarkable, but which seems to exercise a great attraction on children. There is no other exit from the park, so go back across the footbridge to follow the Avenue des Peupliers through the centre of the island. The walk takes you past secluded houses, each of which is built in a different style, from 1960s modern to traditional French rustic. The river can sometimes be glimpsed through the trees. The Avenue de la Ferme, reached via the Avenue des Uzelles on the left, is even more rural and it is difficult to believe that you are not far from Paris.

Cross onto the Ile Brise Pain via the footbridge and follow the Allée Centrale to the **Domaine Sainte Catherine**, a 19th-century farmhouse hidden by trees which has been converted into a restaurant and tea room. It is bigger than it looks and the shady garden extends to the river. The menu is not particularly original but you can stop here just for a drink at the friendly bar or for tea in the garden overlooking the Marne.

Follow the Allée Centrale past the swimming pool and turn left across a series of footbridges which will bring you via the Allée des Coucous to your starting point at the Chemin du Bras du Chapitre, a favourite place for animals and people to congregate. You are likely to see swans, ducks and a beaver-like creature called the coypu, (*ragondin* in French) originally intro-

Coypu at Créteil

duced from South America to be bred for its fur, which has happily colonised the islands. The engaging little muzzles and whiskers of these animals are usually visible just above the waterline. They are fed titbits by the local children, although they do considerable damage to the river bank. Take the Chemin de Halage (towpath) to the right, past weeping willows, swans, ducks, benches and fishermen. At the bridge take the steps up to the busy Pont de Créteil and follow the road to the right, across the Marne to St Maur. A ten-minute walk along this main road will bring you to the **RER station** at St Maur Créteil. This is slightly shorter than the walk back to the Métro at Créteil-Université, although the traffic presents a disconcerting contrast to the oasis of calm you have just left.

Distance from Paris: 11 km (7 miles)
Depart: Métro line 8 or RER Châtelet-les-Halles
Arrive: Métro: Créteil-Université
Journey time: 20 minutes approx
Length of visit: Half day
Alternative return from: RER St Maur Créteil
Carte Orange Zone: 3
Single ticket (RER): 2.10€
Distance from Métro to islands: 1½ km (1 mile)
Distance from islands to St Maur: 1 km (½ mile)

Getting there

Métro line 8 to Créteil-Université.

RER A2 trains to Boissy St Leger, stopping at St Maur Créteil leave Châtelet-les-Halles every 10 minutes. The last train back to Paris is at 12.29 am.

Car: A4 from Porte de Bercy, then A86 to Créteil. N19, then N186 to the Pont de Créteil or Chemin Bras du Chapitre.

Boat: 'Paris Canal' cruises: full day's cruise along the Marne from Paris, Musée d'Orsay to Chennevières, stopping for two hours at lunchtime at the Domaine Sainte Catherine. (See below).

When to go

A mild sunny day would be ideal, when the light is reflected on the water and you could share a picnic with the fish, ducks and copyu.

NB: You could easily combine a visit to the islands at Créteil with a visit to the Ile du Martin-Pêcheur at Champigny, only two stops from St Maur on the same line.

Boat trip along the Marne

Paris Canal cruises, Bassin de la Villette, 19–21 Quai de la Loire, 75019 Paris, tel 01 42 40 96 97, fax 01 42 40 77 30, www. paris-canal.com. Reservation essential. Cruises leave the Quai Anatole France, next to the Musée d'Orsay at 9.45 am, stop at the Domaine Sainte Catherine from 12 noon–2 pm for lunch and follow the Marne to Chennevières, arriving back in Paris at around 5.15 pm. I have yet to try this cruise, discovered in an obscure leaflet, but it is still running. Every weekend in July and August, 58€ per person, including lunch.

Restaurant/tea room

Domaine Sainte Catherine, 22-24 Allée Centrale, Ile de Brise Pain, tel 01 42 07 19 18. www. domaine-ste-catherine.com.

Closed all day Monday and on Sunday evenings. Reservation advisable at the weekend. Menu 30€ or à la carte.

6. Ecouen

A walk through the forest leads to the fairy-tale
setting of the château of Ecouen, with its
collection of Renaissance treasures.

If you are interested in the French Renaissance, there is no need
to travel as far as the Loire. One of the most elegant examples
of this style in France, the 16th-century château of Ecouen, is
the setting for the furnishings and objets d'art that make up the
collections of the National Museum of the Renaissance, some
of them from the Musée de Cluny. If you go on a Saturday afternoon, you can hear the music of the period played on the
16th-century organ in the chapel.

Although it is very close to Paris by train, the château,
surrounded by a 17-hectare **park** covered with snowdrops in
early spring, is gratifyingly under-visited. The full impact of
its hilltop site overlooking the grain-producing *Pays de France*
is only revealed when you approach it on foot from the Forest
of Ecouen. I first went there by bus from the station and actually failed to recognise it as the same place when I went there
again via the forest some years later, so different were the two
impressions. The château gradually rises into view as you
approach it from the woodland path and is suddenly revealed
in all its stateliness as you emerge on to the vast flat lawn at the
top. This back view, much more imposing than the front,
includes a balustrade to the left overlooking a sharp drop.
From here there is a sweeping view of the plain below, just like
the hazy, stylised landscapes in medieval paintings.

The château was built for Constable Anne, Duke of Montmorency (1492–1567), the owner of over 130 châteaux and
one of the wealthiest and most powerful men in France (see the
chapters on Chantilly, p. 56, and Montmorency, p. 127).
Completed in 1555, it is in the High Renaissance style, a

Château d'Ecouen

development of the Early Renaissance style of the châteaux of the Loire built during the reign of François I. The architecture, the grounds and the interior all reflect the new taste for a château as a place for gracious living rather than a medieval fortress. Painted friezes decorate the windows and walls and dreamy Biblical or classical scenes are painted on the chimneypieces. From the upper floor windows there are superb views of the park, the roofs of the houses descending the steep hill to Ecouen and the rolling countryside beyond.

The château was saved from destruction after the Revolution by Napoleon, who turned it into a school for the daughters of members of the Légion d'Honneur in 1806. The rooms now contain a fine selection of furniture, tapestries, glass and china made in France, Italy, Germany and the Netherlands in the 16th and early 17th centuries, representative of the Renaissance taste for elegance and refinement. The most famous exhibit is a Brussels tapestry, woven *c.*1515, which extends over three rooms on the first floor and tells the story of David and Bathsheba, dressed, of course, in 16th-century clothes. The other highlights are the Charles V clock in the form of a golden ship, complete with clockwork crew, *c.* 1580, on the ground floor and the beautiful Ottoman pottery from Iznik, inspired by Chinese models, on the second floor.

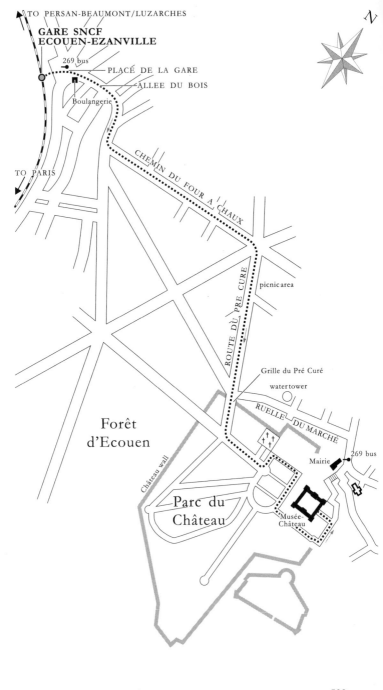

TO PERSAN-BEAUMONT/LUZARCHES

**GARE SNCF
ECOUEN-EZANVILLE**

269 bus

PLACÉ DE LA GARE

ALLEE DU BOIS

Boulangerie

TO PARIS

CHEMIN DU FOUR À CHAUX

ROUTE DU PRE CURE

picnic area

Grille du Pré Curé

water tower

Forêt
d'Ecouen

RUELLE DU MARCHÉ

Mairie

269 bus

Parc du
Château

Château wall

Musée-
Château

Ecouen

0   500 metres

Suggested walk to Ecouen from the station

Cross the Place de la Gare to the right of the **station**, turn right at the *boulangerie* into the Allée du Bois and follow it into the forest.

Turn right into the Chemin du Four à Chaux (paved) which curves left gently uphill and comes out at the junction of several paths. Follow the sign to the Museum 'par la Forêt' past the picnic area on your left. This unpaved road rises gently uphill to a gate set in the château wall, *la grille du Pré Curé*. (Should the gate be closed, which it is from late May to early July, follow the footpath which parallels the château wall, as shown on the map.) Go through the gate, then uphill past the signboard showing a map of the grounds and you will come out at the back of the château with the **view** from the balustrade on your left. Walk round the back to the right to find the main entrance on the other side.

Distance from Paris: 19 km (12 miles)
Depart: Gare du Nord
Arrive: Ecouen-Ezanville
Journey time: 23 minutes
Length of visit: Half day
Carte Orange Zone: 4
Single ticket: 3.50€
Distance from station to château: 1¼ km (¾ mile)

Getting there

SNCF trains from Gare du Nord (*Ile de France*) to Luzarches or to Persan-Beaumont via Montsoult stop at Ecouen-Ezanville every 15 minutes on weekdays, every half hour at weekends and return up to nearly midnight.

You can use a Paris métro ticket on the 269 **bus** from the station to Garges-Sarcelles, but the wait can be long and you will miss the pleasure of the approach to the château from the forest. If you take the bus, get off at the *Mairie d'Ecouen* stop and follow pedestrian access signs for the château via steps leading to a little footpath.

Car: A1 from Porte de la Chapelle, then exit 3, Pierrefitte/Sarcelles. Follow signs for Sarcelles/Beauvais (N401, then N1), then the N16 towards Sarcelles/Chantilly.

When to go

Avoid Tuesdays when the château is closed. As it is so close to Paris it would also be suitable for an afternoon visit in winter. The walk through the park in the snow, which remains intact here long after it has all melted in Paris, is a magical experience. Free concerts of Renaissance music are held in the chapel of the château every Saturday at 3 and 4 pm. No need to book.

Useful information

Musée National de la Renaissance, Château d'Ecouen, 95440 Ecouen, tel 01 34 38 38 50 (recorded information), tel 01 34 38 38 52 (bookings), www. musee-renaissance.fr. Open from 9.30 am–12.45 pm and 2–5.15 pm every day except Tuesdays and 1 January, 1 May and 25 December.

Closes at 5.45 pm from April to September. Guided visits at weekends at 11 am and 3.30 pm.

The **park** surrounding the château is open all year round, except from late May to early July, from 8 am–6 pm, 6.30 pm in summer, admission free. Admission to museum 4.50€, 3€ on Sundays and for those under 25. Free to teachers on proof of status, to visitors under 18 and to everyone on the first Sunday of the month.

Restaurant/tea room

La Plaine de France in the château, tel 01 34 04 07 93. Open daily except Tuesday 11 am–5.15 pm. Menus 19€, 23€.

Café de la Gare, opposite the station. Open to 9 pm every day except Sunday, when it closes at 4 pm.

7. La Ferté-Milon

Cruise or walk along the prettiest stretch of the Canal de l'Ourcq through the little town of La Ferté-Milon, dominated by its magnificent ruined castle

Ferté means a stronghold, and certainly the most impressive sight in La Ferté-Milon is the 14th-century castle crowning the hill above the Ourcq valley. The River Ourcq has always been important to Paris, originally supplying the city with grain and wood from the rich duchy of the Valois and still supplying part of its drinking water. At the invitation of François I, Leonardo da Vinci was the first to experiment with the idea of turning it into a canal. The oldest part of the Canal de l'Ourcq, which enters Paris at Porte de la Villette, is the ten-kilometre stretch between Mareuil and its termination at Port-aux-Perches, which had been completed by the 16th century. It is also the prettiest and least-visited part of the whole canal and you are likely to meet only local people on the towpath or on

The château at La Ferté-Milon

the weekend pleasure cruises from Port-aux-Perches. To my mind, this alone makes it worth the journey. You could combine a cruise from La Ferté-Milon to Port-aux-Perches and back with a beautiful walk along the canal to the little town of Mareuil, from where you can take the train back to Paris.

The sleepy little town itself conceals several surprises. The 'ruined' castle is in fact a magnificent sham in the sense that it was never completed. Had it been, it would have been the largest and grandest castle in France. The assassination in 1407 of its owner, the Duke of Orléans, by the henchmen of Jean Sans Peur sparked a civil war which enabled the English to re-invade the country, and the building work was abandoned. Henri IV ordered its demolition in 1594 during the Wars of Religion, although the magnificent façade was spared. Jean Racine, France's greatest dramatist, was born in La Ferté-Milon in 1639 and La Fontaine, author of the celebrated *Fables*, married Racine's cousin in the Eglise de Notre Dame in 1647, the same church in which Racine had been baptised. The elegant iron footbridge across the Ourcq in the town centre was built by a young engineer from Paris, unknown at the time, called Gustave Eiffel. La Ferté-Milon is the archetypal provincial town, no bigger than a large village, but the province could only be that of Paris.

Suggested visit to La Ferté-Milon

On leaving the **station** turn right into La Chaussée, the main street leading into the old town, which is clustered round the castle on the hill. The 15th-century **Eglise St Nicolas** is on your left. Ignore the first door, which is locked, in favour of the smaller one, which is not. If, exceptionally, both doors are locked, knock or ring the bell at the *Pompes Funèbres* (funeral parlour) across the street, where the key is kept. Although the church is not as impressive as the one near the castle, it is of more interest inside, possessing a particularly lurid set of Renaissance stained glass windows depicting the Last Judgement, right of the altar. The red devil shoving the damned into

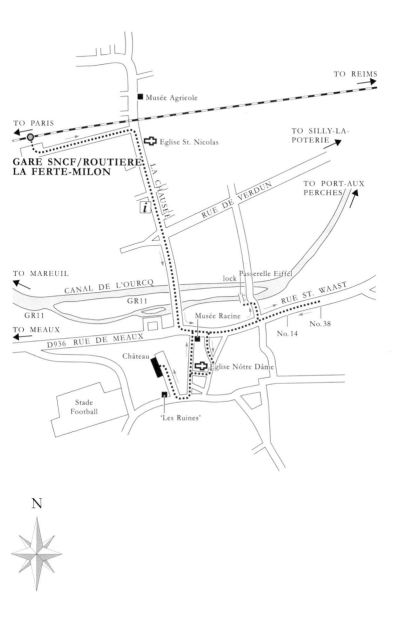

TO REIMS

TO PARIS

Musée Agricole

Eglise St. Nicolas

TO SILLY-LA-
POTERIE

GARE SNCF/ROUTIERE
LA FERTE-MILON

LA CHAUSÉE

TO PORT-AUX
PERCHES

RUE DE VERDUN

TO MAREUIL

Passerelle Eiffel

lock

RUE ST. WAAST

CANAL DE L'OURCQ

GR11

GR11

No. 38

TO MEAUX

Musée Racine

No. 14

D936 RUE DE MEAUX

Château

Eglise Nôtre Dâme

Stade
Football

'Les Ruines'

N

La Ferté-Milon

0   250 metres

the flames apparently bore a strong resemblance to Cardinal Mazarin, an observation which the young Louis XIV found so funny when he passed this way in 1654 that he nicknamed his cardinal the Red Devil. Apparently the name stuck.

The **Office du Tourisme** is further along, on the right. Continue past the canal and the pretty Passerelle Eiffel (footbridge) on the left and turn left into the Rue des Bouchers to visit the **Musée Jean Racine**, the little house in which Racine grew up. There is a poetic video reconstructing his life at La Ferté-Milon, as well as a few landscapes by Corot, who stayed here in 1858, but very little about the history of the town. History is rather taken for granted in these parts.

If you feel like doing some historical research of your own, continue along the Rue St Waast, to the 16th-century Hotel Racine. Behind it, the old Port au Blé, where boats were once loaded with wood for Paris, leads to the Eiffel footbridge and the lock. The curious round tower next to the footbridge is a remnant of the medieval ramparts.

Further along the Rue St Waast, no. 14 on the right has a semi-legible plaque stating that it belonged to Jean Racine's 'ancestors', although it actually dates from 1850. Just beyond,

Passerelle Eiffel

at no. 38 on the same side and of more authentic interest, is a house with a barely readable sign, the owner's name having been painted over at least twice:

Epicerie Mercerie *Md DE VINS* *LOGE à PIED et à CHEVAL*	Grocer Haberdasher WINE MERCHANT LODGING for those on FOOT and HORSEBACK

Return along the Rue St Waast and climb the steep cobbled streets on your left leading to the **Eglise Notre Dame** where La Fontaine was married. The outside is actually more impressive than the interior and this may be a comfort, as it is usually locked. The porch dates from the 12th century and the tower from the 16th. The 16th-century stained glass windows of the same period were destroyed by German artillery in 1918, when the town was at the heart of the Battle of the Marne.

Continue climbing, past the Café des Ruines to the **castle** behind it. Seen close up, its sheer size is breathtaking, as no doubt Louis d'Orléans intended it to be, its medieval solidity contrasting with the flowing bas relief above the main gate. This represents the Coronation of the Virgin and the style already shows the first stirrings of the Renaissance. But the biggest contrast of all is with the finished appearance of the façade and the emptiness behind it. From here there is a sweeping view over the town and the Ourcq valley. It is a dramatic place in which to picnic, or lunch at the **Café des Ruines** before making the descent to the town and the canal.

At this point you have several options: returning to the station, following the canal towpath to Port-aux-Perches two kilometres away and returning to La Ferté-Milon, or following the towpath in the other direction to Mareuil-sur-Ourcq. If you have arranged to join the boat cruise at La Ferté-Milon lock, you could combine part of a cruise with a walk. The towpath walk to Mareuil, although far longer, is much prettier than the same towpath to Port-aux-Perches.

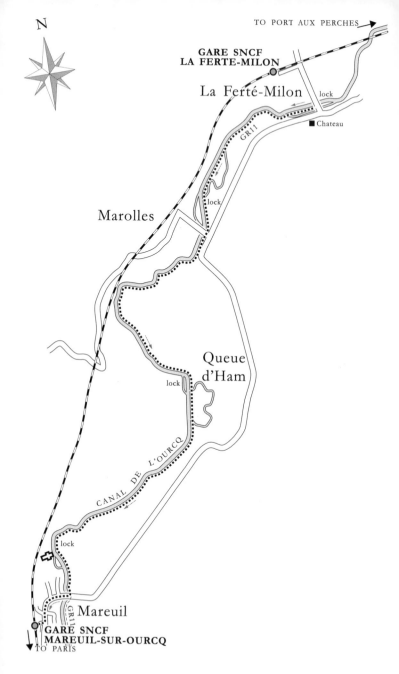

TO PORT AUX PERCHES

**GARE SNCF
LA FERTÉ-MILON**

La Ferté-Milon

lock

GR11

■ Chateau

Marolles

lock

Queue
d'Ham

lock

CANAL DE L'OURCQ

lock

GR11

Mareuil

**GARE SNCF
MAREUIL-SUR-OURCQ**

TO PARIS

0   500 metres

La Ferté-Milon to
Mareuil-sur-Ourcq

7 km canal-side walk to Mareuil-sur-Ourcq

This walk is part of the GR11 (see p. 239), a winding thickly-wooded stretch, where scarcely a boat passes to disturb the waterfowl. You pass the locks at Marolles and La Queue d'Ham before coming to the lock at Mareuil. You will know you are nearly there when you see the 13th-century church at Mareuil gradually coming into view, rising above the canal on your right. It is an imposing sight but rather bare inside, and usually locked. Continue along the towpath, past the church, until you come to a road crossing the canal. Cross the road to the other side of the canal and continue as it curves left and becomes the Rue de Meaux (D936). The **station** at Mareuil is just past the *Mairie,* on the opposite side of the road. There are two cafés near the station, both open on Sundays.

Distance from Paris: 70 km (44 miles)
Depart: Gare de l'Est
Arrive: La Ferté-Milon
Journey time: 66 minutes
Length of visit: Full day
Alternative return from: Mareuil-sur-Ourcq
Carte Orange Zone: Not applicable, outside Ile de France (Aisne)
Single ticket: 12€
Distance from La Ferté-Milon to Port-aux-Perches: 2 km (1¼ miles)
Distance from La Ferté-Milon to Mareuil: 7 km (4¼ miles)
Pop.: 2,372

Getting there

SNCF trains to Reims from Gare de l'Est (*Ile de France*) run twice on Sunday mornings, stopping at Meaux and La Ferté-Milon. On other days there are three morning trains but you have to change at Meaux (5–15-minute wait). The last train back to Paris, with a change at Meaux, leaves La Ferté-Milon at 6.40 pm on weekdays, 7.06 pm on Saturdays and 8.13 pm on Sundays.

You may be eligible for a 25% reduction on this ticket. See p. 235 in the 'Getting Around' chapter. This line stops at several canal-side towns on the way to La Ferté-Milon so it would be easy to start at one station, walk along the canal towpath (GR11) and leave by another. See p. 241

for details of how to obtain the free canal map.

There is a regular **bus** service, line 65, to La Ferté-Milon from the station at Meaux, which runs more frequently than the trains on weekdays. Ring Cars Marne et Morin on 01 60 61 26 40 for details, or visit www.marne-et-morin.fr.

Car: Autoroute A4 or N2 to Meaux, then D405 and D936 to La Ferté-Milon.

When to go

Choose a weekend if you want to combine a visit to La Ferté-Milon with a canal cruise. It is best to make an early start so that you can visit the church, castle and museum and perhaps lunch at the aptly named ivy-clad Café des Ruines next to the castle before setting off on a cruise and/or a walk.

Useful information

Office du Tourisme, 31 rue de la Chaussée, 02460 La Ferté-Milon, tel 03 23 96 77 42. Open 2–6 pm Monday to Friday, 9 am– 12 noon and 2–6 pm on Saturday, 9 am–12 noon on Sunday and public holidays. For information outside these times, ring the *Mairie* on 03 23 96 70 45.

Musée Jean Racine, 2 rue des Bouchers, tel 03 23 96 77 77. Open 10 am–12.30 pm and 3–5.30 pm at weekends from April to October and on the public holidays of

1 May, 8 May, 15 August and 11 November. Admission 4€, concessions 3€, free for children under 10.

Musée Régional du Machinisme Agricole (Museum of Agricultural Machinery), 68 bis rue de la Chaussée, tel 03 23 96 29 85. Same times and admission as the Musée Jean Racine.

Boat trips on the Canal de l'Ourcq

Le Port aux Perches, 2-4 rue François Mitterrand, Port-aux-Perches, 02460 Silly la Poterie, tel 03 23 96 41 25, www.portaux-perches.com. Reservations necessary. Narrowboat, taking up to 60 passengers. *Croisière Promenade* of around 2 hours from Port-aux-Perches to Marolles and back. Leaves at 4 pm, stops at La Ferté-Milon lock at approximately 4.30 pm, turning round just before Marolles lock at 5 pm, returning to La Ferté-Milon lock at 5.30 pm and Port-aux-Perches at 6 pm. Every weekend in the summer months, adults 7€, children under 12, 5€.

Croisière Déjeuner lunch cruise of approximately 3 hours from Port-aux-Perches to Marolles (5 km before Mareuil) and back. Every Sunday in summer, leaving Port-aux-Perches at 12.15 pm and passing La Ferté-Milon lock on the way back at around 2.45 pm. Cruise plus three course menu including aperitif, wine and coffee, 45€, children's menu 30€.

NB: When you book, explain that you are arriving at La Ferté-Milon by train. They can arrange for a car to pick you up at the station at midday for the *Croisière Déjeuner* cruise and they will get you back to La Ferté-Milon by car or by boat. This service is free and one of the staff speaks English.

I have tried the *Croisière Déjeuner* twice, once being met by car at the station and another time joining it by special arrangement at La Ferté-Milon lock at around 12.45 pm. The boat was filled with French families in holiday mood, who broke into a spontaneous cheer when we stepped on board at the lock. Most of the cruise is taken up with lunch, which is honest, although not spectacular, traditional fare. The close-up views of wildlife on the canal, varied with the changing views of the castle in the distance, as well as the pleasure of being the only foreigners on board, are the real attraction of the cruise, especially if you prefer to sightsee while sitting down. And you can leave the boat at Marolles lock and continue on foot along the towpath to Mareuil.

Cafés and restaurants

Les Ruines, 2 place du Vieux Château, 02460 La Ferté-Milon, tel 03 23 96 71 56. www.lesruines.com. Open Tuesday to Sunday for lunch and on Friday and Saturday evenings. Weekend menus 23€, 32€ and à la carte. 12€ menu on weekdays. Sedate atmosphere and traditional, although not inspired, cooking. Generous portions. Dramatic location, with a pretty enclosed garden if you prefer to eat outside.

8. Ile du Martin-Pêcheur

Join in one of the most enjoyable of French popular traditions – eating, drinking and dancing at a *guinguette* in the open air by the river. This one is on a tiny island, reached by a footbridge

When you cross the bridge onto this particular island on the Marne, less than half an hour away from Paris, you step into the timeless world of the *guinguettes*.

Guinguettes are so called because *le petit blanc,* the modest but lively white wine of the Paris region they used to serve, made people *giguet* (ready to dance a jig). Scores of open-air restaurants serving this wine and its traditional accompaniment, *la petite friture* (fried whitebait) opened along the banks of the Seine and the Marne in the 19th century, attracting the working people of Paris, who continued to go there right up to the Second World War. They would spend Sunday afternoons beside the river, eating, drinking and listening to traditional French songs sung to the accordion, until they felt ready to get up and dance. Popular with artists as well as with artisans, the *guinguettes* recall the atmosphere of the inter-war years, evoked by the songs of Edith Piaf, the films of Marcel Carné and the novels of Georges Simenon, all of whom came under their spell, and they have never entirely disappeared from the affection of Parisians.

In the last ten years or so there has been a revival of the tradition, with the older *guinguettes* such as Chez Gégène at Joinville now featuring in the guidebooks and the *bal musette* waltz being taught at dance classes. The *guinguette* on the Ile du Martin-Pêcheur (Kingfisher Island) dates from 1991 and is less celebrated. However, it is already so popular that you will need to book your table and when you get there, you will see why. The few yards separating the island from the mainland

N

Ile de
l'Abreuvoir

PONT DE
CHAMPIGNY

RUE DU 11 NOVEMBRE

RUE ROCHAMBEAU

**GARE RER
CHAMPIGNY**

Place
de la Gâre

BOULEVARD DE CHAMPIGNY

AVE. DE LA
FONTAINE

QUAI VICTOR HUGO

RIVER MARNE

Ile du
Martin-Pêcheur

RUE
MARCHAUDON

RUE ROLLAND
FAUCARD

RUE DE LA PLAGE

TO N33 BUS

TO PARIS

Ile du
Martin Pêcheur

0   250 metres

make all the difference. As soon as you cross the bridge, you are instantly drawn into a sense of happy complicity with your neighbours – you are all escapees from the mainland and the rhythm of everyday life. Seated at long tables outside, people of all ages, some with their children, exchange smiles of enjoyment. Everyone is relaxed, savouring the pleasure of the moment, whether they intend to dance or not.

The first time I went, the service was so slow that we had to leave without dancing, to catch the midnight train back to Paris. We were overtaken on the towpath by the young couple from the next table, who insisted on giving all four of us a lift back to Paris in their tiny car, with two of us illegally perched on our partners' knees. It was their first visit too, and we all agreed that we would be going back.

I did go back, on a cold, wet Sunday afternoon in August. All the tables inside were full and it felt like being on a cosy, old-fashioned cruise ship, an impression heightened by the dripping weeping willows and the green water outside. A kingfisher flashed past as the band struck up 'Le P'tit Bal de la Marine', and people started to leave their tables to dance, rather well, to numbers such as 'Be Bop a Lula' and 'Je ne veux pas travailler'. We seemed to be the only foreigners. Charmed, we sat on there, talking, eating, drinking, and occasionally dancing, for five hours, a record even by French standards. If you

Guinguette, *Ile du Martin-Pêcheur*

want to dance, I would add a word of advice, copied from a notice at another guinguette:

> *Adoptez l'esprit guinguette!*
> *Pas de jeans ni baskets!*

(Get into the spirit of the guinguette - no jeans, no trainers!)

¾ km walk from the station to the guinguette

Take the 'Sortie Boulevard de Champigny' exit to the buses outside the station and turn left into the Place de la Gare. Turn right into the Boulevard de Champigny and continue across the bridge, the Pont de Champigny. Take the steps down from the bridge on the left and follow the Quai Victor-Hugo or the towpath for about ten minutes until you see the bridge.

Distance from Paris: 13 km (8 miles)
Depart: Châtelet-les Halles
Arrive: Champigny
Journey time: 20 minutes approx
Length of visit: Half day
Carte Orange Zone: 3
Single ticket: 2.80€
Distance from station to island: ¾ km (½ mile)

Getting there

RER A2 trains to Boissy St Leger, stopping at Champigny St Maur, leave Paris every ten minutes. The last train back is at 12.25 am.

Car: A4 from Porte de Bercy to Joinville, then cross the bridge onto Avenue Gallieni which becomes Avenue Roger Salengro.

Just before the railway viaduct take the Rue de la Plage on the right, then turn left onto the Quai Victor Hugo.

Getting back

The stop for the Noctilien **night bus** N33 is on Avenue Roger Salengro. Take the Rue de la Plage, following the railway line to the third road on the left. Cross to the other side of the Avenue for the bus stop to Paris. It takes 35 minutes to reach the Gare de Lyon. Every hour from 12.44 am.

When to go

A Sunday afternoon in summer is best if you want to experience the *guinguette* at its most traditional. Saturday evenings attract a younger crowd and tend to be so popular that you may have to book several weeks in advance.

NB: You could easily combine a Sunday afternoon at the *guinguette* with a morning stroll and lunch at the Domaine Sainte Catherine in Créteil, two stops away on the same RER line. See p. 87.

Useful information

For more about *guinguettes* in the Paris region, visit www.culture-guinguette.fr

Restaurant/*guinguette*

L'Ile du Martin-Pêcheur, 41 Quai Victor-Hugo, 94500 Champigny, tel 01 49 83 03 02 (restaurant reservation is advisable), www.guinguette.fr. It is the only building on the island. Open May to August for lunch, 12 noon-7 pm on Sunday, noon-5 pm on Saturdays in July and August, and for dinner 8 pm–2 am from Wednesday to Saturday. In winter open on Saturday evening and for Sunday lunch in April and October. Closed January to March.

The music varies from traditional French songs played on the accordion at the tables to live bands on the dance floor playing rock and roll, tango, waltzes, reggae, swing, blues and jazz.

Free admission to the bar/dance floor if you don't want to eat. Two-course *formules* at 20€ and 26€. The traditional *petite friture* is available as well as more standard fare and some imaginative fish dishes. Wine from 15€ a bottle. The food and wine was good value, and the service has greatly improved.

9. Luzarches

**An old town with good country restaurants and walks
and a delightfully provincial atmosphere**

Luzarches is one of my favourite places. Surrounded by good walking country, it has a memorable 12th century church, a medieval gateway, and a choice of restaurants. Best of all, it is accessible in every sense of the word. Although it is at the end of a direct line from Paris, Luzarches is no dormitory suburb but a real community, where the inhabitants, without exception, are friendly and welcoming. It is a town where the shopkeepers will unbar their shutters and open up for you during Sunday lunch.

Set on a hill rising slightly above the Seine and the Oise in the *Pays de France*, Luzarches has had its fair share of excitement. Beseiged in 1102 by the future king of France, Louis VI, liberated from the English by Joan of Arc in 1429, it became the 'chef-lieu du canton' (county town) just before the Revolution, soon after which its abbeys were sold off. In September 1914 it marked the nearest point of the German army's advance on Paris.

The entire town, including the church and the medieval gateway leading off the 12th-century market place, can be comfortably visited in less than two hours, but it would be a pity not to linger in one of the restaurants over Sunday lunch, surrounded by local families enjoying themselves.

Or you can ramble across country to Seugy and take the train back from there or go even further south to Viarmes or Belloy-en-France, the next two villages on the line back to Paris.

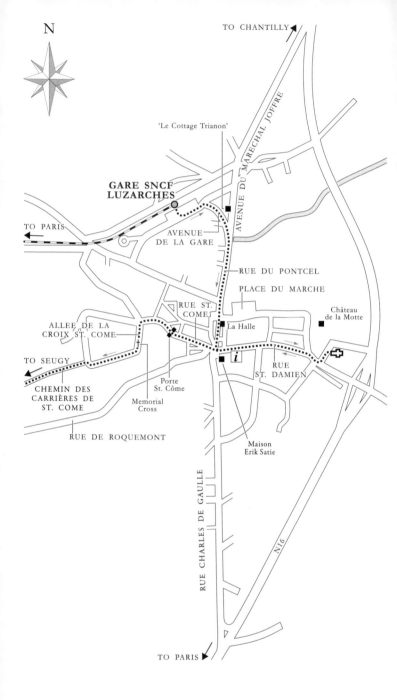

N

TO CHANTILLY

'Le Cottage Trianon'

GARE SNCF
LUZARCHES

AVENUE DU MARÉCHAL JOFFRE

TO PARIS

AVENUE
DE LA GARE

RUE DU PONTCEL

PLACE DU MARCHE

RUE ST.
COME

Château
de la Motte

ALLEE DE LA
CROIX ST. COME

La Halle

TO SEUGY

i

RUE
ST. DAMIEN

CHEMIN DES
CARRIÈRES DE
ST. COME

Porte
St. Côme

Memorial
Cross

RUE DE ROQUEMONT

Maison
Erik Satie

RUE CHARLES DE GAULLE

N16

TO PARIS

Luzarches

0   500 metres

Suggested visit to Luzarches

From the **station** the town straggles uphill along a main street which leads to the market place in the centre. The market building itself, **La Halle** dates from the 12th century and is in the busiest part of the town, with most of the shops and cafés grouped around it.

Just past the Rue St Damien, at no. 17 Rue Charles de Gaulle, is the house of the composer **Erik Satie** (1866–1925) who lived in Luzarches from 1904 until his death. The house is now the public library. Follow the Rue St Damien, past the **Syndicat d'Initiative**, to visit the massive **church** with its 12th-century bell tower and 16th-century façade. It is even more impressive from the back (go round the cemetery behind it). Unusually for the Ile de France, this church seems to be always open. It is dedicated to Saints Cosmas and Damian, two martyred brothers, patron saints of doctors and surgeons, whose relics were brought to Luzarches by the crusader Jean de Beaumont in 1160. There is an interesting medieval statue of the Virgin to the right of the altar, the oldest part of the church.

The imposing building behind a locked iron gateway next to the church is the **Maison Départmentale du Tourisme**, formerly the château de la Motte, also known as the château d'En Bas. It looks interesting but in fact there is not much to see of the original 13th-century château, apart from some ruins in the rather pretty grounds.

On the way back along the Rue St Damien, near the Syndicat d'Initiative, there used to be another little café called La Renaissance. It looked so humble and also, well, *local*, that we only ventured inside because I had developed a blister and had to stop. After some silent sizing up as we sat at the bar (there was no one at the tables) one of the customers eventually pushed a plate of freshly grilled sardines he had brought across the counter to us. I politely ate them all and a plateful of *crevettes grises*, the delicious tiny brown shrimps, followed the sardines. The chemist had just closed and I will never forget the matter-of-fact way in which the *patronne* produced a plaster from behind the counter when I hesitantly asked if she had such a

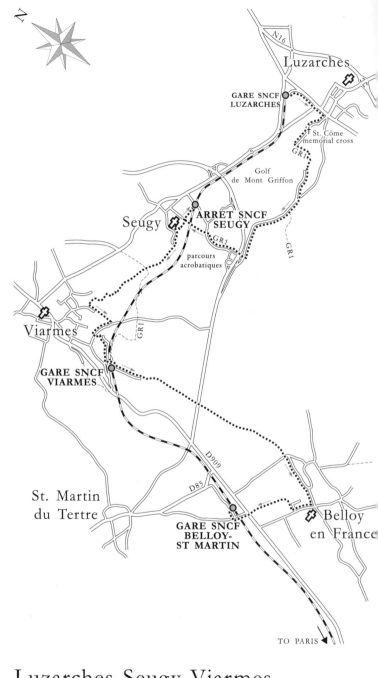

Luzarches-Seugy-Viarmes
-Belloy en France

thing. Alas, the café has now become become a cocktail bar, Au Bout du Monde, evidently considered more of a crowd-puller, even in Luzarches.

As for traditional French restaurants, the choice is between the **St Côme** near the market place or the more distant and more upmarket **Cottage Trianon** near the station. Both establishments have changed hands since the first edition of this book. I have revisited the St Côme and can report that the *petit salé* was generous and well-made. The Trianon was more expensive but had some imaginative dishes, such as a *demi pigeonneau* (half a roast pigeon).

Opposite the Rue St Damien, the Rue St Côme climbs gently uphill, framed by the **Porte de St Côme** at the top. This medieval gateway is all that is left of the former ramparts, but through the gateway on the right there are some fascinating little alleys descending to the town below, skirting thick stone walls that must date from the same period. The large entrance on the left is to the château d'En Haut, which can be neither seen nor visited, but there is a good hilltop view from here, before turning left into the pretty green Allée de la Croix St Côme. It skirts the garden walls of the château and leads to a **memorial cross** to Saints Cosmas and Damian, put up in 1874. It is a good place for a picnic.

3 km walk from Luzarches to Seugy

If you feel like rounding off your visit with an exploration of the surrounding countryside, the shortest and prettiest walk is to the village of Seugy, the next station on the line back to Paris.

From the **memorial cross** to St Côme take the GR footpath (see p. 239). Follow the Chemin des Martyrs downhill, which becomes the Chemin des Carrières de St Côme, cross the Rue de Roquemont and turn right, ignoring the GR, which turns left further on. Follow the road for half a mile until you see a roundabout ahead and the Restaurant de Mont-Griffon on your left. At the pedestrian crossing there is a little sign, 'Golf restaurant', at a slip road on the right which leads to an underpass. Take the underpass. You will see the GR sign on your left as you emerge, with the Mont-Griffon golf course on your right. Follow the GR past a sign on the left for *parcours acrobatiques dans les arbres* (glorified tree climbing for adults) keeping the golf course on your right and then follow the GR footpath downhill on your left, across the railway line into Seugy, coming out into the pretty Ruelle du Four leading to the **church** and the **café**. There is a short cut from the church to the **station**. See map of Seugy, described in the visit to Royaumont, on p. 180.

2¼ km walk from Seugy to Viarmes

You are unlikely to meet a soul on this walk along a neglected old road across the fields, in which you can experience how people reached the next village before the coming of the car transformed the local landscape.

Take the Chemin de la Madeleine south of the church at Seugy, past a *lavoir* (wash house). Continue straight on through the fields at the crossroads, ignoring the GR signs telling you to go left, and after about 15 minutes you will come out into the Chemin de la Fontaine aux Moines leading into Viarmes. For the **station**, which is at the top of a very steep hill, continue along the Chemin de la Fontaine, turn left into the Ruelle de la Chaumette, then left into the Ruelle de la Douaire and left again into Rue de la Nourrie. I have found Viarmes itself of little interest, apart from a now almost illegible notice on the wall of the 12th-century church of St Peter and Paul, 'Défense d'uriner'.

3 km walk from Viarmes to Belloy-en-France

There is a café in Belloy but unfortunately it is not open on Sunday and the walk is not particularly remarkable. However, if you want to prolong your walk, Belloy itself is something of a curiosity, a real Sleepy Hollow on the railway line to Paris.

Turn right outside Viarmes **station** and take the first right to cross the railway line. Turn right along the Rue des Reservoirs. When you come to two concrete circular reservoirs take the

Renaissance porch,
Belloy-en-France

grassy path on the left (unmarked) which continues alongside a field, then across a country road and more fields. You will see the church spire of Belloy on your right. When you come out on to the road go straight across into the Rue des Carreaux, which leads to Rue Faubert and the church, the **Eglise St Georges**.

It has a remarkable Renaissance porch to the left of the main entrance. Look for the fire-breathing salamander carved on the façade, the emblem of François I. The church is usually locked, but is open on Sunday afternoons in May and June for guided visits and the *curé*, who lives opposite, can be wheedled into opening up at other times. On the wall to the left of the altar there is an unusual stone sculpture of a man's head, with three faces looking in different directions, which may represent the Trinity. The church dates from the 12th century and its foundations conceal an earlier one, traces of which came to light when pipes were being laid for the central heating. But, the *curé* told us, the finds were quickly sealed up before the historical experts in Paris could get wind of it. Otherwise, he added conspiratorially, they would no doubt still be waiting for the central heating.

There is a short cut via Rue du General Leclerc and the Avenue de Carmen which crosses a field and then the D909 to the **station** at Belloy St Martin.

Distance from Paris: 32 km
(20 miles)
Depart: Gare du Nord
Arrive: Luzarches
Journey time: 48 minutes or less
Length of visit: Half or full day
Alternative return from: Seugy,
Viarmes or Belloy St Martin
Carte Orange Zone: 5
Single ticket: 4.80€
**Distance from Luzarches to
Seugy:** 3 km (2 miles)
**Distance from Seugy to
Viarmes:** 2¼ km (1½ miles)
**Distance from Viarmes to Bel-
loy-en-France:** 3 km (2 miles)
Pop.: 3,940

Getting there

SNCF trains to Luzarches (terminus), calling first at Belloy St
Martin, Viarmes and Seugy, leave
the Gare du Nord (*Ile de France*)
once or twice an hour on weekdays, once an hour at weekends
and make the return journey every
hour up to approximately 11.30
pm.

Car: N16 (Chantilly).

IGN maps: 2412 OT for
Luzarches, Seugy and Viarmes,
2313 OT for Viarmes and Belloy-
en-France.

When to go

Sunday is the best day if you want
to see inside the church and enjoy
the relaxed atmosphere of a small
French town on Sunday morning. Everyone seems to be either
shopping, in a café or in church,

and they are all looking forward
to lunch. The church and the shops
generally stay open until 1 pm. If
you go on a weekday, there is a
market on Wednesday and Friday
mornings, the bigger one being
on Friday.

Useful information

Syndicat d'Initiative, 6 Rue St
Damien, 95270 Luzarches, tel
01 34 09 98 48, www.tourisme-
luzarches.org. Open 10.30 am–12
noon Friday, Saturday and Sunday
3–5 pm Saturday. An exceptionally well-stocked and helpful office.

Maison du Tourisme, Château
de la Motte, Rue François de
Ganay, 95270 Luzarches, tel 01 30
29 51 00, www.val-doise-tourisme.
com. Open 9 am–12.30 pm and
1.30–5.30 pm on weekdays, (4.30
pm on Friday). It has general information on the Oise region.

Restaurants

Le Cottage Trianon, 5 Avenue
du Maréchal Joffre, tel 01 34 71 09
29. Closed Sunday evening and on
Monday. Weekday menu 12.50€,
à la carte at weekends. Main dishes
from around 15€, wine from 14€
a bottle. Traditional cooking. The
only restaurant in Luzarches where
you can eat outside, in a pretty
wisteria-framed courtyard.

Le Saint-Côme, 26 Rue du
Cygne, tel 01 34 71 04 63. Closed
on Mondays, Sunday evening and
on Tuesday evening in winter.
Weekday menus 12.50€, 16.50€,

22€ and 30€ and à la carte at weekends. Half-litre carafe of wine 6€. Centrally located, popular restaurant with a delightfully old-fashioned atmosphere.

Cafés

Luzarches

There are several friendly cafés near the market, open on Sunday.

Seugy

Le Rendezvous des Chasseurs, Rue de la Fontaine. Closed on Tuesday. Described in visit to Royaumont on p. 181. One of the few traditional cafés in the Ile de France that seems to be flourishing, having expanded into larger premises since my last visit.

Viarmes

Auberge de la Gare, 2 Place de la Gare, tel 01 30 35 48 79. A friendly family-run establishment with a garden, next to the station. Opening hours variable but always *looks* closed. Ring the doorbell. Specialises in couscous and does generous *merguez* sandwiches to take away. *Merguez* are spicy sausages, a typical ingredient in North African couscous dishes.

11. Montfort-l'Amaury

Home to the composer Ravel and other artists, the picturesque little town of Montfort conceals a dramatic and violent past which encapsulates the history of the Ile de France

Montfort is one of those well-kept medieval towns that seem too good to be true. Its narrow streets of picturesque houses are built on the slopes of a citadel crowned by the ruined walls of a castle and encircled by the remnants of medieval ramparts. A stately church dominates the town centre, its clock chiming the quarters, and the shops cater for residents with leisure and taste.

Many of them are Parisians who own second homes in and around Montfort. Perhaps the best-known resident was the composer Maurice Ravel, whose house has been turned into an eerie museum, preserved exactly as it was when he died in 1937. Colette, with whom he collaborated on *L'Enfant et les Sortilèges* in 1925, had a house in nearby Méré. A later resident, the film director Henri Georges Clouzot, made Montfort the setting for two of his films, and until quite recently the Auberge de la Moutière restaurant was a favourite venue for fashionable Parisians.

But there is more to Montfort than its picture-postcard charm and its artistic residents. I originally went there to see Ravel's house, but it was the mystery of the citadel and the ramparts which drew me back. The more I found out about the town's past, the more I realised that it is the story in miniature of the Ile de France and the role it has played in the shaping of modern France.

History of Montfort

It is a story of violence, constant adaptation and triumphant continuity; and it begins with the Roman road from Beauvais to Chartres, which crosses the town from north to south before entering the Forest of Rambouillet. The hill overlooking this strategic route was fortified in 996 on the orders of Robert the Pious, son of Hugues Capet, the first king of France. The village became a fortress (*Mont Fort*) with a castle surrounded by ramparts, its defence entrusted to the descendants of the builder, who became Counts of Montfort.

Amaury, the first of these, gave the town its name, and founded a dynasty which included Simon IV de Montfort (1165–1218), notorious for his brutal leadership of the Albigensian Crusade against the Cathars in the South of France. His defeat of the heretics enabled Louis VIII to add the Earldom of Toulouse to the expanding kingdom of France. His son, Simon V de Montfort (1192–1265) married the sister of Henry III of England and is credited with the founding of the first English parliament in opposition to his brother-in-law. The 700th anniversary of this event was celebrated in Montfort with great pomp in 1965. In fact, the history of the rulers of Montfort is so entangled with the fortunes of the Capetian kings of France and the Plantagenets of England that it is difficult to separate them. What does emerge is the fragility of the French kingdom, constantly threatened by unruly vassals and

Ravel's house, Montfort-l'Amaury

with invasion by the English, themselves descendants of a powerful neighbour, William of Normandy.

As the Plantagenets were linked by marriage to the Mont-fort family, both the king of England and the king of France laid claim to Montfort in the 14th century and a lengthy war ensued, during which the castle and most of the ramparts were razed by the English. Two fragments of the castle walls ('Les Tours') are all that remain. Through an earlier connection by marriage with the rulers of Brittany, Montfort eventually passed to Anne de Bretagne (1477–1514), whose subsequent marriages to two French kings definitively established the town as part of the kingdom of France.

The ruined stone and brick tower on the hilltop was part of the Renaissance château built by Anne de Bretagne, who also began the enlargement of the 11th-century church. A second set of ramparts was built in the 16th century at the instigation of Charles IX, who promised the town a charter of independence in return. It became an important administrative centre for the region, which included the Forest of Montfort (it became Rambouillet under Napoleon I) and the little village of Versailles.

However, the expansion of Versailles under Louis XIV led to a decline in the importance of Montfort, which passed to the Duc de Luynes. During the Revolution the 11th-century chapel on the hill was requisitioned from the magistrate to whom it had been sold off, for use as a prison for the Chouans – participants in the counter-revolutionary uprising led by Jean Chouan in the Vendée from 1793 to 1800. They died there of starvation in conditions so atrocious that the owner had it demolished after the fall of Robespierre in 1794, so that such scenes could never be repeated in Montfort. Under Napoleon the administration of the district was transferred to Rambouil-let and Montfort suffered the further indignity of occupation after the French defeat at Waterloo in 1815. The occupation was presumably by the Prussians – the local history is understand-ably vague on this point.

In the 19th century the 16th-century ramparts were demol-ished, in the mistaken belief that the population would continue to expand. Montfort's popularity with artists and writers dates from this period, Victor Hugo's Romantic poem to its ruined castle setting the fashion, which has continued to the present day:

Je vous aime, ô débris!   Et surtout quand l'automne
Prolonge en vos échos sa plainte monotone.
Sous vos abris coulants je voudrais habiter,
Vielles tours, que le temps l'une vers l'autre incline,
Et qui semblez de loin sur la haute colline,
Deux noirs géants prêts à lutter.

(I love you, oh ruins!   And most of all, when autumn
Prolongs in your echoes its monotonous lament.
I would like to live in your crumbling shelter,
Old towers, which time has inclined towards each other,
And which seem from afar on the high hill,
Two dark giants, ready to fight.)

Victor Hugo, *Ode aux ruines*, 1825 (My translation)

Suggested tour of Montfort-l'Amaury

You can phone for a taxi from the **station** or turn left to cross under the N12 to walk for three kilometres along the D76, the straight tree-lined Roman road to Montfort, which eventually becomes the Avenue General de Gaulle and then the Rue de Paris. You will pass several large houses on the way, the elegant modern houses gradually giving way to elegant 17th-century houses as you near the town. There is a restaurant, which I have not tried, called Chez Nous at 22 Rue de Paris, recommended by Michelin and the tourist office.

Turn left into the Rue Normande to reach the **Place Robert Brault**, formerly the Place Royale, and the centre of Montfort. Partly bordered by the remains of the medieval ramparts overhead, this largely traffic-free little *place* was, and still is, a communal meeting place, where the Marché aux Femmes – a hiring fair for servant girls – was held in the 19th century. It is the best place in which to linger for a drink or for lunch, either

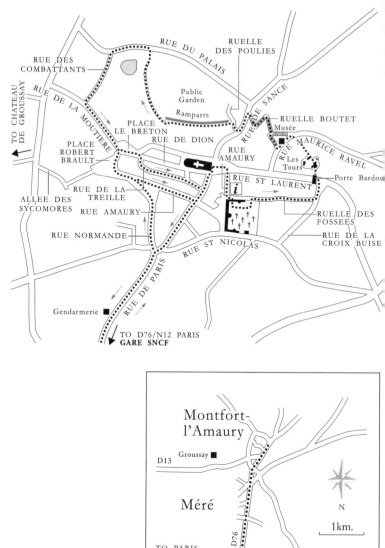

RUE DU PALAIS

RUELLE DES POULIES

RUE DES COMBATTANTS

RUE DE LA MOUTIÈRE

TO CHATEAU DE GROUSSAY

Public Garden

Ramparts

RUELLE SANCE

RUELLE BOUTET

Musée

RUE MAURICE RAVEL

PLACE LE BRETON

RUE DE DION

PLACE ROBERT BRAULT

RUE AMAURY

Les Tours

Porte Bardou

RUE ST LAURENT

ALLÉE DES SYCOMORES

RUE DE LA TREILLE

RUE AMAURY

RUELLE DES FOSSEES

RUE NORMANDE

RUE ST NICOLAS

RUE DE LA CROIX BUISE

RUE DE PARIS

Gendarmerie

TO D76/N12 PARIS
GARE SNCF

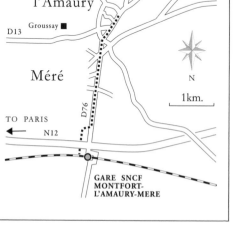

Montfort-l'Amaury

D13 Groussay

Méré

D76

TO PARIS
N12

N

1km.

GARE SNCF
MONTFORT-L'AMAURY-MERE

N

Montfort-l'Amaury

0   200 metres

at the long-established **Café de la Poste** or at the restaurant next door. Both have tables outside, overlooking tree-shaded benches where a few locals quietly gossip. The soothing provincial atmosphere makes it hard to believe that this was also once the place where public executions were carried out, Montfort being the county town up to the time of Napoleon.

Take the Rue Amaury to rejoin the Rue de Paris which leads to the imposing **Eglise de St Pierre et St Paul**. Although it was founded in the 11th century, most of it was built in the late 15th century at the initiative of Anne de Bretagne with some later additions, and both the late medieval and early Renaissance styles are represented in the vaulting and stained glass of the interior and the flying buttresses and gargoyles of the exterior. Light and spacious inside, it looks like a miniature cathedral.

From the Place de la Libération in front of the church, turn right into the Rue Amaury to find the helpful **Office de Tourisme**. Ask for the *Randonnée Culturelle*, a free map of the town which shows every building of historical interest. The English translation is rather quaint, so it is worth taking the French one too. If you are interested in ending your visit with a short walk to a beautiful park and lake, ask for the leaflet on the nearby Château de Groussay. They will show you on the map how to get there and from there back to the station.

The Office de Tourisme is situated right opposite the unusual walled and arcaded **cemetery** which actually looks like a cloister. It was constructed in the 16th and 17th centuries, when the original cemetery next to the church became too small for the expanding population. It is entered through a Renaissance doorway with an inscription which reads:

> Vous qui ici passez,
> Priez Dieu pour les trépassez,
> Ce que vous êtes, ils ont étez
> Ce que sont, un jour serez.

> (You who pass by
> Pray for those who have passed away.
> What you are, they have been,
> What they are, you will be.)

In the modern upper part of the cemetery some of the graves bear a notice which is more amusingly typical of present-day France, addressed to those families who have not kept up their grave-plot payments:

Le propriétaire de cette concession
est prié de se présenter
d'urgence en mairie.

CONCESSION EXPIREE

(The owner of this concession
is requested to go
immediately to the town hall.

CONCESSION EXPIRED)

From the cemetery turn right into the Ruelle des Fossés, left into the Rue de la Croix Buisée and look left for an impressive view of the church and the town at the foot of the hill, framed in the stone arch of a ruined gateway, the **Porte Bardoul**. It was the gateway to the château in the 16th century and the entire hilltop site is now a public **park**. Beside the gateway steps lead to a twisting path to the top of the hill, past the demolished chapel, up to the two fragments of wall romantically covered with ivy known as **Les Tours**. They are all that remain of the 11th-century castle keep, demolished by the English in the 14th century. The stone and brick turret with Renaissance carving next to them is known as the **Tour d'Anne de Bretagne**, the sole remnant of the 15th-century château. There is a splendid **view** of the church, the town and the surrounding countryside from here, 182 metres above sea-level.

Steps leading down from the hill will bring you to the little **Musée Maurice Ravel** on the left in the street named after him. Ravel was born in 1875 and lived here from 1921 to his death in 1937. He remodelled the house, which he called the 'Belvedere', until it fitted his requirements perfectly, making some of the rooms even smaller and decorating them himself. They are filled with little toys and objects that appealed to his imagination and the total effect is of entering a private universe, playful and rather self-consciously 'artistic'. Admirers of the famous *Bolero*, which he composed here in 1928, will be intrigued to discover that it was actually inspired by a visit to a factory.

From Ravel's house take the steps down the tiny Ruelle Boutet leading to the Rue de Sancé, the continuation of the original Roman road through the town. The house of the playwright Jean Anouilh (1910–1987) is at no. 9, where his niece still lives. Turn right into the Ruelle des Poulies, the

Tour d'Anne de Bretagne, Monfort-l'Amaury

local name for the medieval **ramparts**, which are below Anouilh's house on the left of the public garden. They are entered through a massive stone archway and the ten-minute narrow walk surrounded by huge walls on either side, with not a soul in sight, gave me the uncanny feeling that I had stepped straight back into the 11th century.

Follow the Rue des Combattants and turn left into the Rue de la Moutière. No. 8 was formerly the Auberge de la Moutière run by the owner of Maxim's in Paris from 1947 to 1975, attracting the fashionable world to Montfort. The Rue de la Moutière leads back into the Place Robert Brault. If you have time, I strongly recommend the walk of just over a kilometre to the **Château de Groussay**, which has only recently been opened to the public. Start north-east of the Place, then take the Allée des Sycomores and cross the main road into the Ruelle des Prés, a pretty woodland path which skirts the château walls until you come to the entrance.

The château itself, which dates from 1815, can only be visited

Montfort: view through the Porte Bardoul

by groups, but the park *à l'anglaise* is worth the entrance fee for the tranquillity of the light reflected in the lake, the enormous carp and the harebells and wild thyme dotting the grass. The rather kitsch *fabriques* (follies) – a Chinese pagoda, a Palladian bridge, a Temple of Love and so on – actually enhance its appeal. It was a favourite of Cecil Beaton's, who often stayed there.

It is about four kilometres (two and a half miles) from the château to the station at Montfort, following the Rue Roger Vannier which becomes the Rue St Blaise, to rejoin the Avenue du Général de Gaulle.

If you decide to stay in Montfort, three little medieval streets with timbered houses – Rue Petau de Maulette, Rue de Dion and Rue de la Treille – lead from the Rue de la Moutière back to the Rue de Paris. The most interesting-looking house, at **no. 9 Rue de la Treille**, is where Victor Hugo stayed and wrote his ode to the castle ruins.

From the Rue de la Treille turn right into the Rue de Paris for the walk back to the **station**. If you wait for the tourist office to close, the kindly staff have been known to give lifts to visitors, but this is strictly outside their official duties.

Distance from Paris: 40 km (25 miles)
Depart: Gare de Montparnasse
Arrive: Montfort-l'Amaury-Méré
Journey time: 40 minutes
Length of visit: Half or full day
Carte Orange Zone: 6
Single ticket: 6.70€
Distance from station to Montfort: 3 km (1¾ miles)
Distance from Montfort to Château de Groussay: 1 km (½ mile)
Distance from château to station: 4 km (2½ miles)
Pop.: 2,800

Getting there

SNCF trains to Houdan or Dreux, stopping at Montfort-l'Amaury-Méré, leave Gare de Montparnasse (*Ile de France*) four times in the morning on weekdays, once on Saturday and twice on Sunday. Note that some *Grandes Lignes* trains to Dreux from Montparnasse stop at Montfort. The last train back to Paris is at approximately 10 pm on Sundays and at around 8.30 pm the rest of the week.

Taxi from the station to Montfort: tel 01 34 86 08 80 or 01 34 86 89 75.

Car: Autoroute A13, then A12 and N12 (Dreux).

When to go

To make the most of your visit, go towards the end of the week, as Maurice Ravel's house is closed on Monday and Tuesday. Good weather is preferable for this largely outdoor visit.

Useful information

Office de Tourisme, 6 Rue Amaury, 78490 Montfort-l'Amaury, tel 01 34 86 87 96, email: tourisme@ ville-montfort-l-amaury.fr. Open 10 am–12 noon and 2–6 pm daily and on public holidays except 25 December and 1 January.

Musée Maurice Ravel, 5 Rue Maurice Ravel, tel 01 34 86 00 89. Reservation necessary. Open 2.30–6 pm in summer, 2.30–5 pm in winter, from Wednesday to Friday and also in the mornings at weekends and on public holidays except 25 December and 1 January for guided visits. Guided visits (in French) start at 10 am, 11 am, 2.30 pm, 3.30 pm, 4.30 pm and 5.30 pm, for a maximum of seven visitors at a time. Admission 7.30€, 3.70€ for visitors aged under 18.

Château de Groussay, tel 01 34 86 94 79. Open 1 April–30 October, 10 am–7 pm from Wednesday to Sunday, including public holidays. Admission to the park 6€, 15€ for group visits to the château and park.

Cafés and restaurants

Café de la Poste. 16 Place Robert Brault, tel 01 34 86 01 93. Closed on Wednesday. Generous *plats du jour*, around 12€.

La Treille, 16 Place Robert Brault (no connection with the café), tel 01 34 84 31 52. Closed Sunday evening. *Plats* 14-25€, more upmarket than the Café de la Poste next door.

11. Montmorency

The quiet little house and garden in which Rousseau produced his most famous work

Montmorency, as its name suggests, is built on a hill; it is 130 metres (426 feet) above sea-level. From the 11th to the 17th century it was the seat of the Montmorency family, who built the church with its spectacular view over the Seine valley in the 16th century. Its sloping narrow streets and wide boulevards are mainly residential, rarely visited by foreigners, and its medieval market place still has an almost provincial atmosphere.

However, the real interest of a visit to Montmorency is the house of Jean-Jacques Rousseau, which has been sensitively restored and is now the Museé Rousseau. Perhaps because it is so close to Paris, it tends to be overlooked by visitors and you are likely to have the place to yourself. If you are a Rousseau fan, the contrast between the domestic peace of the little house and garden and the revolutionary consequences of the books that Rousseau wrote here makes it well worth the journey.

The town itself began as a hill fort on a site overlooking the rich *Plaine de France,* which had been inhabited well before the Neolithic period. From the early 11th century its strategic importance was defended by a family of barons with a chequered history of loyalty to the French crown, who took the name of Montmorency. They produced six Constables of France, twelve marshals and four admirals, the most famous being Constable Anne, Duke of Montmorency (1492–1567) who built the châteaux of Ecouen and Chantilly. His descendants preferred these châteaux to the hilltop fortress of their ancestors, which eventually fell into ruin along with the 12th-century fortifications of the town, their destruction helped along by invasions by the English in the 14th century and massacres during the Wars of Religion in the 16th. In the 19th century a

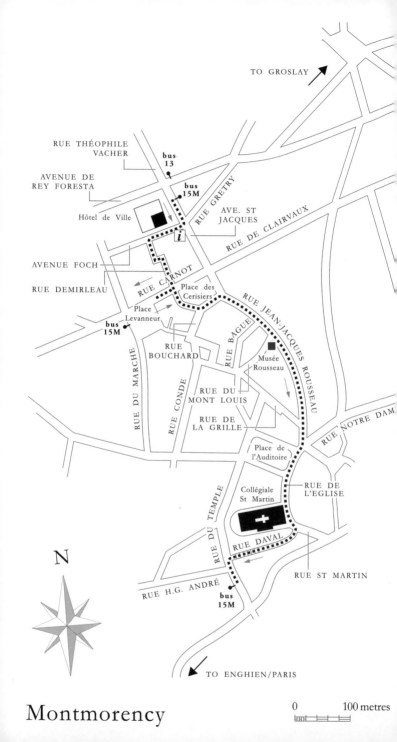

TO GROSLAY

RUE THÉOPHILE VACHER

bus 13

bus 15M

AVENUE DE REY FORESTA

RUE GRÉTRY

AVE. ST JACQUES

Hôtel de Ville

RUE DE CLAIRVAUX

AVENUE FOCH

RUE CARNOT

RUE DEMIRLEAU

Place des Cerisiers

RUE JEAN-JACQUES ROUSSEAU

Place Levanneur

bus 15M

RUE BAGUE

RUE BOUCHARD

Musée Rousseau

RUE DU MARCHE

RUE CONDE

RUE DU MONT LOUIS

RUE DE LA GRILLE

RUE NOTRE DAM

Place de l'Auditoire

RUE DE L'EGLISE

RUE DU TEMPLE

Collégiale St Martin

RUE DAVAL

RUE ST MARTIN

RUE H.G. ANDRÉ

bus 15M

N

TO ENGHIEN/PARIS

Montmorency

0   100 metres

mass grave of victims of the massacre of 1589 was discovered in the market place.

By the 17th century the Montmorency line had come to an end with the execution of Henri II de Montmorency in 1632 for plotting against Richelieu, and the town began to take on its present character as a favoured residential site, conveniently close to Paris. Charles Le Brun, the painter chosen by Louis XIV to decorate Versailles, built an elegant house here in 1673 (no longer standing) and by the 18th century Montmorency had become home to a fashionable society of writers, artists and wealthy patrons.

Rousseau first came to live here in 1756 at L'Ermitage (no longer standing), a house built for him by Madame d'Epinay, but he proved a difficult guest and in 1757 moved to Montlouis, the house which is the present museum. The publication of *L'Emile*, his startlingly original treatise on education, was followed by an order for the author's arrest. His great patron, the Maréchal de Luxembourg, helped him to escape Montmorency during the night of 8 June 1762, never to return there. He fled to Switzerland, only returning to France in 1767.

The town continued to attract wealthy Parisians and the railway line serving Enghien-les-Bains, a fashionable spa, was extended to Montmorency in 1866, attracting even more residents and visitors. If only it still existed! Its closure in 1954 has contributed to the town's preservation as a bourgeois residential enclave, innocent of new commercial or industrial buildings. It has also preserved the village-like charm of the market place. Because of its isolation on a hill, Montmorency doesn't get many tourists, although the bus service from Enghien has greatly improved since the first edition of this book.

Suggested visit to Montmorency

From the 15M *Mairie* bus stop in the Rue Théophile Vacher, continue in the same direction as the bus towards the **Office de Tourisme**, on the corner of Avenue Foch. Go along Avenue Foch, past the Hotel de Ville in the park on your right, turn left into the Rue Dr Demirleau and then right into the Rue Carnot, which will take you to the the former Place du Marché (market place) now known as **Place Roger Levanneur**, the heart of the town. The market itself is small and extremely attractive. I haven't been able to resist buying certain varieties of peaches and apples here that I rarely see in central Paris. It is an ideal place in which to stop at a café for an aperitif and watch the leisurely, good-humoured shoppers from a table outside.

The **Museé Jean-Jacques Rousseau** opens at 2 pm, giving you plenty of time to get there. Return to the Rue Carnot and turn right into the Rue Dr Demirleau, leading to the Place des Cerisiers (Montmorency used to be famous for its cherry trees). Cross the Place diagonally and turn right downhill into the Rue Jean-Jacques Rousseau. The museum is just past the Rue Bague on your right.

The modest two-storey house, which Rousseau rented from 1757 to 1762, appears to the visitor very much as it did to Rousseau. The **garden** is of particular interest, having been reorganised by the philosopher so that he could work there. The hexagonal table and the stone bench on the upper level were installed at his request and he turned the little annexe at the very end of the path into his study, naming it the 'Donjon' (castle keep). Containing only a stone fireplace and two tables and completely isolated from the house, it is a writer's dream cell. It was here that he wrote *La Nouvelle Héloise*, *Le Contrat Social* and *L'Emile*. The *toilettes* are placed discreetly next to it, a pleasing touch.

The **house** itself consists of only three small rooms and the furniture Rousseau left to Thérèse Levasseur, the laundry-maid who eventually became his wife in 1768. The tiny kitchen, complete with a table laid for two, is next to her bedroom on the ground floor, with wooden stairs leading to Rousseau's bedroom (and the alcove containing his *commode*) on the floor above. The house did not extend beyond this room in Rousseau's time, and the smaller window looked out on to a view of Paris, now blocked by a 19th-century building. It feels as if you have stepped into the 18th century to intrude into Rousseau's private life. Understandably, all visitors must be

Rousseau's 'Donjon'

accompanied by a member of the museum staff, one of whom speaks English.

On leaving the museum continue downhill along the Rue Jean-Jacques Rousseau, from where you can sometimes see the Eiffel Tower 15 kilometres away. The street leads into Rue Notre Dame and the Place de l'Auditoire, downhill on your right. The 18th-century *auditoire* (courtroom) building is surmounted by a clock. The ruins of the old ramparts of the town are a steep climb just behind this building, should you be feeling energetic.

Rue Notre Dame continues into Rue de l'Eglise, which leads to the **Collégiale St Martin**, the church built by the Montmorencys between 1520 and 1563 as a family mausoleum, perhaps the largest funerary chapel ever built. If it is locked, ask at the presbytery opposite for the key. Most of the tombs were destroyed during the Revolution; those of Constable Anne and his wife were saved and are now in the Louvre. The stained glass windows, notably those nearest the altar which date from the Renaissance, represent the family in contemporary costume at the height of its power and fame.

On no account leave the church without going round to the back and seeing the magnificent **view** over the Seine valley. The doors at the back are sometimes open on to this view, which gives you the impression that the church is perched over a sheer drop. A sunny late afternoon, or better still, sunset, would be the ideal time.

Take the narrow path to the right behind the church, opposite the Rue St Martin with a bollard in the centre, which leads sharply downhill, ending in steps which will bring you on to the Rue du Temple. The 15M bus stop for Enghien is a few yards further downhill. I cannot resist adding that I managed to just miss this bus and after waiting for ten minutes, gave up and set off in the rain along the tedious road that goes all the way to Enghien. Another, quite unscheduled, bus came roaring past and to my amazement stopped for me without being asked. I was back in Paris 20 minutes later.

Distance from Paris: 15 km (9 miles)
Depart: Gare du Nord
Arrive: Enghien-les-Bains
Journey time: 15 minutes
Length of visit: Half day
Carte Orange Zone: 4
Single ticket: 2.80€
Distance from Enghien-les-Bains to Montmorency: 2 km (1¼ miles)
Pop.: 21,000

Getting there

SNCF trains to Persan-Beaumont via Valmondais or to Pontoise, stopping at Enghien-les-Bains, leave Gare du Nord (*Ile de France*) every 15 minutes, returning up to about midnight.

From Enghien station, Paris trains connect with **bus** no. 15M to Montmorency (*Mairie* stop) which operates every half hour, returning up to about 8 pm and takes around 12 minutes to get you to within a few yards of the tourist office. On Sundays it is replaced by the Ligne Verte. The no. 13 bus will also take you to Montmorency from Enghien station (get off at the *Rey de Foresta* stop) but the service is less frequent. You can use a Paris Métro ticket on these buses.

On leaving the train, walk towards the first carriage to find the underpass exit ('sortie Gare Routière') for the buses on the other side of the station. For the return journey, take the 15M from the market place (*Place Levanneur* stop), near the Disque Bleu café) or near the church (*Luxembourg* stop). The timetable is posted at the bus stops.

Taxi from Enghien to Montmorency, around 15€, tel 01 39 64 04 45.

Car: A1 via Porte de la Chapelle, exit Beauvais.

When to go

As the main attraction of Montmorency is the Jean-Jacques Rousseau Museum you could go at any season of the year, avoiding Mondays when the museum is closed. It is worth timing the trip to begin with a visit to the little market, which is held on Wednesday and Sunday mornings up to around 1 pm.

Useful information

Office de Tourisme, 1 Avenue Foch, 95160 Montmorency, tel 01 39 64 42 94. Open all year 8.30 am–12.30 pm and 2–5 pm, Tuesday to Friday, 8.30 am–noon and 2–4.30 pm on Saturday and 9.45 am–12.45 pm on Sundays in the summer.

Musée Jean-Jacques Rousseau, 5 Rue Jean-Jacques Rousseau, tel 01 39 64 80 13. Open all year Tuesday to Sunday 2–6 pm. Closed on Mondays, 1 May, and from 25 December to the first week in January. Guided visit of approximately ¾ hour. Admission 4€ adults, 2€ if aged 13–25, children under 13 free.

Restaurants

Le Disque Bleu, 8 Place Roger Levanneur, tel 01 39 64 95 28. Open to 8 pm every day except Thursday, and Sunday when it closes at around 2 pm. Lunch up to around 2.30 pm except Sunday, when you can get a sandwich. A modest, friendly *café-brasserie* overlooking the market place. *Plats du jour* around 9€.

Al Vicolo, 5 Rue Carnot, tel 01 39 89 15 30. Closed Sunday evening and on Tuesdays. *Plats du jour* around 12€. I have not tried this relatively new Italian restaurant in a little street off the market place, but it looks attractive.

12. Moret-sur-Loing

An inspiration to Impressionist painters,
the old border town of Moret is guarded by its fortified
bridge across the River Loing. A peaceful riverside walk
leads to the 11th-century port of St Mammès

> Moret was in those days an old-fashioned town of
> one street at the edge of the Forest of
> Fontainebleau... [Philip and his friends] spent all
> day painting. Like most of their generation they
> were obsessed by the fear of the picturesque, and
> they turned their backs on the obvious beauty of
> the town to seek subjects which were devoid of a
> prettiness they despised.
>
> Somerset Maugham,
> *Of Human Bondage*, 1915

In choosing Moret for an inexpensive holiday from Paris, the
art student Philip Carey, Maugham's autobiographical hero, was
following in the steps of the Impressionists: Pissarro, Monet and
above all, the English painter Alfred Sisley (1839–1899). Sisley
spent the last years of his life in Moret, fascinated by the changing light which he captured in paintings of the old bridge with
its fortified gateway, the river Loing and the poplar-bordered
canal.

The magical quality of the light has not changed and nor
has the old part of the town, which still consists of one main
street entered at each end through a medieval gateway. The tiny
town overlooking the river was originally encircled by ramparts
and only accessible through its two gates. These precautions
were necessary, because Moret was a border town in the 11th
century, part of the kingdom of France which it protected
from the neighbouring rulers of Champagne, until the marriage

St Mammès

of Philippe le Bel to Jeanne de Navarre in 1284 put an end to the threat.

You could spend a pleasant afternoon exploring the old part of the town around the bridge made famous by Sisley, perhaps venturing across the river to glimpse the house where the French statesman Georges Clemenceau (1841-1929) spent his retirement, and returning to Paris the same way you came.

However, if you share Philip Carey's horror of the obvious, you can make a short but little-used detour along the towpath of the river Loing to its confluence with the Seine. There you will discover the 11th-century river port of St Mammès, also painted by Sisley, but only well-known to boatmen. On the way, you can lunch in a riverside restaurant where the décor, the quality of the food and the prices seem unchanged from the 1950s, and then relax on a three-hour cruise along the Seine beside the Forest of Fontainebleau, returning to St Mammès to catch the train. As very few visitors seem to know about the existence of this station, your detour will bring you into contact with local people who treat you with a warmth you can only dream of in Paris.

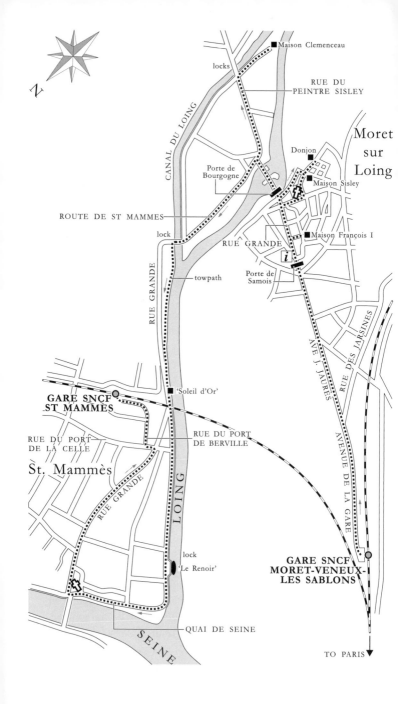

Moret-sur-Loing

Suggested visit to Moret

On leaving the **station** a two-kilometre walk along the Avenue Jean Jaurès will take you to the **Porte de Samois**, the medieval gateway to Moret. You are now in the Rue Grande, with the **tourist office** on your left. Further along on your right, a plaque at no. 24 commemorates the house where Napoleon spent part of the night of 19 March 1815 on his way back from Elba. Turn right through the porch of the *Mairie* into a small courtyard, where you will find an impressive Renaissance façade on the left, the **Maison de François Premier**, so called because his emblem, the salamander, is carved over the door.

Continue along the Rue Grande and through the **Porte de Bourgogne**, the second gateway, which is still part of the town's medieval fortifications. It leads to the bridge over the peaceful River Loing, overlooking two old mill-houses in mid-stream. Go down to the quayside on your right, where marks and dates on the rampart wall record the levels to which the river rose in previous centuries. This is known as the Quai des Laveuses, presumably because it was where the townswomen used to do the family wash.

Walk through an alleyway into Rue de la Tannerie and follow the steps at the end into the Rue du Donjon. The house of the painter **Alfred Sisley** is opposite, at no. 9. Sisley died there in poverty, but the local landscapes which he painted are now world famous. Continue along the Rue du Donjon, where there is indeed a **Donjon** (castle keep), built in 1128. Its most famous prisoner was Nicolas Fouquet, the finance minister Louis XIV jailed for corruption.

Return along Rue du Donjon to the **Eglise de Notre-Dame**, the chancel of which dates from 1166. The transept and the nave were constructed later and the bell tower was added in the 15th century. Opposite the church in the Place Royale is the Maison du Bon Saint Jacques, the medieval pilgrim's inn from where the nuns sold the *sucres d'orge*, the barley sugar that has become a speciality of Moret.

Follow Rue de l'Eglise back to the Rue Grande and cross the bridge over the Loing on to the Route de St Mammès on your left. You can compare the view from the riverside park here with Sisley's painting, *Le Pont de Moret*, 1893, which hangs in the Musée d'Orsay in Paris.

From here, you could either return to Moret, go on to St Mammès or continue to the **Maison Georges Clemenceau** by turning right on to the Rue du Peintre Sisley. The riverside 'cottage' built in 1926 for the retired Prime Minister is no longer open to the public, but makes a pleasant short walk.

2 km riverside walk to St Mammès

Turn left along the Route de St Mammès which soon curves right to cross the Loing Canal. Cross the bridge to join the towpath on the left.

Just before the railway bridge you will pass a neglected building which appears to have once been a café or restaurant. Do not be deceived by appearances. It still is a restaurant, the **Auberge du Soleil d'Or**. Climb the steps further along on your right up to the road from where you will see the entrance. The unassuming exterior conceals a well-run family establishment which offers honest home cooking, a surprisingly extensive wine list, ridiculously low prices and an unrivalled view over the Loing. The 11€ menu includes charcuterie, grilled trout, crisp fried potatoes and a generous serving from the cheese board, prepared by the *patronne*, a comfortable lady in slippers. When I commented that the restaurant was practically invisible to strollers on the towpath below, the reply was that it could be seen by the boats on the river. Clearly, local custom has kept the place going for the 30 years that the family have been here. Nothing has changed since my first visit ten years ago, except that the establishment is no longer a hotel.

A ten-minute walk along the towpath will bring you to the *Renoir* which is moored at the lock in front of no. 10, Quai du Loing. Although the boat can take about 70 passengers, there are rarely more than 20 on Sundays and the loudspeaker commentary is mercifully sporadic. It is owned by a friendly couple, both boating enthusiasts with more conventional weekday jobs. They will ply you with free coffee or orange juice, answer all your questions about navigation and even let you take the wheel, should you feel so inclined. Although they have lived in St Mammès for years they told me that they had never been inside the Soleil d'Or, put off by its unprepossessing exterior, although they had heard the food was good. Intrigued by my recommendation, they finally went and were pleasantly surprised.

On leaving the boat, continue along the towpath and turn right on to the Quai de Seine, the point at which the Loing flows into the Seine. You will find several geranium-framed cafés here, with friendly locals and provincial prices, overlooking the huge barges moored along the quay. The presence of these barges in such a small town seems surprising but in fact St Mammès is still an important river port and is the scene of a busy **market** on Sunday mornings. I highly recommend the quality of the cheese sold there.

At the end of the Quai de Seine is the austere little 11th-century **Eglise de St Mammès**. It is rarely open but if you manage to go inside, there is a 13th-century stone statue of handsome, long-haired St Mammès, the patron saint of those with stomach ailments. He is shown holding what looks like a coil of spaghetti but actually are his guts, as he was martyred by a lance thrust into his stomach. The falcon on his left hand symbolises nobility and fidelity. The statue above him is of St Nicolas, patron saint of sailors, with what looks like a little laundry basket of people at his feet. Presumably they are shipwreck survivors.

Continue along the Rue Grande, cross Rue du Port de la Celle and turn left into Rue du Port de Berville which becomes a footpath leading to **St Mammès station**, hidden at the edge of the town. Like many small stations in the Ile de France, it has no staff on Sundays, so you will need enough change for the ticket-vending machine, or better still, a return ticket. My friend and I once missed the train while struggling with the machine and were given a lift to Moret by a sympathetic local – a gesture which left us with an even warmer memory of St Mammès. That impression has not changed on my subsequent visits.

Distance from Paris: 70 km (44 miles)
Depart: Gare de Lyon
Arrive: Moret-Veneux-les-Sablons
Journey time: 55 minutes or less
Length of visit: Half or full day
Alternative return from: St Mammès
Carte Orange Zone: 6
Single ticket: 7.90€
Distance from station to Moret: 1½ km (1 mile)
Distance from Moret to St Mammès: 2 km (1¼ miles)
Pop.: 4,402

Getting there

SNCF trains (*Grandes Lignes*) to Nemours or Montereau leave Gare de Lyon roughly every hour, stopping at Fontainebleau before Moret-Veneux-les-Sablons. The last train back from Moret is at around 9.45 pm, 10.30 pm on Sundays.

Fontainebleau is a popular destination on summer weekends so it is a good idea to buy your ticket in advance, as there will be queues at the booking office and at the ticket-vending machines. At Moret, a surprisingly large station, take the exit marked 'sortie Moret-billets-information'. If you decide to return from here, allow enough time to find the correct platform, as both local and express trains stop at Moret. Fast trains back can take as little as 35 minutes.

If you plan to return from St Mammès, it is simpler to buy a return ticket in Paris. On arrival in Moret, ask for a *fiche horaire* for St Mammès–Paris. Trains from St Mammès run up to 8.30 pm, 10.30 pm on Sundays, but there are fewer trains than from Moret.

NB: The 's' is St Mammès is not sounded, so pronounce it 'Mammay'.

Taxi from the station to Moret, approximately 5€, tel 01 60 70 46 04.

Car: Autoroute A6 , N37 to Fontainebleau, N6 to Moret.

When to go

If you want to take the boat trip from St Mammès, go on a Sunday between Easter and October. A hot, sunny day would be ideal. There is also a market at St Mammès on Sunday mornings. Otherwise, Saturday is probably the best day on which to enjoy the flavour of a provincial town. On some Saturdays during the summer there are street pageants arranged by the tourist office.

Useful information

Office de Tourisme, Place de Samois, 77250 Moret-sur-Loing, tel 01 60 70 41 66. Open daily 10 am–12.30 pm and 2.30–6.30 pm in summer, 10 am–noon and 3– 5 pm in winter.

Musée du Sucre d'Orge, (Barley Sugar Museum), 5 Rue du Puits du Four, tel 01 60 70 35 63. Devoted to the history of the manufacture and sale of the barley sugar originally made by the Benedictine nuns established in Moret in 1638 and still made by the traditional labour-intensive process. You can buy pretty little tins of these sweets in the local *pâtisseries*, an unusual and lightweight present. Open 3–7 pm on Sundays and public holidays from Easter to 1 November and on Saturdays from June to September and 3–5 pm on weekdays in July and August. Admission 1.60€, 0.80€ for children under 10.

Boat trips along the Seine

Larguez les Amarres, Denis and Marie-France Duburque, 5 Quai du Loing, 77670 St Mammès, tel 01 64 23 16 24. Reservation preferred or arrive 15 minutes early. Cruise of approximately 3 hours from St Mammès to Samois-sur-Seine and back. Includes *goûter* of orange juice or coffee and cakes. The *Renoir* leaves from the Quai du Loing at St Mammès at 3 pm, goes through the lock at Champagne-sur-Seine and stops for 20 minutes at Samois, an attractive village with a waterside café at 5 pm, before returning to St Mammès at about 6 pm. Every Sunday in summer from Easter to 31 October, adults 20€, children under 12, 10€.

Restaurants

Auberge de l'Ecluse, 1 Route de St Mammès, 77250 Moret-sur-Loing, tel 01 60 70 50 85. Open every day for lunch and dinner. Moroccan specialities: menus 16.20€ and 20€, reasonable house wine. *Petite friture* (fried whitebait – the traditional riverside dish) is sometimes available. You can eat in a pretty garden beside the lock, but service can be leisurely.

Auberge du Soleil d'Or, 156–158 Rue Grande, 77670 St Mammès, tel 01 60 70 53 31. Open every day except Wednesday for lunch and dinner, but it is a good idea to ring first to check. Closed in August. It is best to arrive before 1.30 pm for lunch, although you can linger until around 3 pm. No credit cards. Menus 11€, 15€ and à la carte, drinkable house wine at 3.50€ for 37 cl.

Cafés

There are several cosy little cafés along the Quai de Seine at St Mammès, overlooking the barges and the Sunday morning market on the quay.

13. Poissy

A surprising combination of old-fashioned pleasures is clustered around the river at Poissy, five minutes' walk from the bland modernity of the station and town centre

In turn royal city, religious, agricultural, commercial and industrial centre, Poissy is in many ways a typical town of the Ile de France. It is a modest place, familiar to most Parisians only as the name of a terminus on the RER line serving the north-western suburbs. In fact, its historical importance dates from the 11th century and there are some interesting discoveries awaiting the visitor.

The buildings near the station reminded my American companion of California and the nearby town centre is deceptively modern-looking. But this bustling part of Poissy is only minutes away from the quiet, rather faded charm of the Esturgeon restaurant overlooking the Seine, the ruined medieval bridge, and a pre-war world of artists, islands and *guinguettes*.

Poissy's other unexpected attractions include its imposing 12th-century church, the model Villa Savoye designed by Le Corbusier in the 1920s and the winding walk through the remnants of the medieval Abbey grounds to the Musée du Jouet, the small and engaging Toy Museum. It is on the edge of the Parc Meissonier, designed *à l'anglaise* to include a lake bordered by wild flowers instead of the usual formal walks and flowerbeds. There is an open-air swimming pool on an island of the Seine opposite the park.

It is possible to stroll along the river to Villennes, which has an excellent restaurant and is on the SNCF line to Paris, or even to walk as far as Médan to glimpse the château with its memories of Ronsard and Maurice Maeterlinck and visit Emile Zola's country house.

Poissy's location, on the edge of the Forest of St Germain

The Seine at Poissy

next to a bend of the Seine and within 28 kilometres of Paris, accounts for its early importance in French history. Robert II, son of Hugues Capet, the founder of the royal dynasty which was to unify France, had a castle there and in 1014 laid the foundation stone of a church pre-dating the present Collégiale Notre Dame. It was in this church, rebuilt in the early 12th

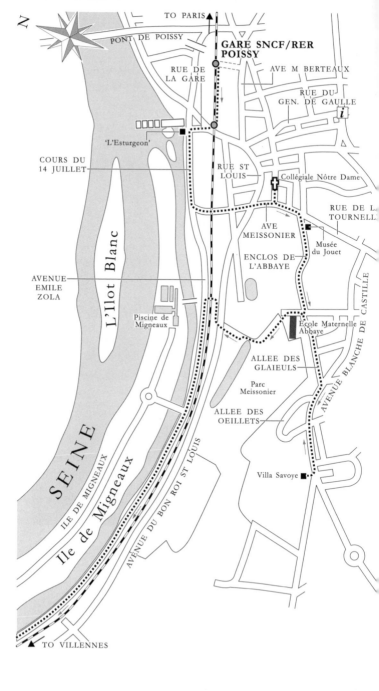

N

TO PARIS

PONT DE POISSY

GARE SNCF/RER POISSY

AVE M BERTEAUX

RUE DE LA GARE

RUE DU GEN. DE GAULLE

i

'L'Esturgeon'

COURS DU 14 JUILLET

RUE ST LOUIS

Collégiale Nôtre Dame

RUE DE L TOURNELL

AVE MEISSONIER

Musée du Jouet

L'Ilot Blanc

ENCLOS DE L'ABBAYE

AVENUE EMILE ZOLA

Piscine de Migneaux

Ecole Maternelle Abbaye

AVENUE BLANCHE DE CASTILLE

ALLEE DES GLAIEULS

Parc Meissonier

SEINE

ILE DE MIGNEAUX

Ile de Migneaux

ALLEE DES OEILLETS

AVENUE DU BON ROI ST LOUIS

Villa Savoye

TO VILLENNES

Poissy

0   500 metre

century, that the future St Louis, son of Blanche of Castille and Louis VIII, was baptised in 1214. St Louis had the town's first stone bridge built and also created the cattle market, initiating Poissy's development in the Middle Ages as an important agricultural and commercial centre supplying Paris.

Poissy remained a royal residence until the 13th century, the site of an important abbey and a Dominican priory built by Philippe le Bel. For two months in 1561 the Abbey was the scene of an intense debate, the 'Colloque de Poissy', a last-ditch and doomed attempt to reconcile the doctrinal differences between French Catholics and Protestants, held in the presence of Charles IX.

In the 20th century Poissy's agricultural activities were replaced by industry, with the installation of the Peugeot-Talbot car factory on the banks of the Seine north of the town. *Le Noyau de Poissy*, a liqueur distilled from apricot kernels and said to have been first made at the Dominican priory, is still produced at the Distillerie du Noyau de Poissy.

Suggested visit to Poissy

From **Poissy station** take 'sortie Rue de la Gare', which is the exit at the very end of the platform, with steps down leading to the road and the river. The café **Au Bon Coin** in Rue de la Gare on the left is easily overlooked, but is the typical local corner café that is becoming increasingly rare in Paris. Turn left past the café into the Cours du 14 juillet, bordering the river, and cross on to the old stone bridge, which extends about a quarter of the way across the Seine. In front of you stretch a series of stone bases, all that is left of the 13th-century toll bridge, which had 37 arches and a drawbridge, closed by a solid gate at each end. Part of the town's medieval defences, the bridge was also a thriving centre for various trades associated with the river and its two ports: fishermen, sailors, tanners, millers and washerwomen. Destroyed and rebuilt several times in the course of various wars, the bridge survived until 26 May 1944, when it was finally destroyed by the Allied bombardment.

Musée du Jouet, Poissy

The Pont de Poissy to the right is the modern replacement.

Just below the old bridge is the terrace of the restaurant **L'Esturgeon**, named after a gigantic sturgeon caught by its owner at this very spot in 1839. The restaurant was at the height of its popularity in the 19th century, when patrons were rowed across to an annexe on the islet opposite. Manet, Corot, Matisse, Renoir, Pissarro, Zola and Maupassant all enjoyed the romantic view of the river from its green-tinted glass terrace, framed by weeping willows and the old bridge. The *Salon de Thé* sign outside dates from the 1930s and no longer applies, so you will have to have lunch if you want to sit on the terrace. Or you could head for **La Goujonnette** opposite, where the first-floor dining room looks out on to the same view. I have not tried this relatively new restaurant but it seems to be popular.

Continue past the restaurants along the tree-lined riverside walk for a few minutes and then turn left under the railway bridge into the Avenue Meissonier leading to the church, the **Collégiale Notre Dame**. The oldest part is 12th-century, and there are Renaissance additions, but the church owes its present appearance to heavy restoration by Viollet-le-Duc in the 19th century. The most notable sights are considered to be the remnants of the baptismal font of St Louis and a 16th-century sculpture of the entombment of Christ, but I was particularly taken by a curious tombstone at the very back of the church, on the left as you face the altar. The Latin inscription recounts how Rémy Hénaut, who died 'around 1630', had already been laid in the tomb when his son 'by human arts and also the intercession of Saint Geneviève' restored him to life. 'A new Lazarus', having lived and died twice (*bis vivus, bis mortuus*) 'he was from then on known as the Resurrected One.' The tomb contains both his remains and those of his son.

Outside the church there is a **statue of St Louis,** simply recording his birth in Poissy in 1214 and his death in Tunis in 1270, a reminder of the dangers of going off to the Crusades. Continue along the Avenue Meissonier, with the river behind you. The barracks-like building facing you, with the Poissy coat of arms and the tricolour flag over the gate, is actually the prison. Cross the road to the right of the prison and go through an arched medieval gateway into the cobbled **Enclos de l'Abbaye**. A plaque set in the wall beneath the gateway, put up by the Societé de l'Histoire du Protestantisme Français in 1931, records that this was the site of the 'Colloque de Poissy'. Nothing now remains of the Abbey and its once extensive lands but this rambling walk and a field of grassy ruins, covered with wild daffodils when I was there, visible from the top floor of the Musée du Jouet.

The **Musée du Jouet** on the left is housed in a 14th-century fortified building which was once part of the Abbey. The exhibits of children's toys and games from 1850 to 1950 are grouped by theme: dolls, teddy bears and toy soldiers on the ground floor, games and magic lanterns on the first floor, and train sets on the second floor. I expected to be bored, but was fascinated and ended up pressing buttons to make the trains move and trying out a

The Villa Savoye

19th-century fortune-teller's board, remarkably accurate in its predictions. The first public museum of its kind to open in France, the Musée du Jouet is toy-sized itself, but its collection is surprisingly rich and very well-displayed.

Continue past the museum under three more gateways, past La Grange, once part of the Abbey buildings, now an arts centre, and turn right, slightly uphill, into the residential Allée des Glaïeuls, opposite the *école maternelle*. Continue uphill until you reach the main road, Avenue Blanche de Castille, and turn right, past the Allée des Œillets. The **Villa Savoye** is a little further on, entered through a white wire gate set back from the road. Press the button to be buzzed in. Le Corbusier was commissioned to build the villa as a summer residence for a banker and his wife in 1929, the only stipulation being that it should be light, have good views, and offer an easy approach by car, as Madame Savoye did not know how to reverse. Given a free hand, Le Corbusier applied his famous rules for modern architecture to the construction of the villa: 'The materials of urban architecture are the sun, the sky, the trees, steel, cement, in that hierarchical order.'

The result looks strangely familiar: a white box set on stilts of reinforced concrete, allowing cars to drive right up to the door, an uninterrupted façade of windows and an interior ramp leading to the airy principal rooms on the first floor and the roof garden. So many architects have copied this style that it is something of a surprise to see the distinctly thirties sunken curved bath of blue mosaic tiles and the sliding cupboards in the kitchen, the last word in modernity at the time, and to imagine how much the house must have startled some of Le Corbusier's contemporaries.

From the villa, retrace your steps along the Allée des Glaïeuls until you reach the *école maternelle*. The entrance to the **Parc Meissonier** is opposite La Grange, so discreetly placed that you would never suspect the existence of a park *à l'anglaise* around the corner, with untamed expanses of grass and trees leading to a lake. The Dominican priory founded by Philippe le Bel in memory of his grandfather, St Louis, once stood here. It was famous for the beauty of its gardens and something of the restful atmosphere of a priory garden still clings to the park. Go downhill, keeping the pretty lake with its swans, ducks and wild flowers on your left, and past the statue of Ernest Meissonier, Poissy's resident Victorian painter, facing the park entrance. Take the pedestrian crossing over the main road, the Avenue du Bon Roi St Louis, leading to the car park opposite.

Bear right past the cars until you come to a small pedestrian underpass beneath the railway line, which leads straight to the Avenue Emile Zola and the footbridge to the **Piscine de Migneaux,** the swimming pool on the Ile de Migneaux. It is set in its own park so that you can sunbathe on the grass and the outdoor pool boasts two enormous waterslides, so it is popular with knowledgeable Parisians. If you want to explore the island, access is by a proper bridge a little further along the Seine on the left. Go past the footbridge and Le Bon Vivant restaurant (mentioned in Gault-Millau 2001, but always closed when I have passed by).

From here you could return along the river to the **station** at Poissy or continue to Villennes.

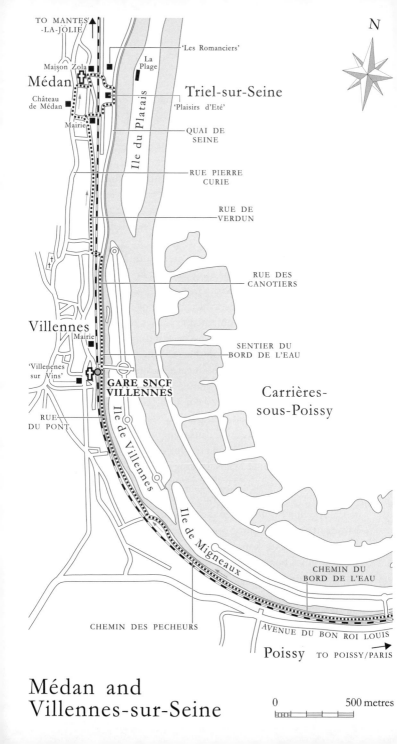

Médan and Villennes-sur-Seine

3 ½ km walk to Villennes

The bridge to the long narrow **Ile de Migneaux** is a few steps further on. The island is exclusively residential, the home of several celebrated recluses, among them Shung, the former artistic director of the Opéra Bastille in Paris. The only public building, apart from the swimming pool, is a youth hostel to the left of the bridge, the gardens of which have an uninterrupted view of the Seine. You can only catch frustrating glimpses of the river between the big houses built in a bizarre variety of styles which line the island's only road, so it is actually more rewarding to continue the walk by the river along the mainland path, the Chemin du Bord de l'Eau.

This road eventually deteriorates into a slightly muddy, pot-holed path used by a few friendly locals, with attractive views of the gardens and boats belonging to the island residents opposite. When you have passed the end of the island the path turns back into a proper road, leading through a boatyard and to a gate barring access, as it has now become a private road. The gate is to stop cars, not pedestrians, so if it is closed simply scramble up the railway embankment around it and down on the other side. I owe this invaluable tip to a municipal surveyor, who by great good luck happened to be testing the railway underpass next to the gate when I arrived.

The private road, peaceful and pretty, leads past houses whose gardens stretch to the water's edge, allowing irregular glimpses of the river. It ends at a bridge which goes to another long narrow island, the **Ile de Villennes**, which presents even more of a closed face to non-residents than the Ile de Migneaux. You can cross the bridge and the little park beyond to enjoy the refreshingly wide view of the Seine but there is little else of interest to walkers. **Villennes station** is opposite the bridge. The town and the ticket office are on the other side of the tracks, accessible by a level crossing and a footbridge over the line. The striking 11th-century church next to the station is open, thanks to the enthusiasm of local volunteers, although rather bare inside. There is a café opposite which is also usually open, should you have to wait for a train.

A restaurant with the unpromising name of **Villennes sur Vins** has recently opened opposite the church. Intrigued by several local recommendations, I tried it out for Saturday lunch with friends who live nearby. We were agreeably surprised, not only by the restaurant, but also by the village-like charm of Villennes on a Saturday afternoon. There are some market stalls, several cafés and restaurants, and a few people were enjoying a game of *pétanque* (bowls) in the tiny centre of town, which is surrounded by little streets of pretty old houses.

The restaurant itself is in the former *quincaillerie* (hardware store) with a beautiful mosaic tiled floor dating from the 1920s, of which the present owners are justifiably proud. The décor inside is cosy and traditional, but we sat at tables outside to sample an excellent *blanquette de veau* (the classic French housewives' dish of veal, mushrooms and carrots stewed in cream), accompanied by well-chosen wine and followed by simple, delicious desserts. The salads were made with good olive oil and the wine glasses were thin and elegant. The service is friendly, with a lack of ostentation unusual for cooking of this quality.

As Zola's house in Médan is not far from Villennes but is only open on weekend afternoons, I would recommend a separate visit. You could start with lunch in Villennes, which is easily accessible from Paris, before the half-hour walk to Médan, and back.

1 ¾ km walk to Médan

On arriving at **Villennes station**, cross the footbridge over the line and turn left into the Sentier du Bord de l'Eau, which parallels the railway on the left and the Seine on the right. It is slightly muddy, but you can glimpse the river between the trees and actually hear the birds singing, as only residents' cars have access. A ten to fifteen-minute walk will bring you to an underpass beneath the railway line. Do not take the Rue des Canotiers which continues along the river, inviting though it looks, as you will find access barred after a certain point. Go through the underpass and turn right into the Rue de Verdun, a not very exciting but reasonably quiet road, and continue, past the *Mairie* at Médan, until you come to the Rue de la Victoire on your left.

Go up this road, which will bring you out on to the Rue Pierre Curie (D164). Turn right and cross the road to the **château de Médan**, a former hunting lodge with a long history of literary and artistic associations. The property of the Abbey of St Germain des Prés in Paris in the 9th century, its subsequent owners included Jehan Perdrier in the 15th century, a friend of the poet François Villon, and Jehan Brinon, whose generosity as a host to Ronsard and the poets of the Pléiade bankrupted him in the 16th century. Cézanne, staying at Zola's house nearby, painted the château in 1880 and in 1924 it was bought by Maurice Maeterlinck (1862–1949), the Belgian playwright, whose play *The Blue Bird* was performed here. The château was occupied by the Germans during the Second World War and then used as a printing press in the 1950s by the newspaper *Combat*, which had started life as a Resistance paper founded by Albert Camus. The closure of the paper in 1974 led to the abandonment of the château, its dereliction and its eventual seizure by the URSSAF, the dreaded state authority responsible for collecting national insurance contributions from self-employed workers. In 1977 it was bought by the present owners and then entirely restored over ten years, ironically with state help.

The vicissitudes of the château and its heavily restored 17th-century appearance are in sharp contrast to the neighbouring 19th-century home of the novelist Emile Zola (1840–1902). The rambling house is almost entirely as he left it, all the alterations to the original building having been initiated by Zola himself. In 1905 his widow gave it to the *Assistance Publique*, the French public hospital authority, who used it as a convalescent home for disadvantaged children for over 60 years and are the current owners.

Turn left from the château and cross the road into Rue Buquet on the right, past the 16th-century **church** (usually locked, but with an interesting façade and bell towers). Turn left into the Rue Pasteur to reach **Zola's house** on the right, part of which is open to the public as a museum. He bought it in 1878 with the proceeds from *L'Assommoir* and lived there for about eight months of the year until his death 24 years later. His growing success enabled him to improve and enlarge the house to his own design, adding two towers, extending the garden and finally buying the Ile du Platais opposite. It was reached by a boat called *Nana* belonging to Maupassant, who ingenuously explained to Zola's wife that it was so-called 'parce que tout le monde montera dessus'.

Zola spent the later, successful years of his life at Médan, the acknowledged leader of the new 'naturalist' school of writers, whose members included Flaubert, the Goncourts and Maupassant. An early champion of the Impressionists, among them his old friend Paul Cézanne, a generous host and a fighter against injustice, he was also a tireless worker, whose house reflected his lifestyle. It was here that he wrote *Nana, Germinal, La Terre* and *La Bête Humaine*, the latter inspired by the railway line to Rouen which passes the house. The success of *Germinal* led to the construction of another tower housing the billiard room, but the tower containing his study had been built first. He would write there every day from 9 am to 1 pm, 'never an hour more, never an hour less' (the exact schedule later adopted by Somerset Maugham). Above the chimney-piece in the enormous study overlooking the river is the writer's motto:

Zola's house at Médan

Nulla dies sine linea ('Not a day without a line').

Zola, by Manet

In the room given over to the Dreyfus Affair there is an interesting exhibit of the first three handwritten pages of Zola's famous 1898 article, *J'accuse*. It succeeded in re-opening the case and getting Dreyfus acquitted, though not before Zola himself had had to flee the country for a year. The handwriting is firm and decisive, with scarcely any crossing out; the 39th and last page is almost as clear as the first.

The peaceful routine at Médan was suddenly interrupted in 1888 when Zola, like Rousseau, fell in love with his laundrymaid. He later installed her and their two children in a neighbouring village and would cycle over to visit them in the afternoons. His wife seems to have forgiven him, because a stipulation of her gift of the house to the *Assistance Publique* was that it should be preserved 'in its present state, as far as possible.'

You could make a nostalgic detour to reach the river by turning left from Zola's house into the Avenue Emile Zola, which crosses the railway line to become Quai de la Seine. **Les Romanciers** (The Novelists), a popular hotel-restaurant which until recently had a boat service to **La Plage**, the now defunct 1930s swimming pool on the Ile du Platais opposite, has recently closed down, victim of changing tastes in popular entertainment and new health and safety regulations which made the boat service unprofitable. The other restaurants along the river have also closed down, apart from **Plaisirs d'Eté**. It is the only source of food and drink in Médan and is open sporadically, depending on the whim of the owners, a retired couple.

Follow the Quai de la Seine into the Rue de la Seine and take the underpass to cross the railway line back to the Mairie and the return route to **Villennes station**.

Distance from Paris: 28 km
(17 miles)
Depart: Châtelet-les-Halles or
Gare St Lazare
Arrive: Poissy
Journey time: 20 minutes (St
Lazare); 33 minutes (Châtelet)
Length of visit: Half or full
day or two visits
Alternative return from:
Villennes-sur-Seine
Carte Orange Zone: 5
Single ticket: 4.10€
**Distance from Poissy to
Villennes:** 3½ km (2 miles)
**Distance from Villennes to
Médan:** 1¾ km (1 mile)
Pop.: 35,815

Getting there

RER A5 trains to Poissy leave
Châtelet-les-Halles and other
stations in central Paris approximately every 20 minutes or less,
every 30 minutes at weekends,
returning up to midnight.

SNCF trains from Gare St
Lazare (*Départs Ile de France*) to
Mantes-la-Jolie, stopping at
Poissy and Villennes-sur-Seine
run approximately every half hour
on weekdays, every hour at weekends, returning up to midnight.

Car: N13 or A13 to Rouen,
exit Poissy or A14 from La
Défense to Orgeval, exit Poissy.

When to go

The walk along the Seine is particularly enjoyable in fine weather.
Avoid Monday when the Toy

Museum and the Villa Savoye are
closed. Choose a weekend if you
want to visit Zola's house at
Médan, a Saturday if you want to
lunch in Villennes first.

Useful information

Office de Tourisme, 132 Rue du
Général de Gaulle, 78300 Poissy,
tel 01 30 74 60 65. Open 8.30 am–
12.30 pm and 2–5.30 pm Monday
to Saturday, all year round.

The local liqueur, **Le Noyau
de Poissy**, can be bought at 105
Rue du Général de Gaulle, near
the tourist office or sampled at
the café Au Bon Coin (see below).

Villa Savoye, 82 Rue de
Villiers, tel 01 39 65 01 06. Open
daily except Mondays, 10 am– 6
pm from May to August. Closes
at 5 pm in March, April, September and October. Open 10 am–1
pm and 2–5 pm November to
February. Closed on I January, 1
May, 1 and 11 November and 25
December. Admission 5€ or 3.50€
to visitors aged under 26 and
teachers on proof of status. Free
on the first Sunday of the months
between October and April.

Muséé du Jouet, (Toy
Museum), 1 Enclos de l'Abbaye,
tel 01 39 65 06 06. Open daily
except Mondays and public holidays, 9.30 am–12 noon and 2– 5.30
pm. Admission 4€, 3€ for children
aged under 10.

Piscine de Migneaux, (covered
and outdoor swimming pool), Ile
de Migneaux, tel 01 39 65 06 07.
Accessible by footbridge from
Avenue Emile Zola. Complicated

opening hours (ring first) but generally open in summer until at least 7 pm. Admission 5.50€ adults, 4.50€ children.

La Maison d'Emile Zola, 26 Rue Pasteur, 78670 Médan, tel 01 39 75 35 65. www.maisonzola-museedreyfus.com. Open 2–6 pm at weekends and public holidays except 24 and 25 December and 31 December–1 January. Guided visits on Saturdays at 3 pm and 4.30 pm, Sundays 2.30 pm, 3.30 pm, 4.30 pm and 5 pm. Admission 5€ adults, 2.50€ visitors aged 12 to 18, children under 12 free.

Château de Médan, Rue Pierre Curie, tel 01 39 75 86 59. A 1½ hour guided visit, conducted by the owners, can be arranged for groups of 20 or more. 7€ per person. Reservation essential.

Restaurants

L'Esturgeon, 6 Cours du 14 juillet, Poissy, tel 01 39 65 00 04. Open every day except Thursday and Sunday evenings. Closed in August. Menus at 35€, 50€ and à la carte. A preponderance of not very exciting fish dishes, such as *bar au laurier braisé beurre blanc* (bass with bayleaves braised in butter). Rather formal atmosphere.

La Goujonnette, 17 Cours du 14 juillet, Poissy, tel 01 30 06 47 39. Open Monday–Saturday for lunch and dinner. Closed in August. Menus at 15€, 19€ and à la carte. A traditional French restaurant, set back from the river, opposite L'Esturgeon.

Au Bon Coin, 6 Rue de la Gare, Poissy, tel 01 39 65 03 53. Open Monday to Friday to 7.30 pm, Saturday to 2 pm. An old-fashioned café near the station and the river, patronised by local working people. Tables outside and a busy, friendly atmosphere. *Plats du jour* around 7€, sells Le Noyau de Poissy.

Villennes sur Vins, 51 Place de l'Eglise, 78670 Villennes sur Seine, tel 01 39 08 04 73. Closed Sunday and Monday. Traditional French cooking at lunchtime, gourmet specialities in the evening. Two-course *formule* 15€, menu 19€, à la carte in the evenings. Wine 3-4€ a glass, 17-20€ a bottle.

Plaisirs d'Eté, 4 Quai de la Seine, 78670 Médan, tel 01 39 75 45 72. Closed Sunday evening and on Mondays. *Plats* 14-18€, wine 4€ a glass or from 16€ a bottle.

14. Provins

> Once the third largest city in France,
> 'Provins the Magnificent' rose above the flat Brie
> countryside, crowned by spires and encircled by
> five kilometres of walls and ramparts

The city, still crowned by its dome and fortress, has preserved its early medieval layout more or less intact. Massive ramparts, comparable to those of Carcassonne and unique in the Ile de France, still surround the Ville Haute (upper town) on the hill. The old city walls have been replaced by a canal which encloses the Ville Basse (lower town) and separates it from the surrounding plain.

Provins is a city apart, untouched by modern industry, and cradling a glorious but long-distant past. Despite its summer influx of visitors, a strong medieval atmosphere clings to the Ville Haute, while the Ville Basse exudes a gentle provincial charm. It is over an hour by train from Paris but the journey is easy and the ramparts alone are worth the trip. It is possible to avoid part of the summer crowds, which are becoming more international since the town's UNESCO listing as a World Heritage site in 2001, by following the route given here, which takes the back streets and follows the ramparts downhill until they become the canal encircling the Ville Basse. The Ville Haute with its dome and fortress rises magnificently to the right, while the silence of the tree-lined walk along the water is only broken by a few *boules* players and locals out for a stroll.

Although the site was occupied as early as 5000 BC, the first recorded mention of the city was in AD 802. The transfer of the relics of St Ayoul to Provins in 996 marked the beginning of its importance as first a religious and then a political and commercial centre. In the 11th century the Counts of Champagne moved their capital from Troyes to Provins. Under their

*The ramparts
at Provins*

enlightened rule the town became famous for the great medieval fairs held three times a year which attracted traders from Flanders, Germany, Lombardy, Provence and Catalonia. Provins had its own system of weights and measures, its own currency and its own cloth industry. The ramparts were built in the 12th and 13th centuries to protect the growing population of bankers, merchants and artisans and to defend the road to Paris, which passed through the Ville Haute. The town was visited by the great medieval scholar Abelard in 1122 and no fewer than seven different religious foundations, including the Knights Templar, were added to the existing orders between 1193 and 1269. The city's emblem of a red rose dates from 1228 when it was brought back from the Middle East by Thibault IV le Chansonnier, the poet-Crusader and Count of Champagne. It was adopted by Edmund of Lancaster when he married the heiress of Champagne in 1275 and became the red rose of Lancaster, opposing the white rose of York in the Wars of the Roses.

The decline of the city was almost as sudden as its rise. In 1285 Philippe le Bel, husband of the heiress of Champagne, became king of France. The proud city of the Counts of Champagne became incorporated into his expanding kingdom, whose capital, Paris, soon completely eclipsed Provins. Heavy taxes, the Black Death and the disaster of the Hundred Years' War sealed the fate of the medieval city, whose population continued to shrink. It was occupied by the English in 1417 and again in 1432. The chronology in a local history I consulted remarks laconically 'Pillage' next to this date and is equally reticent about the events surrounding other key dates, perhaps because they would apply to most towns in the Ile de France: the town's capture by Henri IV in 1585, the setting up of a Comité Révolutionnaire in 1793, when the statues in the churches were systematically decapitated, the presence of Cossacks in the city in 1814, its occupation by the Prussians in 1871, and again by the Germans from 1940 to 1944.

The destruction of more than ten churches during the Revolution gave Provins the decor of picturesque ruins prized by the Romantic writers. Nineteenth-century visitors included Victor Hugo, Lamartine, Sainte-Beuve, Jules Verne, and Balzac, who used the city as the setting for one of his novels, *Pierette*. In the 20th century Proust set part of his posthumous novel, *Jean Santeuil*, in Provins. Tourism has continued to increase but the few local industries – wine-growing and clay-mining – disappeared completely in the 19th and 20th centuries respectively. Today, many of the city's inhabitants work in Paris.

Suggested visit to Provins

Provins station is at the end of the line. The first impression of having arrived at a medieval outpost in the middle of nowhere is confirmed by the flat, empty countryside to the right of the tracks and the two distinctive towers dominating the hill on the left, rising above the exit from the **station**.

The Ville Basse

Turn left from the station across the Avenue Jean Jaurès, which parallels a little stream. This is the canal, aptly known as La Fausse Rivière (the False River) which follows the line of the old city walls encircling the Ville Basse. Take the little footbridge across the stream on the left, marked by the sign 'Cité Medié-vale, accès piétons' indicating pedestrian access to the historic town centre, and follow it as it bridges another little stream. This is **La Voulzie**, one of the two rivers running through Provins which used to cause periodic flooding until the construction of the Fausse Rivère in the 18th century. Turn right, following the sign 'Centre Ville' into the Rue Guyot de Provins and follow it round, turning left into the Rue Victor Arnoul, a much busier road, which eventually becomes the Rue Edmond Nocard just past the Caisse d'Epargne.

At the end of this street turn right into the Place St Ayoul. You will be immediately struck by the slightly lopsided medieval church on the right, the **Eglise de St Ayoul**, and rightly so, for it marks the beginning of the city's fame as a reli-gious centre and its subsequent prosperity and development. The 10th-century discovery here of the relics of St Ayoul, Abbé of Lérins martyred in 675, led to the building of a Bene-dictine priory on the sacred spot in 1048, a priory in which Abelard taught from 1120 to 1122. The church is now all that remains of the priory and it presents a most curious appearance. The main doorway, with its mutilated statues, dates from the 12th century, when the church was repaired following a terri-ble fire in 1157. The curious bronze central pillar, which seems in perfect harmony with the doorway, is actually the work of a modern sculptor, Georges Jeanclos, and dates from 1990. Inside, almost every period is represented, from the 12th to the 19th century. During the Revolution it became a place from which fodder was sold to a cavalry regiment but it has a quiet, mysterious atmosphere which only hints at its turbulent past.

On leaving the church a few steps to the right will bring you to the **Tour Notre Dame**, built in 1544, and incongruously surrounded by houses. You naturally look for the church

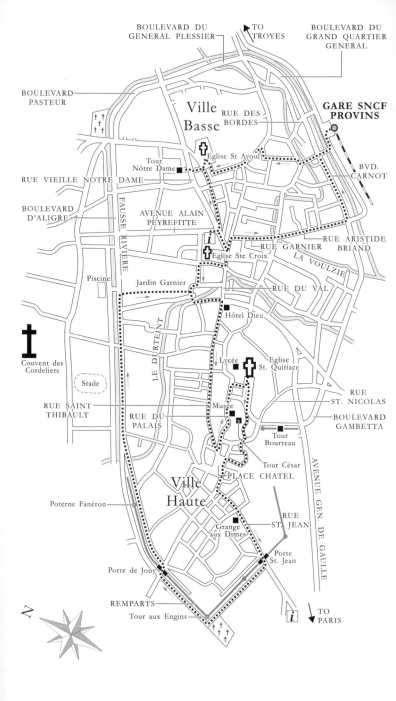

Provins

0   200 metres

which should be attached to it, in vain, as it was most efficiently razed in 1793. The imposing archway of the tower, in the roof of which house martins have built their nests, leads to a square which is now a car park, but whose regular shape betrays its origin as the cloister which once belonged to the church.

Retracing your steps along the Rue Notre Dame, turn right into the Rue de la Cordonnerie (Cobbler's Street) which still contains shoe-shops, as it is the main shopping street in Provins. It leads past a useful branch of the **tourist office** in the Avenue Alain Peyrefitte to the right. There is a public lavatory next to it, one of the many which used to feature on the official *Guide du Visiteur* map before the UNESCO listing. Provins is a town endowed with more well-kept public conveniences than any other I have visited, even the cemetery in the Ville Haute being provided with two. It also lives up to its emblem of the red rose, which is planted in every public garden and is on sale in the form of rose petal jam.

Rue de la Cordonnerie leads straight into the Rue du Val, a pedestrianised street which is the centre of the Ville Basse, lined with shops, cafés and restaurants. Turn right down the quiet little Rue Ste Croix, which leads to another curious old church, the **Eglise Ste Croix**, named after a fragment of the True Cross brought back from the Crusades by Thibault IV in the 13th century. The church has been undergoing 'restoration' for years and is permanently locked, but the late medieval doorway in this street is worth the slight detour for its bizarre sculptures of mythical beasts. During the Revolution the choir became a 'Temple de la Raison', the rest of the church being used for the manufacture of saltpetre, and it seems to have been quietly crumbling ever since. Serious restoration is planned to start in 2008.

Go past *La Poste* opposite the church and turn left into the Rue Toussaint-Rose, then right into the Rue Valentin Abeille, named after a local Resistance hero, passing the doorway to the **Jardin Garnier**, a pretty public garden. It extends down to the Fausse Rivière, where there is a good place to stretch out on the grass, but you will pass this part of the garden on the return walk. Turn right into the little Rue du Durteint and take the footbridge across the **River Durteint**, which is no bigger than a stream, overhung by picturesque houses and window-boxes. Turn left from the footbridge into the Rue du Moulin de la Ruelle which leads back to the pedestrianised thoroughfare of the Rue du Val.

The Ville Haute

Go up the steep but not impossible Rue St Thibault, the old road to Paris and the Ville Haute. Once lined with inns, the road is still a thoroughfare, trudged by a steady stream of visitors in the summer who are rewarded by the increasingly impressive views of the Ville Basse and the valley of the Durteint as they climb past the medieval houses on either side.

On the left is the 12th-century **Hôtel Dieu**, once a palace of the Counts of Champagne, then a hospital and now the start of the visit to the underground passages of the Ville Haute, **les Souterrains**. Some of these were quarries for fuller's earth, used in cloth-making, others served as military or private communication links between the houses. The graffiti show that they were also used as meeting places by various secret societies.

One of the steep little streets winding down to the valley on the right is called Rue de la Pierre Ronde and the 13th-century round stone is still there on the pavement, just after the Rue des Blancs Manteaux. It is a *pierre de cens*, a stone on which the townsfolk paid feudal taxes and church tithes. On the left, the fortifications enclosing the Ville Haute rise into view and at the top of the hill on the right, marking the entrance to the Place du Chatel, there are the ruined stone columns of the **Eglise St Thibault**. You can make out the outlines of the rest of the church, incorporated into a neighbouring house. It was abandoned in the Middle Ages, victim of an early road-widening scheme to ease the passage of traffic along the road to Paris. *Plus ça change…*

Once in the Place du Chatel, turn sharp left into the Rue du Palais, past the *école maternelle* on the left until you come to an old building on the right, the Maison Romane which houses the **Musée de Provins**. The 11th-century building, one of the oldest houses in Provins, was originally a Jewish school, later a synagogue. Its cellar, even older than the house, is linked to the network of underground passages running beneath the Ville Haute. The museum itself contains a rather sketchy assortment of artefacts. However, there is an evocative painting of Provins as it appeared before the Revolution, absolutely bristling with church spires, and a portrait of the city's last public executioner, Cyr-Charlemagne Sanson (1748–1794), looking calm and gentlemanly. He was the first in the region to receive the newly-invented guillotine, and it was his brother, the public hangman for Paris until 1795, who executed Louis XVI.

Continue past the museum and the pretty little Jardin des Brébans on the left, with its roses and view of the Ville Basse. The entrance to the Lycée Thibaud de Champagne is opposite the garden. The lycée is housed in the 12th-century former palace of the Counts of Champagne, next to the **Eglise St Quiriace**. Turn down the narrow Rue Pierre Ythier to reach the Place St Quiriace, shaded by lime trees, which was formerly the cloister. The main entrance to the church is on the left. The building was begun in 1160, with financial help from the incumbent Count of Champagne, and contained the head of St Quiriace, brought back from the Crusades around 1209. But the ambitious plans of its builders had to be modified to fit the straitened means of the community. By the 13th century only the transept and part of the nave had been completed and an 'economic' façade was finally given to the building in the 16th century. In 1689 the bell-tower collapsed, following a fire some years earlier, and the Gothic church was given the 17th-century slate dome that now dominates the skyline of the medieval city. In spite of this anachronism and the fits and starts in its construction, never fully completed over the course of the centuries, the general impression on entering the church is one of simplicity, spaciousness and harmony. It is light and airy, almost bare of decoration, apart from the stained glass windows recounting the lives of various saints. One of them is dedicated to St Edmund of Abingdon, who died in Provins in 1240 and whose cope is preserved in the local museum. To his left

St Thibault, Eglise
St Quiriace

St Thibault, the pious knight turned hermit who died in 1066, is shown leaning pensively on his sword, looking positively Byronic. It was in this church that Joan of Arc and Charles VII heard Mass on their way through Champagne in 1429.

On leaving the church, cross the Place St Quiriace and take the winding Rue de la Pie to the **Tour César** opposite. This is the octagonal fortress whose towering silhouette alongside the dome of St Quiriace dominates the city and it is equally imposing seen close up. It dates from at least 1137 but its connection with the Romans is spurious, the name 'César' having been given to it in the 19th century. Before that, it was known as the 'Grosse Tour' and served various functions at different periods, as a lookout tower, as a prison, and as the bell-tower for the church of St Quiriace. In 1432 it was the defendants' headquarters when the town was besieged by the English. There is a branch of the **tourist office** in the former bell-ringer's house within the tower, where you can buy tickets allowing you to climb to the top. The spiral staircase is steep and narrow and you may have to wait to let other visitors descend, one by one, before you can continue to the top, where there is a viewing table. There is a less spectacular view, free, from the ramparts at the Porte de Jouy.

On leaving the Tour César, continue along the Rue de la Pie which leads into the Rue Jean Desmarets. If you turn left you will soon see a very steep GR footpath on the right leading down the hill (see p. 238). Known as the 'Sentier du Bourreau' (Hangman's Footpath), it leads to the **Tour du Bourreau**, the public executioner's house outside the city walls. It is a solitary, grim-looking structure, last occupied in 1788 by Cyr-Charlemagne Sanson, the gentleman whose portrait is in the museum.

It is a steep climb back up the hill, so you may prefer to turn right along the Rue Desmarets and then left and left again to follow the quiet, winding Rue Maufranc back into the tree-lined **Place du Chatel**, the animated centre of the Ville Haute. Most of the restaurants and cafés are concentrated here and around the Rue Couverte on the left, which leads to the Rue St Jean. A medieval tithe barn in this street, the **Grange aux Dîmes**, has been converted to house a display of various trades and crafts practised in Provins in the Middle Ages. The **Table St Jean** opposite is a good place to stop for a leisurely lunch.

The ramparts

The Rue St Jean leads to the **Porte St Jean**, the 12th-century gateway guarding the road to Paris and the entrance to the city, currently being restored. It is the best point from which to start a walk around the ramparts. The main **tourist office** is located just outside the gateway, as this is where the medieval tournaments and displays are held in summer. The path outside the ramparts on the left eventually peters out, but the walk along the tree-lined path above the dry moat on the right is truly spectacular, the high point being the round **Tour aux Engins**, opposite the cemetery. As you saunter past, the alternating

Porte St Jean, Provins

square and round towers seem like an army of giants marching with you, until you reach the massive corner Tour aux Engins which marks the point at which the wall swings north. From here, there is a silhouetted view of the ramparts extending both north and west of the city, the towers seeming to stride into the distance almost as far as you can see. Tradition has it that in 1432 the English successfully pierced the defences of Provins at a weak point along the northern ramparts, but you wonder how they managed it.

Follow the ramparts as far as the **Porte de Jouy**, once, like the Porte St Jean, equipped with a portcullis and drawbridge, which leads back to the Place du Chatel. To the right of the gateway, steps lead up to a turret, from where there is a view of the Brie countryside. Continue the walk inside the ramparts, which leads steeply downhill, through the massive stone arch of the **Poterne Faneron** framing the valley below. Although it is not particularly difficult, this part of the walk does not attract many visitors. The series of towers punctuating the ramparts eventually peters out, but one of them, known as the 'Trou au Chat' (Cat's Hole) because of the low archway at the base, allows access to the other side of the wall, from where the view of the fortifications is still impressive. The steep path levels out to become a tree-lined footpath leading to a footbridge across the little River Durteint and the start of the **Fausse Rivière**. From here there is a memorable **view** of the ramparts climbing the hill behind you and of the peaceful, tree-lined canal, crossed by iron footbridges, stretching along the valley in front of you, linking the two worlds of the Ville Haute and the Ville Basse.

The Ville Basse

The canal-side walk seems to be frequented only by a few local people, visiting the allotments, playing *boules* near the War Memorial, studying, flirting or resting on the benches under the trees. The Tour César and the dome of St Quiriace soon rise into view on the right, crowning the roofs of the Ville Haute and framed by trees and gardens, while the square outline of the **Couvent des Cordeliers** rises to the left, dominating a hill outside the town. I do not recommend a detour to the former convent, which is now part of the Bibliothèque Nationale and inaccessible to visitors, but it has an interesting history. It was a monastery before 1248, the date of its official foundation by Thibault IV, and its strategic position just outside the city attracted constant attacks during the wars of the 14th century. In the 16th century Henri IV made it the base for his siege of Provins. In 1743 Louis XV transformed it into a hospital run by the Sisters of Charity, and the building has only recently been rescued from a century of neglect.

Just past the convent and the swimming pool (*piscine*) on the left, the grounds of the **Jardin Garnier** extend down to the canal on the right. The grounds are open until 5 pm from October to March, 8 pm in the summer, so you could walk through the garden to the entrance in the Rue Valentin Abeille and so back through the Ville Basse via the Rue Victor Garnier, which becomes Rue Aristide Briand to the **station**.

However, if you have the time and the inclination, you

could follow the Fausse Rivière right round the Ville Basse to reach the station. The prettiest part of the walk is now behind you but the quietest is along the Boulevard du Grand Quartier Général near the station. The ruins of the old wall and its towers are clearly visible here and there is a good sunbathing spot beside the water, almost invisible from the path, just after the bridge marking the beginning of the Boulevard. There is a little *café-tabac* in the Rue des Bordes, a few minutes' walk from the station.

Distance from Paris: 80 km (50 miles)
Depart: Gare de l'Est
Arrive: Provins
Journey time: 1 hour 20 minutes
Length of visit Full day
Carte Orange Zone: 6
Single ticket: 9.90€
Pop.: 12,091

Getting there

SNCF trains to Provins (terminus) leave Gare de l'Est (*Ile de France*) once in the morning on weekdays and again at around noon at weekends. The last trains back are at around 8 pm. All trains stop for up to nine minutes at Longueville, so do not panic when everyone else seems to be getting off there.

Buying a *Carte Mobilis* for this journey will save you 3.90€ on the return trip. See p. 235.

Car: A4 towards Metz, exit no. 13 Serris-Provins, then D231, or N4, D231, or N19 to Provins-Troyes.

When to go

The most rewarding aspect of a visit to Provins is the town itself and the walk around the ramparts, so you could choose a mild sunny day at any time of the year. Provins attracts a growing number of visitors during the summer, the high point being the *Fête Médié-vale* which is held in the second weekend of June. The Tour César and St Quiriace are open all year round, although in winter the other sights tend to be only open on weekend afternoons.

Useful information

Office de Tourisme (Ville Haute), Chemin de Villecran, 77160, Provins, tel 01 64 60 26 26. www.provins.net. Sells *Le Pass Provins*, a combined ticket to the main tourist attractions below, with a small reduction for *Le Petit Train* and the *Spectacles*, adults 9.20€, children 6.10€. *Le Pass* can also be bought at any of the *monuments*. Open every day except 25 December 9 am–6.30 pm from April to October and 9 am–5 pm from November to March.

Point d'information (Ville Basse), Avenue Alain Peyrefitte, tel 01 64 01 11 45. A helpful, less crowded offshoot of the main tourist office. Open 1–5.30 pm Monday to Friday, 11 am–5.30 pm on Saturday all year.

Tour César, open 10 am–6 pm from April to October and 2–5 pm from November to March. Closed on 25 December and 1 January. Adults 3.40€, children 1.90€.

Musée de Provins, Maison Romane, 7 Rue du Palais. Open noon–5.30 pm every day from April to October, and at weekends in winter, 11 am–6.30 pm in July and August. Closed from Christmas to New Year. Adults 3.50€, children and students 1.50€.

Grange aux Dîmes, Rue St Jean. Open 10 am–6 pm every day from April to August and at weekends in September and October. Open 2–6 pm on weekdays in September and October and 2–5 pm at weekends from November to March. Closed on 25 December and 1 January. Adults 3.40€, children 1.90€.

Les Souterrains, Hôtel Dieu, Rue St Thibault. Entrance to 250 metres of the maze of underground passages beneath the Ville Haute. Open 10.30 am–6 pm at weekends and during school holidays and at 3 pm and 4 pm for guided visits on weekdays from April to October. Guided visits at 2 pm, 3 pm and 4 pm at weekends and during school holidays from November to March. Closed on 25 December and 1 January. Adults 3.70€, children 2.20€.

Le Petit Train makes a 45-minute circuit of La Ville Haute, starting from the tourist office. Daily 11 am–1 pm, 2–7 pm from April to August and at weekends from September to October. Adults 4€, children 2.50€.

Spectacles (shows). Inside and outside the ramparts. Staged displays of medieval falconry, tournaments and an assault on the ramparts during the *Fête Médiévale* in the second weekend of June and throughout the summer, especially at weekends. Detailed programme available from the tourist office. Adults 6-10€, about a third less for children.

Restaurants

La Table St Jean, 3 Rue St Jean, tel 01 64 08 96 77. Open every day except Tuesday evening and Wednesday. Menus at 17.50€, 23€ and 29€, weekday *formule* at 15.50€, bottle of *vin de pays* 13.80€. A cosy, restful restaurant in a 13th-century building, with a log fire and a garden at the back. Traditional, although not inspired, French cooking. Reservation advisable on Sundays.

Au César Gourmand, 1 Place du Chatel, tel 01 60 58 81 65. A modest, well-located café serving light meals, with tables outside at the quieter corner of the busy centre of the Ville Haute.

15. Rambouillet

Summary residence of kings, emperors and presidents,
the château of Rambouillet is set in a delightful park.
Its 17th-century canals lead to the Jardin Anglais:
a hidden wilderness crossed by streams,
concealing a thatched cottage built for a
princess and Marie Antoinette's dairy

Rambouillet is gratifyingly easy to reach from Paris by train,
but you will not have to contend with enormous queues to visit
the château. Parisians tend to head for the Forest of Rambouillet, huge but far too car-friendly and so somewhat crowded, and
foreign visitors are more likely to gravitate to nearby Versailles.

Rambouillet, perhaps because it is an official presidential
residence, does not attract the public on the same scale. In
fact, it is very rewarding to visit, as although only a few rooms
are included in the guided tour, they are good value. The visit
to the 14th-century Tour François I, concealed by the 19th-
century façade, is followed by a tour of Marie Antoinette's
boudoir, Napoleon's astonishing bathroom and the dining
room in which De Gaulle gave General Leclerc the final orders
for the liberation of Paris in 1944. It has been a venue for
international conferences since 1975 when the first G5 summit
was organised by President Giscard d'Estaing. More recently,
the hastily-convened peace conference on Kosovo was held here
in February 1999.

The château overlooks a formal French garden and a
sweeping view of the canals, bordered by statues and rows of
trees. But like the château itself, the stately park conceals some
unexpected surprises. Away from the château, the canal-side
walk becomes more like a country stroll as you pass swans,
ducks and fishermen, and opens out into the Jardin Anglais, a
romantic landscape garden added in the 18th century when the

'back to nature' fashion was at its height. The one at Rambouillet is the most successful imitation of nature I have seen in the Ile de France. A meadow crossed by streams leads via little footbridges to the Chaumière aux Coquillages, (Seashell Cottage), not far from the Laiterie (Dairy) built for Marie Antoinette. In spring the ground is covered with bluebells and the stream is noisy with the sound of fish spawning. The walk back through the old town centre of Rambouillet, past the little Place Marie Roux with its umbrella-shaded cafés, prolongs the sense of leisurely enjoyment, which you could round off by a visit to the model railway museum on the way to the station.

The oldest part of the château dates from the 14th century and the Tour François I is so-called because that king is popularly supposed to have died there in 1547, having been taken ill while hunting in the nearby forest. The canals were mainly constructed in the late 17th century, just before the purchase of the château in 1706 by Louis XIV as a gift to the Comte de Toulouse, his legitimised son by Madame de Montespan. The château stayed in royal hands up to the Revolution, although Marie Antoinette, who was not fond of hunting, was bored there. Louis XVI had the Laiterie built to amuse her and remind her of the Trianon. From 1800 to 1815 Rambouillet was used by Napoleon, who chose to spend his last night in France there on 29 June 1815, on his way to exile in St Helena. It was at Rambouillet that Charles X signed his abdication in 1830, before he too left France for exile in England. The château became an imperial residence again under Napoleon III, and has been a presidential residence since 1896, used to entertain visiting heads of state such as Khrushchev, Eisenhower, Nelson Mandela and Boris Yeltsin. President Chirac ended the long tradition of hunting at Rambouillet, which is no longer considered an acceptable use of public funds. However, state funds are lavished on the park, which was rapidly re-opened to the public, following the temporary closure of the Jardin Anglais and the Laiterie after the great storm of December 1999.

Suggested visit to Rambouillet

From the **station** take sortie A, the main exit. Cross the Place Prud'homme in front of the station and the busy Rue Sadi Carnot, straight over into the Rue Gambetta, the quietest road leading to the château. Take the third street on the left and go past *La Poste* and the 19th-century Gothic **Eglise St Lubin** in the Place Jeanne d'Arc. The entrance to the **Musée Ramboli-train**, devoted to model railways, is a little further down from the church, on the left. Go past the museum, down the little Rue de la République which leads to the straggling main shopping street in Rambouillet, Rue du Général de Gaulle. This is the latest in a series of name changes, from Rue Royale to Nationale, then Impériale and back again to Nationale, reflecting the changes in government.

This part of Rambouillet has pretty old houses which give it a village-like feel, but unlike most villages it is quite lively in a discreet sort of way. Most of the cafés are open on Sunday, the Brasserie du Roi de Rome seeming the most attractive, with tables outside in a quiet cul-de-sac leading to the **Palais du Roi de Rome**. Built in 1784, the two-storey mansion was converted in 1812 to serve as a palace for Napoleon's little son, the Roi de Rome, who only spent a few hours there before leaving in captivity for Austria. It is now used for art exhibitions (free) and has a pretty public garden and a museum of board games, **Le Musée du Jeu de l'Oie**.

Continue along Rue du Général de Gaulle to Place de la Libération and the helpful **Tourist Office**, next to the town hall. The entrance to the park from here is the most direct for the **château**, as the visitors' entrance is at the back. The guided visit includes Marie Antoinette's light and airy boudoir in white and gold and the memorable sight of Napoleon's bathroom, completely covered with imperial motifs in the fashionable Pompeian style (Pompeii had just been excavated when the décor was painted in 1809). Painted medallions recall the triumphs of the First Empire, presumably so that Napoleon could contemplate them from his bath. The bath itself is rather small, to fit the Emperor. The best **view** of the park and its

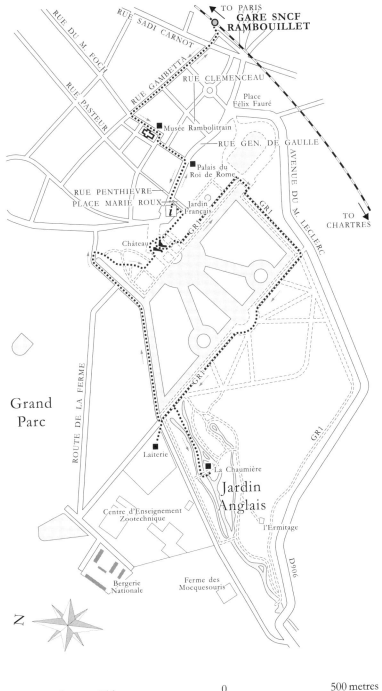

Rambouillet

canals is to be had from the windows of the château.

From the front of the château turn left along the canal, past the formal Jardin Français, then right along the GR1 footpath (see p. 239) alongside another canal. It is a delightful tree-lined walk, popular with fishermen, which follows the trapeze-shaped design of the canals to the meadow leading to the **Jardin Anglais**, the most untamed part of the park. A little stream, crossed by footbridges, leads to the **Chaumière aux Coquillages**, an impossibly English-looking thatched cottage built around 1775 for the Princesse de Lamballe, Marie Antoinette's ill-fated friend. It owes its name to the elegant décor of mother of pearl and marble concealed by its rustic exterior. If you are feeling adventurous you could explore the extreme south-west part of the Jardin Anglais to find another 18th-century pastoral folly on rising ground near the stream, **l'Ermitage**, a chapel that Napoleon had decorated with paintings. It has been so thoroughly restored that it looks quite modern and is not yet open to the public, but the walk to it is extremely pretty. It is covered with primroses in spring, and the stream nearby is loud with croaking frogs.

Retrace your steps past the Chaumière back to the canal and turn left through a gate facing the **Laiterie**, the dairy built for Marie Antoinette in 1785. Its best-known feature is a statue of a nymph and a goat within an artificial grotto. From here, follow the road past the canal on your right back to the **château**. There is a pedestrian exit from the park leading straight to the

La Chaumière aux Coquillages

Place Marie Roux, where there is a cluster of cafés. I particularly like the name of the little one in the Rue Général de Gaulle facing the bigger, busier Le Napoléon – it is called Le Nelson. **Le Napoléon**, a long-established brasserie with tables outside, is your best bet for food on Sundays.

It is possible to leave the

park by another main entrance further on which will bring you out into the Place Felix Fauré, bypassing the Rue Général de Gaulle, but the way you came is the quickest and most attractive route back to the **station**.

Distance from Paris: 50 km (31 miles)
Depart: Gare de Montparnasse
Arrive: Rambouillet
Journey time: 34 minutes
Length of visit: Half or full day
Carte Orange Zone: 6
Single ticket: 6.70€
Distance from station to château: 1 km (½ mile)
Pop.: 26,000

Getting there

Fast **SNCF trains** to Chartres, stopping at Versailles and Rambouillet, leave Gare de Montparnasse (*Ile de France*) approximately every hour on weekdays, every one and a half hours on Sundays. The last fast train back is around 10 pm on weekdays, 8.24 pm on Saturday and around 11 pm on Sunday.

NB: The *Départs Ile de France* information board may show additional trains for Rambouillet but check arrival times carefully, as stopping trains can take over an hour.

Car: From the west of Paris via the A13, A12 and N10, or from the south of Paris via the A6, A10, A11 and N10.

When to go

The park is not particularly crowded, even on public holidays, once you are away from the château and the car access road. A warm, sunny day would be ideal, when you could picnic in the park. **Ring first** to check that the president is not in residence if you want to visit the château, which is closed on Tuesdays, and go later in the week if you also want to visit the Musée Rambolitrain.

Useful information

Office de Tourisme, Place de la Libération, 78120 Rambouillet, tel 01 34 83 21 21. www.rambouillet-tourisme.fr. Open 9.30 am–12 noon and 2.30–5.30 pm every day and from 9.30 am–12.30 pm and 2–6 pm in July and August. Closed 25 December and 1 January.

Château de Rambouillet, main entrance via Place de la Libération, tel 01 34 83 00 25. Half-hour guided visit of part of the lower ground and ground floor, approximately every ten minutes, in French. You can ask for an explanatory brochure in English, to be returned when you leave. Open 10–11.40 am and 2–5.30 pm every day except Tuesday. Closes at 4.30 pm from

October to March. Closed on 1 January, 1 May, 1 and 11 November, 25 December and during presidential visits. Adults 5€, visitors under 25, 3.50€. Combined ticket including the château, the Laiterie and the Chaumière aux Coquillages, 6.50€; ticket for the Laiterie and the Chaumière only, 3€. All visits are free to those under 18.

La Laiterie and the Chaumière aux Coquillages (Dairy and Seashell Cottage). Well worth the walk, even if you don't buy a ticket for the guided visit inside. Open at the same times as the château. The **park** is open every day, entrance free.

Jardin et Palais du Roi de Rome (The King of Rome's palace and garden), Place du Roi de Rome, off Rue Général de Gaulle, tel 01 34 83 10 31. Contact the Tourist Office for details of current exhibitions held in the palace. The garden, which has been restored to the original design of 1812, is open daily from 2–7 pm.

Musée du Jeu de l'Oie, Palais du Roi de Rome, tel 01 30 88 73 73. A collection of board games from the 17th to 20th centuries. Open 2–6 pm from Tuesday to Sunday. Adults 2.50€, children aged 12–17, 1.50€, children under 12 free.

Le Musée Rambolitrain, 4 Place Jeanne d'Arc, tel 01 34 83 15 93. A collection of 4,000 model trains and 400 metres of track. Open 10 am–12 noon and 2–5.30 pm from Wednesday to Sunday and on public holidays, except 25 December and 1 January. Adults 3.50€, children under 12, 2.50€, children under 4 free.

Cafés and restaurants

The park is an ideal place for a picnic and there are also several cafés in Rue Général de Gaulle and Place Marie Roux near the tourist office.

Le Napoléon, 3 Place Marie Roux, tel 01 34 83 03 64. Open daily until 8 pm.

16. Royaumont

A majestic Cistercian abbey surrounded by lovely countryside, an unusual venue for concerts

I can recommend a visit to Royaumont Abbey as being good value. Within easy reach of Paris, the trip can include a pretty countryside walk and if you go on a summer weekend you can also hear medieval music in a perfect setting.

Royaumont is the largest and best-preserved Cistercian abbey in the Ile de France, retaining most of its 13th-century appearance including the cloisters, and flanked by the dramatic ruins of its church, demolished during the Revolution. It is set in an elegant park surrounded by ornamental canals, and now functions as an international cultural centre, with a particular emphasis on music. As its name implies, the Abbey had a royal

The cloisters at Royaumont

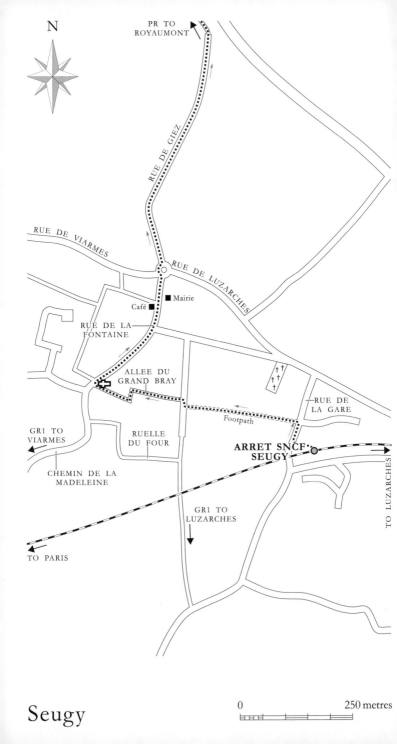

N

PR TO
ROYAUMONT

RUE DE GIEZ

RUE DE VIARMES

RUE DE LUZARCHES

Café   ■ Mairie

RUE DE LA
FONTAINE

ALLEE DU
GRAND BRAY

† †
† †
†

RUE DE
LA GARE

Footpath

GR1 TO
VIARMES

RUELLE
DU FOUR

**ARRET SNCF
SEUGY**

TO LUZARCHES

CHEMIN DE LA
MADELEINE

GR1 TO
LUZARCHES

TO PARIS

Seugy

0   250 metres

founder, Louis IX, who ordered its construction in 1228. This king was also a saint who insisted on waiting on the monks in the Refectory, an austerely beautiful room that is now used for concerts. I have seen a medieval passion play performed to music here, an unforgettable experience.

The best way to appreciate the harmony of the setting is to approach it on foot. There is a PR footpath (see p. 240) from the sleepy little village of Seugy which is on the railway line from Paris, an unusual and satisfying way of reaching the Abbey. The tea room at Royaumont overlooks a canal thick with water lilies and no one tells you to keep off the grass. If you have come for a concert, you can take the free shuttle bus back to the station at Viarmes.

4.3 km walk from Seugy to Royaumont

From the **station** at Seugy turn right into the Rue de la Gare. You can skirt the village to arrive at the roundabout leading to the footpath to Royaumont, but it is more fun to take a little footpath which goes via people's back gardens to the church. Turn sharp left from the Rue de la Gare and follow the path, which emerges at the little **church** on your right.

Go past the church to the Rendez-Vous des Chasseurs, a *café-tabac* selling newspapers which is the only shop in the village and therefore the centre of what activity there is. You will be conspicuous if you step inside, but so would you be if you were French – there are not many unfamiliar faces in Seugy. Savour the sensation of being in *la France profonde* only 45 minutes from Paris.

You are nearly at the end of the Rue de la Fontaine, which leads straight to a little roundabout from where you take the Rue de Giez. From the Rue de Giez there are discreet yellow PR signs all along the route.

The road soon becomes a path which crosses the D922 via a little underpass, emerging alongside a wood. Continue past the riding school (*Centre Equestre*), crossing a tiny stream, l'Ysieux, and passing a little waterfall on the right. A gentle

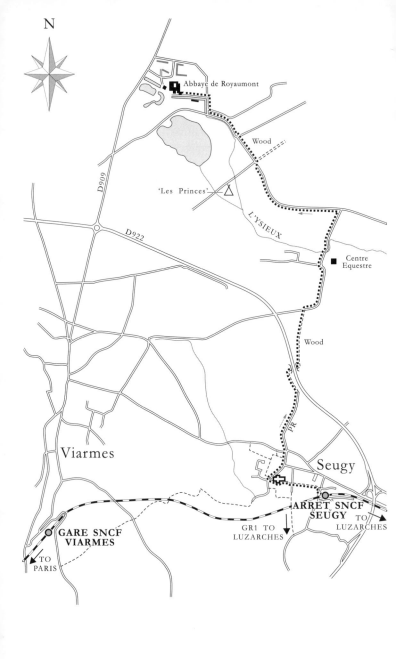

N

Abbaye de Royaumont

Wood

'Les Princes'

L'YSIEUX

Centre Equestre

Wood

PR

Viarmes

Seugy

ARRET SNCF
SEUGY

TO
LUZARCHES

GARE SNCF
VIARMES

GR1 TO
LUZARCHES

TO
PARIS

D909

D922

Seugy to
Royaumont

0   1km.

uphill stretch brings you to the edge of another wood, with a view of rolling countryside below. The path skirts the wood on your right and eventually leads, via a stone bridge on your right, into the Abbey grounds.

The approach to the **Abbey** is particularly impressive, surrounded by parkland with a tree-lined canal in which the arched windows are reflected. On one of my visits a rehearsal for Stravinsky's opera, *The Rake's Progress,* was taking place outside, around a piano perched on the grass. It was watched by a knot of enchanted bystanders, unable to tear themselves away. Overlooking a smaller canal to the left of the Abbey is the discreetly welcoming sight of tables and sunshades, the inspired location of the **tea room**. The Refectory, to the left of the cloisters, is reached via the main entrance in the middle of the building.

Distance from Paris: 35 km (22 miles)
Depart: Gard du Nord
Arrive: Seugy
Journey time: 45 minutes or less
Length of visit: Half or full day
Alternative return from: Viarmes
Carte Orange Zone: 5
Single ticket: 4.80€
Distance from Seugy to Royaumont: 4.3 km (2½ miles)

Getting there

SNCF trains from Gare du Nord (*Ile de France*) to Luzarches stop at Viarmes and Seugy once or twice an hour on weekdays, once an hour at weekends and make the return journey every hour up to approximately 11.30 pm.

Pick up a timetable for trains back to Paris at the Gare du Nord, as there is no ticket office at Seugy or Viarmes.

Royaumont is slightly nearer to Viarmes than to Seugy, but the shuttle bus from Viarmes to the Abbey only connects with certain trains on concert days. (See concert programme for times). The 3 km walk from Viarmes to Royaumont along the D909 is not recommended because of the traffic, and the steep uphill approach to Viarmes station on the way back (see p. 112).

The *navette* (shuttle bus) leaves the car park at Royaumont for Viarmes station after each concert, making several trips if necessary. Keep your concert ticket to show to the driver and be prepared to prevent middle-class Parisians from elbowing you aside when the bus appears.

Car: Autoroute A1 (Lille) from Porte de la Chapelle, exit 3 for N1 (Beauvais), then follow signs for Royaumont.

Taxi from Viarmes: tel 01 30 35 82 28.

When to go

Concerts usually take place in the afternoon or evening at weekends between August and October, although you can visit the Abbey at any time of the year.

Useful information

Fondation Royaumont, 95270 Asnières sur Oise, tel 01 30 35 59 70. www.royaumont.com. Open from 10 am–6 pm in summer and to 5.30 pm in winter all year round. Guided visits at weekends and on public holidays. Admission to the Abbey and grounds 5€, 4€ for children under 16 or students under 26, free to children under 6. **Concert programme and reservations**, tel 01 34 68 05 50. Open 10 am–noon and 2–6 pm Monday to Friday.

You can ask for the brochure to be sent to you or make a credit card booking by phone or at www.concertclassic.com. The brochure will arrive at a Paris address the following day and includes the timetable for the *navette*, enabling you to book your seat when you buy your ticket. Tickets 20€, 15€ students, include entrance to the Abbey and grounds.

Ateliers (workshops) for children aged 8-11 are held to coincide with concert times, and last two hours. 4€ per child, book at the same time as your concert ticket.

Cafés

Bar/tea room at Royaumont, open 12 noon–6 pm at weekends and public holidays.

Au Rendez-Vous des Chasseurs, Rue de la Fontaine, Seugy. Closed on Tuesday. See p. 115.

Auberge de la Gare, Viarmes. Described in visit to Luzarches on p. 115.

17. St Germain-en-Laye

The Symbolist movement is evoked by the former home of the painter Maurice Denis, now a museum, and its delightful garden

St Germain-en-Laye, strategically located on a hill overlooking the Seine and easily accessible from Paris, has always been fashionable with the French ruling classes. The first royal château was built here in 1122 to defend the plain below and the approach to Paris, and when it was burnt down by the Black Prince in 1346, a Renaissance château replaced it. Several French kings were born here, including Louis XIV, who commissioned Le Nôtre to design the terrace with its spectacular view of the valley of the Seine before setting him to design the gardens at Versailles, where the whole court moved in 1682. The château itself was restored in the 19th century by Napoleon III who planned to turn it into a national Gallo-Roman museum, a project which has been completed and extended to include prehistoric exhibits in their international context.

The town and the château are literally on top of the RER express line to Paris, so it is easy to see why St Germain is such a desirable residential area in the eyes of Parisians. I first went there with a friend because the journey from Paris is so easy, intending to combine a breath of fresh air with a visit to the National Museum of Antiquities. But our hearts quailed when we saw the forbidding bulk of the château, and we decided to explore the sunny streets of the little town first. We soon came to what appeared to be a private house on the edge of the town, but actually turned out to be a museum of Symbolist art, the former home of the painter Maurice Denis. Set in a walled garden, it is as different from the grandiose château and its formal grounds as it is possible to imagine. The house itself has an interesting history and its contents are worth a visit, but it

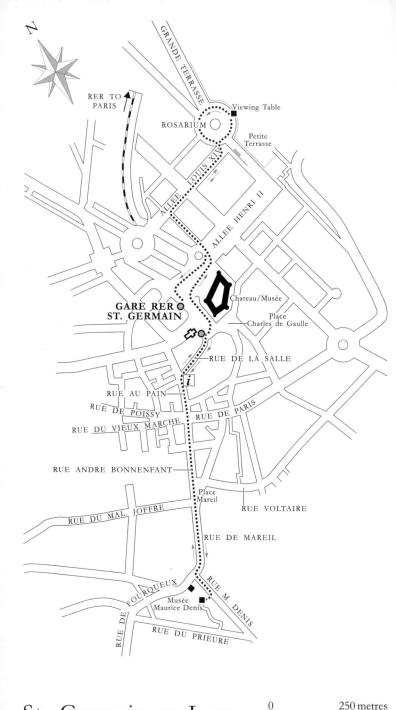

St. Germain-en-Laye

0   250 metres

was the garden, so accessible from Paris, yet so secluded and mysterious, that really appealed to us and has led me to choose St Germain for several return visits.

Suggested visit to St Germain-en-Laye

From the RER **station** take the 'sortie Eglise' which will bring you out at the church near Rue de la Salle. The château will hit you in the eye as you emerge, as will the huge park next to it, which leads to the famous view. Comfort yourself with the thought that you can see the view later. If you are tempted by the National Museum of Antiquities in the château, be warned that, once inside, you will be plunged into prehistoric, Celtic and Roman France, a period far removed in time from the château and the town. There is too much here to be absorbed in an hour and it is best left for a separate visit, unless the weather is cold or wet.

Turning your back on the château, look to the left of the church and head for the town centre by following the Rue de la Salle to the **Office de Tourisme** at no. 38 in the Rue Au Pain. It is a 17th-century house, in which the composer **Claude Debussy** was born in 1862. You can visit the small **museum** devoted to him on the first floor. Several of the houses in this semi-pedestrianised shopping area date from the same period, although their fashionable modern shop-fronts are an effective camouflage.

Follow the Rue Au Pain downhill. You could make a detour by turning right into the **market** in the Rue de Poissy, a good place to buy the ingredients for a picnic lunch. The *fromager* at no. 16 is one of those old-fashioned beautifully tiled shops which are being turned into boutiques in central Paris. It has a mouth-watering display of traditional cheeses. Continue along the Rue André Bonnenfant to the Place Mareil, a quiet little square with a convenient *alimentation* (grocery store) opposite. After this point the town centre appears to come to an abrupt end, with no more shops and hardly any people. As you continue downhill you will see the surrounding countryside coming into view. The **Musée Maurice Denis** surrounded by a high garden wall, is on a corner, with the main entrance on the Rue Maurice Denis.

It is an attractive white building, screened by foliage and it seems rather large for a painter's private house. In fact, it was built in 1688 on the initiative of Madame de Montespan, Louis XIV's longest-reigning mistress, as a hospital and orphanage for the poor – the 17th-century solution to the problem of beggars on the streets. It soon came under royal patronage and was run by the Sisters of Charity until 1803, when they downsized to the hospital in the town centre to save on administration costs. It was a retirement home for Jesuit priests after that, but was unoccupied when Maurice Denis bought it in 1914 and set about turning it into a studio and family home where he could entertain friends such as Roussel, Bonnard, Maillol and Debussy.

Maurice Denis, Self-portrait in front of Le Prieuré

The Prieuré today

The house became a centre for the Nabis, a group of painters calling themselves by the Hebrew word for 'prophet'. Founded by Paul Sérusier in 1888, the painters of this school took their inspiration from Gauguin and were part of the Symbolist movement that was influencing painting, poetry, music, sculpture and architecture at the beginning of the 20th century. Maurice Denis (1870–1943), the main spokesman for the group, lived in the house until his death and undertook the restoration of the **chapel** which he then decorated in pure Art Nouveau style. The chapel has a curious history. Built entirely at the expense of Madame de Montespan, the first stone was laid by the Duc du Maine, her legitimised son by Louis XIV, in a ceremony of great pomp on 12 June, 1698. He was born at St Germain in 1670, exactly 200 years before Maurice Denis, also a native of the town.

The painter's restoration of the house itself is much more restrained than in the chapel: the austerity of its vaulted arches, high windows and parquet floors recall its original function as a 17th-century public hospital. The collection on display, of work by Maurice Denis and his circle, *c.* 1900–1930, offers an intriguing contrast to the setting.

Denis' restoration of the house, which he called 'Le Prieuré' (the Priory) also extended to the 2½-acre hillside **garden**. Steps lead from a broad terrace containing sculptures by Antoine Bourdelle (there is an interesting little museum of his work in Paris, behind the Gare de Montparnasse) past a rose arbour down to a lawn surrounded by trees, 'le théâtre de verdure' (theatre of greenery). Secluded paths lead off on either side to arbours and benches hidden by trees or to a solitary statue. The atmosphere is remote and mysterious, as Denis intended, even on a sunny day when children are playing on the lawn.

More steps lead down past a little pond to the herb and vegetable garden at the foot of the slope. This is in fact the site of the original land and buildings which Madame de Montespan bought in 1682. They soon proved inadequate to the demand (there were a lot of beggars in France in 1682) and were replaced by the present building, with plans for another one which never materialised. This part of the garden, containing apple trees and a water pump, is hardly visited and is an ideal place to spend the afternoon on the grass with a picnic and a book. A gate leads from here into the Rue du Prieuré, but the walk back through the garden is prettier.

You could end your visit to St Germain with a walk through the château grounds to see the view over Paris. The formal grounds, laid out by Le Nôtre, are vast and the walk can seem endless, although it is actually only ten minutes and the view is worth it. Go via the Allée Louis XIV, planted with lime trees, which will bring you to the semi-circular viewing table overlooking a **panorama** of the valley of the Seine and the west of Paris. You can make out Herblay with the help of the viewing table and even the Eiffel Tower on a good day, although the square white Arch at La Défense, clearly visible in the middle, did not exist when the table was placed here. There is a vineyard on the right-hand slope and to your left the elegant balustrade of the Grande Terrasse extends for another 2,400 metres to the Forest of St Germain.

There is a little *buvette* thoughtfully located just behind the viewing table, where you can sit and order a drink before returning to the RER **station** opposite the château.

Distance from Paris: 20 km
(12 ½ miles)
Depart: Châtelet-les-Halles
Arrive: St Germain-en-Laye
Journey time: 35 minutes or
less
Length of visit: Half day or
full day
Carte Orange Zone: 4
Single ticket: 3.50€
**Distance from station to
Maurice Denis Museum:** ¾
km (½ mile)
Pop.: 41,710

Getting there

RER A1 trains to St Germain-
en-Laye leave central Paris from
Châtelet and other stations in
central Paris every ten minutes.
The last train back is at 12.17 am.
Car: N190 via Chatou or N13
via Bougival or A13, second exit,
Versailles Ouest/St Germain-
en-Laye.

When to go

This visit is for a warm day when
you don't have much time or
energy to explore too far afield
and just want to relax in a country garden. It is suitable for
children or older visitors as there
is a choice of activities and not
much walking. Avoid Monday
when the Maurice Denis museum
is closed, and Tuesday if you
want to visit the Musée d'Antiquités Nationales. There is a

market in the Rue de Poissy on
Tuesday, Friday and Sunday mornings, closing at around 1.30 pm.

Useful information

Office Municipal de Tourisme,
Maison Claude Debussy, 38 Rue
Au Pain, 78100 St Germain-en-
Laye, tel 01 34 51 05 12. Open in
summer 9.30 am–1 pm and 2–6
pm on Tuesday and Thursday–
Saturday, 2–6 pm on Monday and
Wednesday, 10 am–1 pm on
Sunday and public holidays. In
winter open 9.30 am–12.30 pm
and 2–5.30 pm on Tuesday and
Thursday–Saturday, 2–5.30 pm
on Monday and Wednesday, 10
am–1 pm on Sunday.
Musée Claude Debussy On
the first floor of the tourist office.
Open 2–6 pm, Tuesday to Satur-
day, closes at 5.30 pm in winter.
Closed on public holidays.
Admission free.
**Musée des Antiquités
Nationales**, Château de St
Germain-en-Laye, tel 01 39 10 13
00. www.musee-antiquitesna-
tionales.fr. Open every day except
Tuesday, 9 am–5.15 pm. Open 10
am–6.15 pm at summer weekends
and on public holidays. Admission 4.50€, 3€ for visitors under
25, and for everyone on Sunday.
Free to visitors under 18 and to
teachers on proof of status.
**Musée Départemental Mau-
rice Denis (Le Prieuré)**, 2 bis
Rue Maurice Denis, tel 01 39 73 77
87. www.musee-mauricedenis.fr.
Open 10 am–5.30 pm from Tues-

day to Friday and 10 am–6.30 pm at weekends and on public holidays, except 1 January, 1 May and 25 December. Admission 3.80€, students under 18 and teachers 2.20€. No charge for entrance to garden.

Musée Bourdelle, 16 Rue Antoine Bourdelle, 75015 Paris, tel 01 49 54 73 73. Open Tuesday-Sunday, 10 am–6 pm.

Cafés and restaurants

There are several cafés and restaurants near the RER station and in the Rue de la Salle.

18. Sceaux

Majestic and serene, Sceaux is the most classical of French parks, and the one which is closest to Paris

Only ten kilometres from Notre Dame, the much sought-after residential suburb of Sceaux has developed around the park designed for Colbert in the 1670s. It is a favourite with Parisians and residents alike but is little-known to foreign visitors, who are more likely to head for Versailles to experience *le Grand Siècle* of Louis XIV.

In fact, *le Grand Siècle* was created as much by his hardworking and able minister as it was by the princely extravagance of the Sun King, and modern France probably owes as much of its identity to Colbert as it does to Louis XIV. Their different but complementary personalities are reflected in the parks surrounding their favourite residences, both designed by Le Nôtre. Although it is on a far smaller scale than Versailles, the sweeping perspectives at Sceaux leave a lasting impression of classical grandeur and sober elegance, very much in the spirit of the age that Colbert did so much to bring into being.

Jean-Baptiste Colbert (1619–1683) bought the manor of Sceaux in 1670 and had the 15th-century château razed and replaced by a magnificent construction designed by Claude Perrault (brother of the writer of fairy tales). Le Brun decorated the chapel and the Pavillon de l'Aurore (Temple of the Dawn) and Le Nôtre was commissioned to design the park. He made clever use of the sloping terrain to create a play of perspectives, culminating in the famous *Grandes Cascades*, a staircase of nine waterfalls and fountains leading to an octagonal pond and prolonged by another green vista.

In July 1677 Colbert invited Louis XIV to Sceaux, having first made sure of a warm welcome for him from the villagers by halving their taxes. The royal visitors were impressed by the 'marvellous cleanliness' of the apartments, unusual for the period, the banquet, the music and the fireworks, followed by a performance of Racine's *Phèdre* in the Orangerie. As he emerged, the king was acclaimed by all the villagers dancing under the illuminated trees of the park. Enchanted, he remarked that he had never been more agreeably entertained.

The good taste and clever management which marked the king's visit continued to be shown in Colbert's expansion and embellishment of his favourite residence. His son added the Grand Canal and the present Orangerie. In 1699 the château was sold to the Duc du Maine, the legitimised son of Louis XIV and Madame de Montespan. The Duchesse du Maine, who had inherited the stylish tastes of her grandfather, the 'Grand Condé' (see the chapter on Chantilly), made Sceaux famous for its elegant parties at the beginning of the 18th century. They became known as the 'Nuits de Sceaux', at which Voltaire and other distinguished writers were frequent guests.

After the Revolution, Sceaux was declared a *bien national* (national property) and sold off. The château was demolished and the park turned into farmland before reverting to semi-wilderness. Some readers of *Le Grand Meaulnes* by Alain-Fournier (1886–1914) think that the park was the mysterious domain described in his celebrated novel, published in 1913. He was a pupil at the Lycée Lakanal from 1903 to 1906, at a time when the park was in a state of romantic neglect. It was rescued from dismemberment in 1923 when it was acquired by the Département de la Seine and most of it restored. The present château, built in 1856 by the Duc de Trévise, now houses the Musée de l'Ile de France.

As with so many of Le Nôtre's parks (the worst, from this point of view, being Chantilly) Sceaux was designed to offer majestic vistas to impress the eye rather than to be easy on the feet. Relentlessly straight paths lead to the Grand Canal, which must be tiresomely circumnavigated, as there is no bridge across. For this reason the suggested route covers only the most visually dramatic parts of the park and offers contrasting walks on the way there and back. There are surprisingly untamed wooded bits, covered with violets in spring, if you

Château de Sceaux

want to branch off the paths or you could walk south or east and leave by either of the other two RER stations shown on the map. The walk back via the old part of Sceaux is, however, by far the most interesting.

I have also included brief directions for a visit to Chateaubriand's house, 2½ kilometres (1½ miles) west of the park. You can walk or take a bus from the house to the RER station at Robinson, one kilometre (just over half a mile) away. François-René de Chateaubriand (1768–1848), the great Romantic poet and statesman, managed to get on the wrong side of both Napoleon and the Bourbons. Fans of the French Romantic movement will be fascinated by the house and garden, which he bought in 1807 when he was forced to leave Paris after criticising Napoleon. He spent ten happy years there, transforming it into a Romantic haven and producing some of his most famous work, notably *Les Mémoires d'Outre-Tombe* from the tower he built in the garden. Allow 2–3 hours for the walk and visit, slightly less if you take the bus.

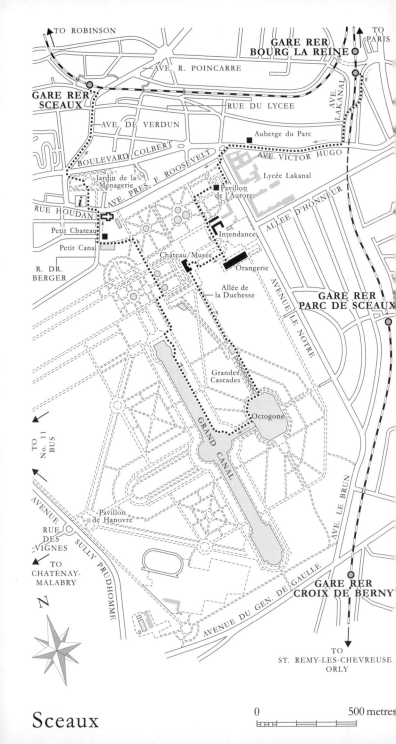

Sceaux

TO ROBINSON

TO PARIS

GARE RER BOURG LA REINE

AVE. R. POINCARRE

GARE RER SCEAUX

RUE DU LYCEE

AVE. DE VERDUN

AVE. LAKANAL

Auberge du Parc

BOULEVARD COLBERT

AVE. VICTOR HUGO

Jardin de la Ménagerie

Lycée Lakanal

AVE. PRES. F. ROOSEVELT

Pavillon de l'Aurore

RUE HOUDAN

ALLÉE D'HONNEUR

Petit Chateau

Intendance

Petit Canal

Château/Musée

Orangerie

R. DR. BERGER

Allée de la Duchesse

AVENUE LE NOTRE

GARE RER PARC DE SCEAUX

Grandes Cascades

GRAND CANAL

Octogone

TO No. 11 BUS

AVE. LE BRUN

Pavillon de Hanovre

AVENUE SULLY PRUDHOMME

RUE DES VIGNES

TO CHATENAY-MALABRY

N

AVENUE DU GEN. DE GAULLE

GARE RER CROIX DE BERNY

TO ST. REMY-LES-CHEVREUSE ORLY

0   500 metres

Suggested visit to Sceaux

Take the 'Sortie André Theuriet' from the **station** at Bourg la Reine. Follow this little street to the right as it parallels the railway line and crosses it into the Avenue du Lycée Lakanal. Turn left to follow this road slightly uphill until it comes out into the main road, Avenue Victor Hugo. Turn right uphill, opposite the grounds of the Lycée Lakanal. The **Auberge du Parc**, further along on the right, is a good place for a drink, a snack or lunch.

Turn left at the roundabout to cross the road, past the Lycée Lakanal, into the Avenue Claude Perrault. The entrance to the **park** is opposite the Lycée, the second gate on the right, facing the **Pavillon de l'Aurore,** an elegant little building crowned by an unmistakeably 17th-century cupola. The work of Claude Perrault, it takes its name from Le Brun's painting of the *Char de l'Aurore* (Chariot of the Dawn) which decorates the ceiling of the dome, and has recently been restored and opened to the public. It is the only building commissioned by Colbert to have survived.

Keep going left, past the 18th-century brick **Pavillon de l'Intendance**, which still houses the administrative offices of the park, until you come to the *entrée d'honneur*, the imposing principal entrance to the park designed for Colbert. The long, tree-lined Allée d'Honneur, impressive to look at but monotonous to walk, leads up to it from Bourg la Reine. It goes straight to the château, but if you want to see the Orangerie, keep on walking past the château on the right. Soon after the *sanitaires* (W.C.) you will come to the stately **Orangerie** built by Mansart in 1686. Racine and Lully wrote the *Idylle de Sceaux* to be performed here for Louis XIV and Madame de Maintenon, and later Voltaire's comedies were put on here by the Duchesse du Maine. Nowadays it is mainly used for concerts, the programme for which can be had from the Musée de l'Ile de France.

Leaving the Orangerie behind you, turn right to the château. The **Musée de l'Ile de France** is on the ground and upper floors, from where there is an excellent **view** of the park.

Apart from the story of the château and its owners, it has a display of paintings and engravings showing the châteaux of the Ile de France as they looked in the 17th, 18th and 19th centuries, including some that no longer exist, such as St Cloud, which was burned down by the Prussians in 1870. Porcelain from Sceaux and Sèvres is on display, as well as a section upstairs devoted to *fêtes populaires* in the Ile de France. There are 19th-century railway posters for the *bal des Canotiers* at Bougival and the *guinguette* at nearby Robinson where, inspired by Defoe's *Robinson Crusoe*, people dined in tree-houses.

There is a little *buvette* next to the château where you can order crêpes before strolling right to admire the **view** in front of the château extending downhill almost as far as the eye can see. Its peculiarly French formality is accentuated by the clipped cone-shaped trees on either side, set off by gay flowerbeds and ornamental ponds. It invariably has a calming effect on the nerves.

Turn left from the *buvette*, following the signs for 'Cascades' down the shady Allée de la Duchesse, one of the pleasantest walks in the park. It eventually divides into two flights of steps on either side of a dramatic staircase of water-falls, the **Grandes Cascades**. Take the steps on the left, past the puffed-out cheeks of the stone masks sculpted by Rodin, through whose lips the water is ejected when the fountains are playing. The sound of rushing water continuously spilling downhill accompanies the descent, a triumph of hydraulic engineering. The waterfalls end in a large octagonal pond, in the middle of which a jet of water spurts up to ten metres into the air. Romantic statues surround the **Octogone**, a restful place which is popular with fishermen and children who are fascinated by the ducks. The statues of two stags flank the continuation of the perspective to the south, which is, however, a fairly tedious walk.

Instead, turn right at the bottom of the steps, following the pond as it joins a little canal which links it to the **Grand Canal**. You cannot but be impressed by this majestic stretch of water which extends for more than a kilometre, almost the full length of the park. The great storm of December 1999 felled some of the poplars which line both banks, but with the state-sponsored efficiency of which Colbert would have been justly proud they were re-planted at record speed.

Turn right to follow the canal back to the château, and cross in front of it, past the horizontal perspective stretching down-hill. Follow the map to the **Petit Canal**, the size of a very long swimming pool. This slightly sunken green-tinted stretch of water was once a carp reservoir for the Petit Château and has only recently been restored. It is a tranquil, mysterious place, almost hidden from view, with only a few people quietly sunning themselves around its grassy verges. If you stand on one of the stone benches half-way along its length you will have a last **view** of the Grand Canal stretching in an unbroken line into the distance. There is a pretty little garden above the canal, which has been restored to its 17th-century design.

The **Petit Château** next to it was built in 1661 and was acquired by Colbert to become part of the park. Later it was the nursery for the children of the Duchesse du Maine before it was separated from the park again and eventually became the public library for the growing town of Sceaux. It now houses the town planning department and is also used for art exhibitions (free).

Leave by the 17th-century gateway into the little Rue du Dr Berger and turn right, past some fascinating side streets, slightly uphill to the **Eglise St Jean-Baptiste**. The 16th-century church is not particularly remarkable but seems to be always open, and this part of Sceaux, around the *place* opposite the church with its two cafés, has an unexpectedly village-like atmosphere that is very attractive.

Opposite the Café de la Paix is the entrance to a small park, the **Jardin de la Ménagerie**, so called because the Duchesse du Maine buried her pets here. The two stone columns mark the tombs of her canaries. Cross the park diagonally to the left, past the small **tourist office** at the entrance, emerging at a busy crossroads. Take the second road on the right, the Avenue de Verdun, which leads downhill to the pretty little RER **station** at Sceaux.

3 ½ km walk to Chateaubriand's house in Châtenay-Malabry

It is possible to take the no. 11 bus, but you may have to wait up to an hour for the 25-minute journey to the *Maison de Chateaubriand* stop, and you will miss seeing the church of St Germain l'Auxerrois. If you do decide to take the bus, leave the park by the Pavillon de Hanovre gate, west of the Grand Canal. Turn right into the Avenue de Sully Prudhomme, skirting the park for 600 metres until you come to a roundabout, the Rond Point de Bergneustadt. The bus terminus is here at the *Coulée Verte* stop.

If you decide to walk, there are occasional pedestrian signs for Chateaubriand's house along the route. Leave the park by the Pavillon de Hanovre gate. Cross the Avenue Sully Prud-homme and take the Rue des Vignes to the end, then its continuation as Rue Ste Catherine which leads to the 11th-century **church of St Germain l'Auxerrois**, which is well worth a visit. It is, unusually, always open. The oldest part is the corner to the left of the altar, where the tops of the pillars depict the medieval stone-masons who built the church, carry-ing the tools of their trade. There is a friendly *café-tabac* opposite the church, contributing to the timeless village-like charm of the place.

Turn left from the church, past Place Voltaire (his parents had a house in Châtenay) and left into the Rue du Dr Le Savoureux, which soon forks, continuing to the right. Cross the main road, Avenue Roger Salengro, and continue slightly uphill into the Rue Chateaubriand, following it all the way as it winds to the gates of the **Parc aux Vallée des Loups**. You buy tick-ets for the visit here inside the left-hand entrance and then follow the path a little way uphill to the **Maison de Chateaubriand**.

Chateaubriand redesigned parts of the house, originally a gardener's cottage, which now sports a portico with caryatids and pillars at the back, as well as some unfortunate recent restoration of the brickwork. It overlooks a small park *à l'anglaise* which he planted with exotic trees to remind him of

Châteaubriand's Tour Velleda

his travels. Some of these are still standing and breathe the pure spirit of Romanticism, as does the **Tour Velleda**, an isolated tower at the back of the park which served as his study. Its stone floor and fireplace are strongly reminiscent of Rousseau's 'Donjon' at Montmorency, although the original crumbling façade has been over-enthusiastically restored. The guided tour of the house can be avoided if you go on a Sunday, which is, however, the most popular day for visitors. The *salon de thé*, which has tables outside overlooking the little park, is a delight.

On leaving, turn left from the park gates down the Rue Chateaubriand. (Ignore the no. 11 *Maison de Chateaubriand* bus stop immediately left of the park gates, which is for buses going the other way.) At the crossroads take the first right, the Rue Eugène Sinet, and consult the timetable at the nearby *Chateaubriand* stop. It is fun taking this luxurious little mini-bus, which feels like a limousine (you can use a Paris Métro ticket) but as it is only two stops to the RER station at

Robinson, it may not be worth the wait. If so, return to the crossroads, take the next road on the right, Rue Anatole France, and follow it until it joins the main road, Avenue des Quatre Chemins. Turn left uphill and the RER **station** at Robinson is a little further, on the right.

Distance from Paris: 10 km (6 miles)
Depart: St Michel Notre Dame
Arrive: Bourg la Reine
Journey time: 15 minutes
Length of visit: Half or full day
Alternative return from: Sceaux or Parc de Sceaux or La Croix de Berny or Robinson
Carte Orange Zone: 3
Single ticket: 2.10€
Distance from Bourg la Reine station to Parc de Sceaux: 1.2 km (¾ mile)
Distance from Parc de Sceaux to Sceaux station: 1 km (½ mile)
Pop.: 19,850

---

on Saturdays. No Sunday service.
Car: N20 or A86, exit 26 for Sceaux.

When to go

The park is at its best on a quiet sunny day. It is busiest on Sunday, but is never uncomfortably crowded. If possible, choose a Wednesday, a weekend or a public holiday, when the fountains of the Grandes Cascades are in action and the Musée de l'Ile de France and Chateaubriand's house are open.

Useful information

Office de Tourisme, Pavillon de Jardin de la Ménagerie, 70 Rue Houdan, 92330 Sceaux, tel 01 46 61 19 03. Open 10 am–1 pm Wednesday–Sunday all year round, 3–7 pm every day except Monday in summer, 3–5 pm in winter.

Domaine de Sceaux, tel 01 41 87 28 60. www.parc-de-sceaux.net. The **park** is open until around sunset, varying from 5 pm in winter to 10 pm in summer. There are almost no restrictions on walking or lying on the grass.

Musée de l'Ile de France,

Getting there

All southbound **RER B trains** (destination Robinson or St Rémy-les-Chevreuse) stop at Bourg la Reine and run at three-to seven-minute intervals, seven days a week. Stops after Bourg la Reine are served every 15 minutes and there are trains back to Paris until after midnight.

Bus no. 11 (the aptly-named *Le Paladin*) from Chateaubriand's house to Robinson RER station runs hourly until 7 pm, 6.30 pm

Château de Sceaux, tel 01 41 87 29 50. Open 10 am–6 pm, 5 pm in winter every day except Tuesday. Closed 1 January, 1 May, and 25 December. Admission free.

The **Pavillon de l'Aurore** is open at weekends, 3.30–5.30 pm in summer, 2.30–4.30 pm in winter. Admission free.

The Museum also has details of concerts at the **Orangerie**. Or telephone 01 46 60 07 79 for the concert programme and 01 47 02 22 29 to make a reservation.

Maison de Chateaubriand, 87 Rue Chateaubriand, 92290 Châtenay-Malabry, tel 01 55 52 13 00, www.maison-de-chateaubriand.fr. Open 10 am–12 noon and 2–6 pm from April to September and 2–5 pm the rest of the year, every day except Monday. Closed in January.The 4.50€ ticket includes admission to the park, an hour's guided visit of the house (in French but there are notes available in English) and a video on Chateaubriand's life. Students and teachers 3€, children under 12 free. Entrance to the park only but including the video, 1.50€. Free admission on the first Sunday of the month. The last visit is 45 minutes before closing. There are no guided visits on Sunday afternoons and public holidays, when entrance to the house and park is 1.50€.

The *salon de thé,* open in the afternoon, is discreetly located in the garden, left of the entrance to the house.

Restaurants and cafés

There are two cafés near the church at Sceaux, one of them open on Sunday, and three *buvettes* in the park. The one near the château sells crêpes.

Les Ecuries de Colbert, 8 Avenue Claude Perrault, 92330 Sceaux, tel 01 46 15 63 09. I have not tried this newly-opened restaurant and *salon de thé*, which is in the park, near the château. It is open from 10 am to 5 pm and has a menu at 20€.

L'Auberge du Parc, 6 Avenue du Président Roosevelt, 92330 Sceaux, tel 01 43 50 35 15. Open until 11 pm seven days a week, this friendly and efficient café/hotel/restaurant is run by a Portuguese family. It offers good value French cooking as well as Portuguese specialities such as sucking pig. The 9€ weekday lunchtime menu includes wine. Dishes à la carte at around 11€. The little *terrasse* with garden tables, plastic chairs and geraniums is particularly inviting. Larger dining room at the back, with another *terrasse* overlooking the pretty garden.

19. Senlis

The lacy spire of the cathedral crowns the royal city of Senlis, birthplace of the French monarchy in the tenth century. Originally a walled town, its narrow cobbled streets enclose a history which stretches back over more than 2,000 years

Senlis is one of the most picturesque towns in the Ile de France, the setting for *Danton* and several other historical films. The ruins of the Roman wall blend harmoniously with medieval and 17th century houses which were once enclosed by an outer set of ramparts, a circuit of just over three kilometres. The tourist office lists 30 buildings of historical interest within this tiny space, a concentration rich enough to cause indigestion. Most visitors solve this problem by sticking to the streets around the Place de la Halle near the cathedral, which are predictably full of cars, boutiques and expensive restaurants.

However, it is very easy to avoid the crowds by simply branching off into the maze of narrow streets and exploring where your fancy takes you. Almost every detour will lead to a rewarding discovery. The route given here combines the most important sights with some that many visitors miss altogether, avoiding the busier streets as far as possible. It has been chosen to offer maximum interest and enjoyment and still leave you enough time for some unplanned exploring or museum visiting. The longer route will take around three hours at a leisurely pace and is highly recommended, but if you are combining a visit to Chantilly with Senlis, the shorter route should take around two hours or less.

Senlis was already an old city in AD 987 when the Frankish nobles met in its Château Royal to elect Hugues Capet, Duke of France and Count of Paris, as their king. Set on a hill between two streams, it was of strategic importance to the

Romans, who occupied it around 8 BC. Judging by the size of the arena just outside the city walls, capable of holding up to 11,000 spectators, Augustomagus, as it was called, was an important town, in whose defence the first set of ramparts was constructed against the barbarian invasions of the third century.

The first bishop of Senlis was St Rieul, credited with converting the town to Christianity in the fourth century. Tradition states that the Merovingian king Clovis visited Senlis in AD 511 to venerate the remains of the saint. Whether this is true or not, it was certainly a favourite place for successive kings to stay, attracted by the pleasures of the hunt. A hunting accident near Senlis ended the Carolingian dynasty and began the long rule of the Capetians, whose little kingdom of France eventually expanded to include the whole country.

The early kings of France continued to favour Senlis, traditionally visiting it on their return from being anointed in Reims. They endowed the town with some of its most prestigious buildings, including the cathedral and the second set of ramparts, built in the 12th century and partially demolished in the 19th. In 1594 Senlis unhesitatingly welcomed Henri of Navarre, the future Henri IV, on his way to Paris to claim his kingdom. But it was the last time that the city played an important part in the history of France.

Today it is a thriving provincial town, whose growing population is housed in satellite suburbs, one of them devoted to high technology. In 1962 the town centre was declared a preservation zone to be protected from unsightly redevelopment and its historic buildings are gradually being restored after centuries of neglect. But there are enough unrestored old buildings still concealed in its narrow streets to reward those who like to make their own discoveries.

Suggested visit to Senlis

Turn left outside the **station** at Chantilly for the bus station next door. The timetable for the Chantilly–Senlis bus is displayed at the bus stop, and it is a good idea to make a note of the times

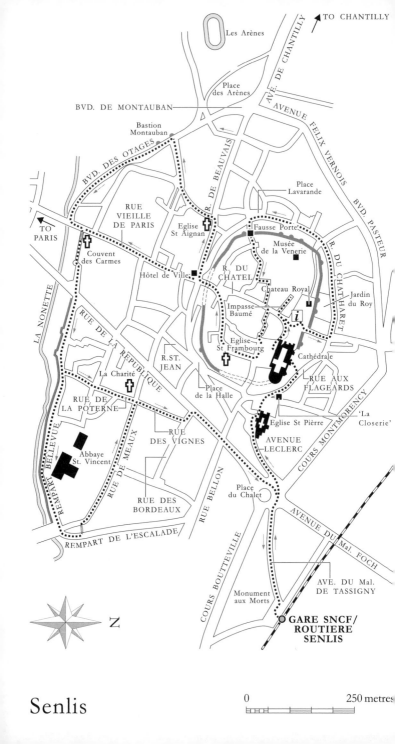

Senlis

0   250 metres

for the return trip, although you can usually pick up a timetable in the bus or at the tourist office at Senlis. There is usually a 10 to 15-minute wait for the bus connecting with the train.

The 25-minute ride from Chantilly is particularly enjoyable. Sit on the righthand side of the bus for the best **views** of the château park and its canals and for a spectacular glimpse of the château itself. The bus finally stops in front of the former railway **station** at Senlis, a toy-like building dating from 1922. Take the path to the right of the War Memorial (*Monument aux Morts*) which leads to a busy roundabout, the Place du Chalet, with a statue of a stag in the middle.

Cross the main road, and take the small second road on the right, past the **Porte de Compiègne** restaurant. This is the Avenue du Général Leclerc, which leads to a striking church, the **Eglise St Pierre**, no longer in use. The oldest parts are 12th century but its curious pepper-pot turret is 15th century and the tall bell-tower beside it was added in the 16th. As for the pious graffiti carved into the wall which you pass on the way to the main doorway in the Place St Pierre, it is impossible to say which century they belong to.

Turn into the Rue aux Flageards opposite the church. This quiet little cobbled street skirts the **Cathédrale Notre Dame** which rises impressively on the left, bordered by a pretty garden. The *terrasse* of **La Closerie**, a discreet tea-room tucked away into the corner of this street, overlooks the garden. Go through the wrought-iron gate leading to the little-used and rather beautiful north doorway. The cathedral seems much smaller than Notre Dame in Paris, which was started 12 years later, but I found it just as impressive, in a different way. Its distinctive spire dominates all the views of Senlis and each of the three doorways gives it a different aspect. It was built between 1151 and 1191 and the spire was added around 1240. In 1504 lightning caused a serious fire and parts of the cathedral were rebuilt, which explains the transition of styles, from the austerity of the 12th century to the lacy stonework of the pre-Renaissance.

Leave by the south doorway, which represents the Assumption of the Virgin. Walk round to the right to see the

Château Royal

west doorway, which represents her Coronation. There is a little sculpture of a man's face with horns (the Devil?) tucked among the carvings at eye level on the right, not to mention the grotesque heads grinning high up near the spire.

The Château Royal is opposite, next to the **Tourist Office**. Go past it, down the cobbled Rue du Chatel, past the massive 16th-century doorway of the Hotel des Trois Pots and turn right into the Impasse Baumé. It leads past a half-derelict building with arched windows and a weed-ridden garden to a medieval doorway. It was once the dormitory of the monks of the Prieuré St Maurice, a monastery founded by St Louis in the 13th century.

Return to the Tourist Office and the entrance to the **Château Royal park**, the ancient heart of the city. It contains the picturesque ruins of medieval buildings of different periods and the best-preserved parts of the Gallo-Roman fortifications, set in a peaceful garden with an atmosphere all of its own. It was probably the site of the Roman forum; the base of a statue to the Emperor Claudius, dated AD 48, was discovered here in 1947. The Château Royal in which Hugues Capet was elected king was built against the Roman rampart and was rebuilt several times before it finally collapsed in the 18th century. The massive tower which remains probably dates from the 12th century but its history is still unclear. Further along the garden the **Musée de la Vénerie** (Hunting Museum) is housed in the 18th-century Prior's House of the Prieuré St Maurice.

On leaving the park, turn left into the Rue de Villevert, past a remnant of the Roman rampart and left into the Rue du Chat-Haret. The entrance to the **Jardin du Roy** is a few steps along on the left. This quiet little park, on the other side of the Roman wall around the Château Royal, has what I consider to be the best **view** in Senlis. The elaborate west façade of the cathedral and its spire rise above the 12th-century ruins of the royal palace built into the Roman ramparts, against a plain grassy foreground. If the park happens to be closed you can still enjoy the view through the railings.

The cobbled little streets which follow skirt the Roman wall, past the Place St Maurice, down the Rue du Puits Tiphaine and past the old houses in the Place Lavarande. The narrow Rue de la Treille to the left is entered through an ancient arch, the postern gate of the Roman wall known as **La Fausse Porte** (the False Gate). Go up this street and turn left into the Rue St

La Fausse Porte

Péravi, where Henri IV once stayed. It continues to the right, leading back to the Rue du Chatel.

Cross Rue du Chatel, which was once the main street through Senlis on the Paris-Flanders route, prolonged by the Rue Vieille de Paris to the south. Take the first street on the left, Rue St Prothaise, which leads back to the cathedral on Place Notre Dame. Turn right into the Place St Frambourg where you will find the modest façade of the oldest church in Senlis, now a concert hall. The original **Eglise St Frambourg**, vestiges of which can be seen in the crypt, was built in the tenth century by Adelaide, wife of Hugues Capet, then razed to make way for a bigger church in 1170, a Gothic masterpiece completed in the 13th century. After the Revolution the church was abandoned and was being used as a garage when the Hungarian pianist Georges Cziffra bought it and restored it as the 'Auditorium Franz Liszt' in 1977.

Continue down the Rue St Frambourg on the right, into Rue de la Tonnellerie, which leads back into Rue du Chatel. Turn left down Rue du Chatel which crosses Place Henri IV and continues from here as the Rue Vieille de Paris. Turn right into Place Henri IV to admire the **Hotel de Ville** on the left, built in 1495.

Shorter route

Continue down the Rue Vieille de Paris. No. 42 on the left is the Hotel du Mouton where **Alexandre Dumas** stayed in 1850. No. 39, formerly the Hôtellerie de l'Ange, has an impressive 16th-century doorway. Further down on the left you will pass the **Couvent des Carmes**, a Carmelite convent and chapel dating from the 14th and 17th centuries which has recently been reconstructed as flats, although the façade has been preserved. Not so the crumbling chapel, which the builders conveniently overlooked, despite their promises to the *Mairie*. Just past the chapel an inconspicuous flight of steps on the left, the Passage des Carmes, leads up to the walk along the outer ramparts, overlooking the River Nonette.

Longer route

Continue past the **Hotel de Ville**, down the Rue Beauvais. You will soon come to the **Eglise St Aignan** on the left, half-concealed by its inconspicuous position among the other houses. Go around the corner to the Rue de la Montagne St Aignan to see the entrance of what was once the parish church of Senlis, dedicated around 1024. After the Revolution the nave, the windows and the capitals of the columns were methodically smashed. The church became a *salle de spectacle* in the 1950s and was in use as a cinema until the 1970s. It was ultimately saved from dereliction by a private individual and is still privately owned, although it has been a listed building since 1981. The curious addition above the main entrance was part of the cinema projection room.

Follow the Rue de la Montagne St Aignan downhill to the edge of the town, the Boulevard Montauban, part of the ring road around Senlis which has replaced the ramparts. Slightly to the right, on the other side of the Boulevard, steps lead up to the grassy **Bastion Montauban**, the remains of a 16th-century tower. There is a bench here and a **view** over the valley of the Nonette, with the round tower of another bastion visible to the left. Facing you, the little street you have just left winds uphill to the city, with the spire of the cathedral rising behind it. It was the route the Roman inhabitants of Augustomagus took to reach the arena, built in the first century AD.

Further along the Boulevard Montauban to the left, the Place des Arènes marks the entrance to **Les Arènes**. The site was discovered in 1865 and is still being restored, so the wrought-iron entrance gates are locked and unfortunately you can see nothing from the road. The gates conceal a grassy path scattered with the bases of Roman columns leading to the arena, which is impressive and strangely moving. The remains of a podium with steps leading down are still visible, as well as a little underground cell with stone arches opening on to the arena. Wild flowers cover the grassy slopes where the spectators once sat and the absolute silence is only broken by birds singing. If you happen to be in Senlis on the first Sunday of the month between

April and October, you can join a guided visit to the arena, which is usually closed to the public. You could return direct to Chantilly from here, as there is a request stop for the Chantilly bus in the Avenue de Chantilly, five minutes' walk from Les Arènes.

Continue along the Boulevard des Otages, whose name commemorates four hostages executed here in 1418, during the civil war between the Armagnacs and the Burgundians. When you reach the bridge across the Nonette, cross the road into the Rue Vieille de Paris and take the little flight of steps on the right, the Passage des Carmes, the point at which you rejoin the shorter route.

Both routes

A short walk along the rampart will bring you to the Rue de la République, a horrible road full of speeding traffic which has effectively cut the town in two, to the detriment of the eastern part. It was built in 1753, apparently at the request of Madame de Pompadour, who found the old Paris road too narrow. Cross the road to follow the quiet, pretty walk along the **Rempart Bellevue** on the other side, where local people like to stroll.

Shorter route

Turn left a few minutes later at the Rue de la Poterne and follow it past the 18th-century **Chapelle de l'Hôpital de la Charité**, where it becomes the Rue des Vignes. Turn left into the Rue des Bordeaux and right to rejoin the Rue de la République which leads back to Place du Chalet and the **station**.

Longer route

Continue along the rampart walk. You will see an impressive 17th-century building rising behind the wall on your left, which is part of the Lycée St Vincent and the reason for the detour. Follow the rampart around to the left and take a narrow path leading to steps down to the Rue de Meaux. Turn right and follow this street slightly uphill to the entrance to the former

Abbaye Royale St Vincent, which is now a school. Wrought-iron gates enclose a pretty garden and a remarkable collection of old buildings, dominated by the 12th-century open-work bell tower. The Abbey was founded in 1060 by Anne of Kiev, wife of Henri I, following the birth of their son, the future Philippe I. Inside, nothing much remains of the original monastery, except the church which dates back to the 12th century, but a strong monastic atmosphere still clings to the place.

The 17th-century Couvent de la Présentation was incorporated into the Abbey buildings and the beautiful cloister enclosing a garden within the school dates from this period. There is another 17th-century cloister, currently used as a sports ground, concealed by the buildings to the right of the gate, but accessible if you keep going. It can also be reached by an underground passage from the building on the right which the caretaker kindly showed me, but I confess that my taste for exploring gave out when the row of lights came to an abrupt end, and I finished my investigations above ground.

Turn left from the gates to continue along the Rue de Meaux until you come to the Rue des Vignes to the right, opposite the 18th-century **Chapelle de l'Hôpital de la Charité**. Follow the Rue des Vignes and turn left into the Rue des Bordeaux, then right into the Rue de la République, which leads back to Place du Chalet and the **station**.

Distance from Paris: 43 km (27 miles)
Depart: Gare du Nord
Arrive: Senlis
Journey time: 1 hour 5 minutes or less
Length of visit: Half or full day
Carte Orange Zone: Not applicable, outside Ile de France (Oise)
Single ticket: 8.60€
Distance from Chantilly to Senlis: 10 km (6 miles)
Pop.: 17,000

Getting there

The railway line from Chantilly to Senlis has been replaced by a bus.

SNCF trains to Creil directly connecting to the bus from Chantilly leave Gare du Nord (*Grandes Lignes*) once in the morning and at lunchtime on Sundays, more often during the week. Return service is more frequent, the last bus for the connecting train to Paris leaving Senlis at around 7 pm.

The **bus** from Chantilly to Senlis is run by Cars Cariane, tel. 03 44 53 25 38. It leaves from the bus station next to Chantilly SNCF station and runs approximately every two hours on Sundays, once an hour on weekdays, stopping by request near the château and at various points en route. The Senlis tourist office has copies of the timetable.

Métro and RER stations do not issue tickets for Senlis, which you must buy at the Gare du Nord. You can pick up a local train timetable at Chantilly station or at the tourist office in Senlis.

It is cheaper to buy a through ticket to Senlis, as it includes the 2.45€ bus fare (show your train ticket to the driver). You may be eligible for a 25 per cent reduction on this ticket. See p. 235.

NB: The final '*s*' in Senlis is sounded, so pronounce it 'Sonleece'.

Car: Autoroute A1 (Lille) exit no. 8 Senlis or N17 (Compiègne).

When to go

Avoid Tuesdays when the Château Royal and all the museums are closed. Good weather is necessary for this mainly outdoor visit.

NB: It is possible to combine a visit to Chantilly in the morning with a visit to Senlis in the afternoon, if you catch the bus near the château at around 1.30 pm. You could lunch in Senlis at the Porte de Compiègne near the station or at La Closerie near the Cathedral, which both serve food at all hours.

Check the bus times at the Senlis bus stop when you arrive at Chantilly station and head for the Musée Vivant du Cheval on leaving the château (see map of Chantilly). The request bus stop, labelled 'DUC', is next to the church, opposite L'Etrier café. The Senlis bus timetable is not shown at this stop, but it does stop there.

Useful information

Office de tourisme, Place du Parvis Notre Dame, 60300 Senlis, tel 03 44 53 06 40. www.ville-senlis.fr. Open 10 am– 12.30 pm and 2–6.15 pm every day in summer, closes at 5 pm in winter. Closed on 25 December, 1 January and 1 May. It is worth asking for the free brochure *Senlis, Ville Royale* in French and English which contains a map with a useful key showing 30 places of interest within the town centre.

Château Royal Next to the tourist office, tel 03 44 32 00 83 (*Mairie*). Open 10 am–12 noon and 2–6 pm on weekdays, 11 am–1 pm and 2–6 pm at weekends. Closed Tuesdays and Wednesday morning and closes at 5 pm from November to January. Combined ticket for the park and the four museums 4.20€, concessions 2.10€, free to visitors under 16. Park only, 0.60€. Guided visits to the Musée de la Vénerie hourly.

Eglise St Frambourg, Place St Frambourg. Tel 03 44 53 39 99

(Fondation Cziffra). The crypt is open 3–6 pm at weekends from May to October and 3–5 pm on Sundays in winter. Admission 4€, concessions 3.50€ and 2€, free to children under 10.

Abbaye St Vincent (*lycée*), Rue de Meaux. The building is a school, so parts of it are inaccessible in term time. Try turning the handle if the gates are shut.

Les Arènes (Gallo-Roman arena), Place des Arènes. The Société d'Histoire et d'Archéologie de Senlis is responsible for the site, which is closed to the public. The tourist office arranges guided visits in French on the first Sunday of the month from April to October, starting from the tourist office at 3 pm and lasting up to 2 hours. 5.20€, 2.60€ for those under 16 or over 60.

The four **museums** in Senlis are all near the cathedral and have the same opening hours as the Château Royal.

Musée d'Art et d'Archéologie, Place Notre Dame, in the former Bishop's Palace, tel 03 44 32 00 83. Contains Roman and medieval finds from Senlis and paintings from the 17th to the 20th centuries.

Musée de l'Hotel de Vermandois, Place du Parvis Notre Dame, tel 03 44 32 00 82. Housed in a 12th-century building, the museum is devoted to the history of Senlis and includes a video on the cathedral.

Musée de la Vénerie (Hunting Museum). In the Prior's House in the Château Royal park, tel 03 44 32 00 81. Contains a collection of paintings, costumes, weapons and trophies associated with hunting.

Musée des Spahis, Place du Parvis Notre Dame, tel 03 44 32 00 81. Devoted to the history of the North African cavalry regiment, part of the French army since 1830, which was garrisoned in Senlis for 30 years.

Cafés and restaurants

A la Porte de Compiègne, 107 Rue de la République, near the station, tel 03 44 53 00 37. Closed on Mondays. A popular, competent brasserie with tables overlooking the Place du Chalet. *Plats du jour* around 9€, *formule* 11.50€, menus from 18€. The salads are made with good olive oil.

La Closerie, 7 Place St Pierre, tel 03 44 53 30 06. Has a quiet, shaded *terrasse* next to the Cathedral gardens. Open 11 am–8 pm except on Wednesdays. Good-value *salon de thé* serving gourmet sandwiches and mixed salads. *Formule* 13€.

20. Villeneuve Triage

Combine a riverside walk with Sunday lunch at the Guinguette Auvergnate, a little-known traditional restaurant on the Seine

The Guinguette Auvergnate is the perfect place to take visitors to Paris, who never fail to be charmed by its friendly relaxed atmosphere, the view of the Seine from its windows framed by potted geraniums and the unpretentious cooking from the Auvergne, the home region of the *patron*. If they are lucky, they will see their fellow-diners waltzing to the strains of the accordion, 'just like a Renoir painting', as a friend once whispered to me. I have arrived as late as 3 pm and still been fed, as Sunday lunch here can last up to 5 pm..

It is a short train ride from Paris practically to the door of the Guinguette, but if you want to show your visitors an under-appreciated aspect of the Paris suburbs, you could start from another station at Choisy-le-Roi, even closer to Paris. From there, you can take them on a pretty 3-kilometre walk along the river, ending with lunch at the Guinguette.

For more about *guinguettes* (pronounced 'gang-ETTE') see the chapter on the Ile du Martin-Pêcheur, p. 102, which is a safer bet if you want to dance. The Guinguette Auvergnate is smaller and less well-known than the ones on the River Marne and attracts a mainly local clientèle. The reason for its survival is probably the geographical isolation of this part of the town of Villeneuve St Georges, with the Seine on one side and the huge *gare de triage*, the largest in Europe, on the other. (A *gare de triage* is a railway station specialising in the redistribution of freight wagons.) They don't hold dances here every Sunday, but the convivial family atmosphere is truly part of the *esprit guinguette*. It is standard etiquette to nod and smile at fellow-

La Guinguette Auvergnate

diners, murmuring 'Bonjour/Au revoir, messieurs et dames' as you arrive or leave.

I discovered the Guinguette by a lucky accident. I went inside what looked like a simple rather old-fashioned café to ask for directions after taking a wrong turn along the river one Sunday afternoon. The long dark interior was surprisingly full of couples and families lingering over coffee and a game of backgammon and immediately reminded me of a boat, a quietly buzzing, happy, laid-back sort of boat. Light poured in from the windows overlooking the river and I glimpsed people dancing at the far end of the room, which led to a terrasse where more people were sitting outside in the sunshine. Charmed, I complimented the *patron* on his establishment. 'Ici, c'est un petit coin du Paradis,' came the reply. Pause, swelling of chest. 'Et moi, je m'appelle Dieu.' ('This is a little corner of Paradise. I'm called God.')

I have been back many times since and can confirm that the Guinguette Auvergnate is indeed a little corner of paradise, if your idea of paradise is a French 1950s timewarp. The menu offers traditional family dishes, varying with the season. I have tried the *souris d'agneau au thym* (roast knuckle of lamb with thyme) and the *saucisse d'Auvergne Aligot* (Auvergne sausage with a purée of potatoes, cheese and garlic) and they were good value. It is worth asking for the *kir Birlou*, an aperitif made with white wine delicately flavoured with a mixture of apple and chestnut, an Auvergnat speciality that avoids the over-sweetness of most *kirs*.

Suggested 3.3 km walk from Choisy-le-Roi station to the Guinguette Auvergnate

Take the steps down from the platform to the main station exit, marked 'Sortie Centre Ville'. There are red and white GR and red and yellow GRP signs (see p. 239) all along the route to the Guinguette, starting from the station. Turn right into a little road which follows the railway track until you come to a pedestrian crossing just before a bridge. Cross the road here and take the steps up to the old station building surmounted by a clock, still bearing the words 'Chemin de Fer d'Orléans' above a pretty decoration of coloured tiles. It is now a 'Maison de la Jeunesse'.

Turn right onto the main road across the Seine, the Pont de Choisy, and stay on the right-hand footpath. Then take the steps down to the right, which lead to the Quai des Gondoles, the riverside footpath. It continues past modern flats and then the gardens of 19th-century houses. However, you may find, as I did, that the route is closed for half a kilometre because of building work being carried out on the river bank. It may be open again by the time you read this. If not, follow the detour left, marked 'Piétons,' at the Rue des Fusillés and turn right at the Boulodrome onto the Avenue de Villeneuve St Georges, a secondary road with not much traffic. When the road becomes a little bridge, crossing water on the left-hand side, turn right, back to the riverside path, which now continues through a small park.

From this point onwards, and especially after the railway bridge, the walk becomes surprisingly rural and peaceful. There

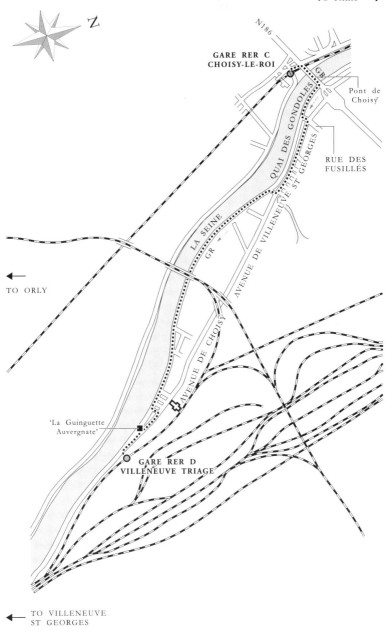

TO PARIS ➜

N186

**GARE RER C
CHOISY-LE-ROI**

GR

Pont de
Choisy

QUAI DES GONDOLES

RUE DES
FUSILLÉS

LA SEINE

GR

AVENUE DE VILLENEUVE ST GEORGES

← TO ORLY

AVENUE DE CHOISY

'La Guinguette
Auvergnate'

**GARE RER D
VILLENEUVE TRIAGE**

← TO VILLENEUVE
ST GEORGES

Villeneuve Triage

0   500 metres

are benches at strategic intervals and people picnic here at the weekends but it does not attract crowds. Weeping willows grow by the water's edge and tiny shingle beaches shelter waterfowl and the occasional silent fisherman. I have seen violets in spring and wild blue and purple convolvulus in autumn. From time to time a huge working barge slides past, but the only sound is likely to be the planes from nearby Orly or a water-skier from the Port de Plaisance further along the river.

Eventually the path goes past a football ground with a church rising behind it, and then passes a *boules* pitch. It comes to an end in a little road which leads to the Avenue de Choisy. Stay on the right-hand side of the Avenue, continuing past the defunct 'Hotel de la Gare' and the *ski nautique* at the Port de Plaisance. You will see the blue and green sign for the RER station at Villeneuve Triage just ahead of you on the left. The **Guinguette Auvergnate** is the café-restaurant on the right, almost opposite the station.

Distance from Paris: 16 km (9 miles)
Depart: Châtelet-les-Halles/Gare de Lyon
Arrive: Villeneuve Triage
Journey time: 15 minutes from Gare de Lyon
Length of visit: Half day
Carte Orange Zone: 4
Single ticket: 2.80€
Alternative depart: St Michel-Notre Dame
Arrive: Choisy-le-Roi
Return from: Villeneuve Triage
Journey time: 14 minutes
Carte Orange Zone: 3
Single ticket: 2.10€
Distance from Choisy-le-Roi to Villeneuve Triage: 3.3 km (2 miles)
Pop.: 30,687

Getting there

RER D trains from Châtelet-les-Halles or the Gare de Lyon to Malesherbes or Melun, stopping at Villeneuve Triage, leave every 15 minutes, at up to 25-minute intervals on Sundays, and return every 15 minutes on weekdays, every 20 minutes or less on Sundays. The last train back to Paris is at 12.19 am.

RER C trains to Massy-Palaiseau, Dourdan-la-Forêt and St Martin d'Etampes, stopping at Choisy-le-Roi, leave St Michel-Notre Dame every 10 minutes.

Car: Porte de Choisy, then N305 to Choisy-le-Roi, and cross the Pont de Choisy onto the Avenue Villeneuve St Georges towards Villeneuve St Georges.

When to go

A day with some sunshine at any time of the year is the ideal weather in which to enjoy the play of light on the river. The Guinguette is at its most relaxed on Sunday afternoon. Go on the second or fourth Sunday of the month if you want to see people dancing.

Restaurant/*guinguette*

La Guinguette Auvergnate, 19 Avenue de Choisy, 94190 Villeneuve St Georges Triage, tel 01 43 89 04 64, www.guinguette-auvergnate.fr Open for lunch every day except Monday and for dinner on Friday and Saturday all year round, and on Thursday evening in the summer. Dancing on the second and fourth Friday of every month from around 8 pm and on the second and fourth Sunday of every month from around 2 pm. See the website for the latest programme.

Weekday menus from 12€, 18€ at weekends, or à la carte. *Plats du jour* around 12€, wine from 12€ a bottle, 50cl *pichet* 4€. Admission to the dance floor without eating but including a drink is 10€.

21. On the Tourist Trail

The most-visited places near Paris are **Versailles, Giverny, Fontainebleau** and **Auvers-sur-Oise,** in that order. You cannot avoid the crowds here, but it would be a pity to miss them on that account. I did, for many years, and was agreeably surprised when I finally went. If you have to choose, I would recommend **Versailles** and **Fontainebleau** as the ones not to be missed.

As tourist brochures can be rather thin on detail when describing access to these places by public transport, here is a brief section on how to get there by train or bus. **Malmaison** is also included, as it is likely to be of particular interest to fans of Napoleon.

Versailles

Louis XIV's magnificent château and park, the quintessence of French 17th and 18th century art, provide the essential context within which to view all the others. The park contains the Grand and Petit Trianons and Marie Antoinette's Hameau, built as royal retreats from court life. The best time of year to visit the château is in winter, when there are fewer people about. At Easter and in July and August, the advice of the local tourist office is to arrive at 9 am if you want to avoid long queues. The park is so vast that you could spend all day there without feeling crowded, even at weekends between April and September, when the fountains play from 11 am–12 noon and 3.30–5.30 pm. (Admission to the park, normally free, is 7€ at these times.) www.chateauversailles.fr.

If you are in need of a republican corrective after the visit, you could stroll over to the Jeu de Paume, in Rue du Jeu de Paume just south of the château (shown on the tourist office map, although it is no longer open to the public). It was here, on 20 June 1789, that the assembled deputies of the Third Estate swore a solemn oath, *le serment du Jeu de Paume*, not to disband until they had given France a constitution.

There is a modest little **restaurant** nearby, opposite the Cathédrale St Louis, serving good Portuguese food to a strictly local clientèle: Chez Pedro, 3 Rue de la Cathédrale, 78000 Versailles, tel 01 30 21 24 34. Open for lunch Monday to Saturday.

RER C5 trains from St Michel and other stations in central Paris to Versailles Rive Gauche (terminus) run approximately every 15 minutes, every half hour on Sundays, taking 40 minutes to arrive. The last train back is at 11.50 pm and a single ticket costs 2.80€.

SNCF trains from St Lazare to Versailles Rive Droite (terminus) run approximately every 15 minutes, taking about 30 minutes to arrive. The last train back is just after midnight and a single ticket costs 3.50€.

The château is a five to ten-minute walk from Versailles Rive Gauche. Turn right outside the station and then left at the main road, Avenue de Paris, which leads to the château. The tourist office at 2 bis, Avenue de Paris, tel 01 39 24 88 88, www.versailles-tourisme. com, is very helpful and has a useful free map.

You could explore the local heart of Versailles by asking them to show you the quartier Notre Dame on the map, where there is a lively market founded by Louis XIV. It is open on Tuesday, Friday and Sunday mornings until 2 pm and there are plenty of bars and restaurants nearby. I recommend Le Ducis, a traditional café-restaurant with tables outside at 13 rue Ducis, tel 01 30 21 93 76, www.leducis.com. Open from 6 am to midnight every day. You could return to Paris via the Versailles Rive Droite station nearby.

NB: The château is closed on Mondays.

Giverny

The famous garden laid out by Claude Monet (1840–1926) has been restored as he designed it, to offer a shifting palette of colours according to the season. Go in July or August if you want to see the water-lilies exactly as Monet painted them.

SNCF trains to Rouen, stopping at Vernon, leave from Gare St Lazare (*Grandes Lignes*), slow trains taking 1 hour 20 minutes, fast trains about 40 minutes. There are three fast trains on weekday mornings, two on Saturdays and four on Sundays. The last train back is at 8.42 pm on weekdays, 9.02 pm on Saturdays and 10.25 pm on Sundays. A single ticket costs 11.90€.

Monet's house is 7 km (4¼ miles) from Vernon but a local bus, the TVS line 240, connects with the train approximately ten minutes later, in the months when the Fondation Monet is open. The last bus back is at 6.25 pm on weekdays, 6.30 pm on Saturdays and 6.20 pm on Sundays.

NB: The Fondation Claude Monet, tel 02 32 51 28 21, is closed on Mondays and from November to March. www.fondation-monet.com.

Fontainebleau

The château of Fontainebleau is crowded even in winter, especially on Sundays, but its unique historical associations with the rulers of France make this visit an unfor-

Fontainebleau

gettable experience. The château was decorated with astonishing brilliance by Italian artists in the 16th century, and enough of their work survives to give an idea of the original magnificence. There is also an important collection of later paintings. The town is surrounded by a vast forest of 25,000 hectares, once a royal hunting preserve and now a favourite haunt of Parisian rock-climbers and hikers. The forest has an entire IGN map to itself, 2417 OT, which shows every footpath and the railway stations.

SNCF trains from Gare de Lyon (*Grandes Lignes*) to Nemours or Montereau, the same line as for Moret-sur-Loing, stop at Fontainebleau-Avon roughly every hour. The journey takes around 40 minutes and a single ticket costs 7.60€. The last train back is at around 9.50 pm, 10.40 pm on Sunday.

NB: There is a halt in the forest just before Fontainebleau-Avon, simply labelled 'arrêt' on the IGN map, where the 9.07 and 10.41 trains stop on Sunday mornings.

The château is 3 km (2 miles) from the station but there is a **bus**, line AB, which connects with the train and leaves the station a few minutes later. The last bus leaves the château at 8.30 pm. It is worth buying the six-zone *Carte Mobilis* for this journey, as it will save you the 1.40€ bus fare both ways, or the *forfait loisirs Chateau de Fontainebleau*, a special ticket at 23€ which combines the return train and bus fare with admission to the château, on sale at the SNCF ticket offices at the Gare de Lyon.

NB: The château, tel 01 60 71 50 70, is closed on Tuesdays. Free admission on the first Sunday of every month and reduced rate on other Sundays. www.musee-chateau-fontainebleau.fr.

Auvers-sur-Oise

The village on the banks of the River Oise has been made famous by the Impressionists, particularly Vincent Van Gogh who died here in 1890. It still feels like a village, with a lively **market** on Thursday and Sunday mornings. The least-visited and most moving part is the humble little cemetery in which Van Gogh is buried, near the church immortalised in his painting.

SNCF trains to Pontoise from Gare du Nord (*Ile de France*) run at least twice an hour. But you need to change at Saint-Ouen l'Aumône for trains to Persan Beaumont, which stop at Auvers-sur-Oise approximately once an hour, involving a wait of between 4 and 25 minutes. Depending on the connection, the journey can take from 55 minutes to an hour and a quarter. The alternative routes from Gare du Nord, changing at Persan Beaumont (*Grande Lignes* departure) or at Valmondois (*Ile de France* departure) both take around an hour and a quarter. The ticket costs 4.80€ and the last train back to Pontoise is at 9.11 pm, 10.44 pm on Sundays.

The SNCF runs a **special direct train in summer** from the Gare du Nord to Auvers-sur-Oise on weekends and public hoidays between April and September, taking 30 minutes. There is one train at 9.56 am, returning at 6.15 pm. Details from the helpful Auvers tourist office, 01 30 36 10 06.

From the station, turn right for the church or left for the tourist office in Rue de la Sansonne and the Auberge Ravoux opposite, where Van Gogh rented a room. It is approximately ten minutes' walk, past the *Mairie*.

NB: The Auberge Ravoux is closed on Mondays and Tuesdays and between November and February.

Rueil-Malmaison

The château was the home of the Empress Josephine and faithfully preserves the memory of the private lives of Napoleon and Josephine.

It is 6 km (3¾ miles) from La Défense. The RATP local maps, *plans de secteur* nos. 5 or 6, cover the local area, including La Défense.

RER A1, A3 and A5 trains to St Germain-en-Laye, Cergy le Haut and Poissy leave Châtelet-les-Halles and other stations in central Paris every few minutes, stopping at La Défense/Grande Arche minutes later. A single ticket costs 2.10€. Or take **Métro Line 1** to La Défense/Grande Arche.

From La Défense follow the exit signs for the 258 **bus** to St Germain-en-Laye which runs at 15-minute intervals, seven days a week, up to midnight. Get off at the *château de Malmaison* stop. Cross the road and turn left down the Avenue du Château de Malmaison which leads to the château, about ten minutes' walk.

NB: The château, tel 01 41 29 05 55, is closed on Tuesdays and 12-1.30 pm on weekdays in winter. www.chateau-malmaison.fr.

Getting around the Ile de France

THE CULTURAL CONTEXT

BEST DAYS TO VISIT

PRACTICAL DETAILS

Getting into the local rhythm

Exploring the Ile de France is an excellent education in itself about what makes France tick – literally. The timing of your trip should be in tune with the rhythm of French provincial life, particularly at lunchtimes, weekends and during holiday periods.

Train timetables: Commuter train timetables reflect the habits of French commuters, so there are longer gaps between trains at lunchtime, at weekends, on Sundays and public holidays, and in August. The last train back to Paris from some places might leave as early as 7.30 pm, although many run up to midnight. The last train on Sundays may run later than on weekdays.

Opening hours: Local tourist offices and the smaller châteaux and museums tend to have extremely complicated schedules, varying according to the day of the week and the season, and are quite likely to close for two hours at lunchtime. **The golden rule is *always* to phone before leaving to check that the times have not changed.** If there is no answer you can always ring the local *Mairie* – outside lunchtime, of course.

Restaurant opening hours outside Paris may be charmingly unpredictable, depending on the number of customers and the mood of the *patron*, as they are often family-run. Generally, they are open at lunchtime from around 11.30 am to 3 pm, but it is risky to place your order after 1.30 pm. The best dishes, or worse still, the chef may have gone by then. Things are more relaxed on Sundays, when you might get away with turning up at 2 pm or even later. Evening opening times are from around 7.30 to 9.30 pm. Traditional French restaurants tend to be closed on Sunday evenings and at least one other day during the week, usually Monday. You can generally get an omelette or a sandwich at a café at any time of the day during the week. On Sundays they tend to be foodless and may close distressingly early, around 7.30 pm.

If you particularly want to visit a restaurant described in the text, it is wise to ring first to check that it will be open.

Restaurant terms: *Menu* means a fixed price menu, usually at least three courses. Wine and coffee are rarely included. A *formule* is a two-course fixed price menu, usually a choice of a first and a main course (*entrée et plat*) or a main course and a pudding (*plat et dessert*), and sometimes including a glass of wine, beer or mineral water. The *plat du jour* is the dish of the day, usually part of the menu, and often a bargain in terms of quality and price. A *pichet* of wine is the house wine, served in 25cl or 50cl jugs (ask for *un quart* or *un demi*), varying greatly in quality depending on the restaurant. A *pichet* of a well-chosen *vin de pays* (local wine from a particular region) may be better value than an expensive but mediocre bottle. The French tend to go for Côtes du Rhône as a safe bet. A restaurant is legally obliged to serve you a jug of tap water free, if you ask for *une carafe d'eau*. If you say *de l'eau, s'il vous plaît*, you are likely to get mineral water.

Weekends: Small towns in the Ile de France tend to be very lively on Sunday mornings, when everyone is shopping for Sunday lunch until about 1 pm. In some villages this may also be the only time in the week when the church is open. Saturdays are also busy, but after about 7.30 pm on Sunday and sometimes even on Saturday, many of these places can seem deserted and you will probably be glad you are staying in Paris.

The pleasures of provincial life

Once you have adjusted to the local rhythm, you will start to appreciate the ways in which life is different, not only from other countries but from Paris as well.

People: People are generally much friendlier than in Paris and it is usual to greet the strangers you pass on a country walk, as well as the people you have commercial transactions with. The formula is 'Bonjour, m'sieur/ madame', rather than just 'Bonjour', which is too abrupt. Occasionally, you may come across someone who treats you with provincial suspicion. Don't take it personally. Remember that you are not just a stranger (bad) but a foreigner (worse), and that even if you were French, it wouldn't make much difference. On the whole, people are extra helpful when they realise you are a foreigner because *any* visitor in some of these places is unusual and a foreign visitor is positively exotic.

Prices: Another pleasant difference is that café and restaurant prices tend to be as low as if you were in a province 300 km rather than just 30 km away from Paris. I always look for the cost of an ordinary cup of coffee (*café express*) taken at the table (*salle*) as a fairly reliable indicator of the local prices. The Paris average is 2.20€, so anything less than this is an encouraging sign.

Food: Not only are restaurant prices generally lower, the quality and quantity of the food is usually superior to Paris fare. A *kir* (aperitif) will be made with a decent wine rather than the cheapest plonk and the ingredients of the dishes are likely to be fresh and properly cooked, rather than frozen and microwaved. This is what French cooking is all about and you should take advantage of the generally non-commercial approach to order traditional dishes you don't often see on Paris menus.

The love of numbers

It may surprise you to know that the royal road to a successful career as a senior civil servant in France is an aptitude for mathematics, and state planning reflects this bias.

Administrative divisions: The entire country is divided into 22 *régions*, subdivided into 100 administrative *départements* which are known by numbers as well as by names. For example, the Ile de France *région* consists of eight *départements*: Paris (75), Seine et Marne (77), Yvelines (78), Essonne (91), Hauts de Seine (92), Seine St Denis (93), Val de Marne (94) and Val d'Oise (95). Every French schoolchild knows the *département* numbers, which always feature as the postcode in the address. For example, 75004 PARIS means the fourth *arrondissement* of the *département* of Paris. These divisions are deep in the national mindset. If you need to phone directory enquiries or ask about train timetables, the first question is likely to be 'In what department?' and it helps if you can rattle off the number, or at least the name.

It is also helpful to keep administrative divisions in mind when reading tourist office maps and literature, which usually organise information on this principle. Likewise, stations outside the Ile de France region and sometimes even stations beyond Zone 6 are not shown on the Ile de France railway map, so it is a good idea to take a Michelin or IGN map with you. The names of the stations, by the way, may consist of two place names, as in 'Moret–Veneux Les Sablons'. This means that they serve two *communes* and will usually be located in the middle, about 2 km away from each of them.

The Métro and RER trains: In theory, the Métro lines are also known by numbers, although in practice people usually say 'Clignancourt–Porte d'Orléans' rather than 'Line Four'. But the RER is always referred to as RER A, RER B or even RER B4. These letters reflect the order in which each line was constructed, so RER E is the latest one.

The French attitude to information

French education, with its emphasis on the formal and abstract, has bred a horror of appearing to patronise people by oversimplifying or stating the obvious. This means that information is often not concrete or detailed enough to satisfy Anglophone tastes. Knowledge is also power, more than in most other countries, so it is rare to find an underpaid bureaucrat pressing more information on you than you have asked for.

As local tourist offices are usually staffed by employees of the *Mairie*, you should bear in mind that tourism is, understandably, usually fairly low on the local council's list of priorities and proceed accordingly. The secret is to know which questions to ask. If you can establish a rapport with the person you are dealing with, so much the better. Beginning with 'Bonjour, madame/m'sieur' rather than 'Je veux savoir...' is a good start.

BEST DAYS TO VISIT

	Markets	*Other Attractions*
MONDAY		
TUESDAY	St Germain-en-Laye Versailles	
WED	Andrésy (Conflans) Luzarches Montmorency	Ferry, Andrésy
THUR	Crécy-la-Chapelle Créteil	
FRI	Luzarches St Germain-en-Laye, Versailles	
SATURDAY	Andrésy	Ferry, Andrésy and Herblay (summer) Rowing, Crécy-la-Chapelle Marne cruise, Créteil Renaissance music, Ecouen Canal cruise, La Ferté-Milon Ile du Martin-Pêcheur (closed Jan-Mar) Concerts, Royaumont (late summer)
SUNDAY	Andrésy Crécy-la-Chapelle Créteil Montmorency St Mammès (Moret- sur-Loing) St Germain-en-Laye Versailles	Ferry, Andrésy and Herblay (summer) Boat trip, Conflans Rowing, Crécy-la-Chapelle Marne cruise, Créteil Canal cruise, La Ferté-Milon Ile du Martin-Pêcheur (closed Jan-Mar) Seine and Loing cruise, St Mammès La Guinguette Auvergnate, Villeneuve Concerts, Royaumont (late summer)

Châteaux/Museums OPEN	*Châteaux/Museums* CLOSED
	Musée Maurice Ravel, Château de Groussay, Montfort; Musée Jean Jacques Rousseau, Montmorency; Villa Savoye, Musée du Jouet, Poissy; Musée Rambolitrain, Rambouillet; Musée Maurice Denis and Musée Claude Débussy, St Germain-en-Laye; Maison Chateaubriand, Sceaux; Château de Versailles; Fondation Claude Monet, Giverny; Auberge Ravoux, Auvers-sur-Oise
	Châteaux: Champs, Chantilly, Ecouen, Fontainebleau, Rambouillet and Rueil-Malmaison Museums: Musée de la Batellerie, Conflans (morning); Musée Ravel and Château de Groussay, Montfort; Musée Rambolitrain, Rambouillet; Musée des Antiquités Nationales, St Germain-en-Laye; Musée de l'Ile de France, Sceaux; Château Royal and museums, Senlis; Auberge Ravoux, Auvers-sur-Oise
Fountains, Sceaux	Château Royal and museums, Senlis, morning
Musée Jean Racine, La Ferté-Milon (summer) Maison Zola, Poissy Fountains, Pavillon d'Aurore, Sceaux Fountains, Versailles (summer)	Musée de la Batellerie, Conflans (morning)
Musée Jean Racine, La Ferté-Milon (summer) Maison Zola, Poissy Fountains, Pavillon d'Aurore, Sceaux Fountains, Versailles (summer)	Musée de la Batellerie, Conflans (morning)

PRACTICAL DETAILS

Public transport in the Ile de France

Paris is the hub of the Ile de France train network, with suburban lines radiating in every direction for up to 80 km. The region is divided into six concentric zones, with Paris itself in zones one and two, a radius of about 8 km from Notre Dame.

The RATP (Régie Autonome des Transports Parisiens) is responsible for the Métro, buses and trams within and often beyond these two central zones and for the most heavily-used suburban express trains, RER lines A1, A2, A4 and B2 and B4, which cross central Paris, terminating up to 21 km away. The state-owned railway company, the SNCF (Société Nationale des Chemins de Fer Français) is responsible for the rest of the RER network and for all the suburban trains. The best map of the system is the *Grand Plan de l'Ile de France*, available free from the RATP (see p. 240) and reproduced on pp. 6-7.

Types of ticket

The admirable co-ordination between the SNCF and the RATP means that you can buy a weekly or monthly *Navigo Découverte* pass at any Métro or SNCF station, covering all forms of public transport in any of the six zones. Paris Métro tickets are valid on all RATP buses, both within and outside Paris. You can also buy a ticket to most SNCF or RER stations in the Ile de France from Métro stations in central Paris and use it to cover the whole of your journey, including the Métro.

If you are staying in Paris for **less than a week** and intend to make several journeys outside zone two, the one-, two-, three- and five-day visitor's pass, *Paris Visite*, offers unlimited travel in up to six zones and some rather limited reductions on entry to a few tourist attractions within and outside Paris. However, it is cheaper to buy a carnet of ten tickets for travel within Paris and to buy separate tickets for visits to the Ile de France from a Métro station. That way, your Métro journey is included in the price of the ticket.

If you arrive early in the week and are staying **three days or more**, it is probably cheaper and certainly simpler to invest in a weekly pass for zones one and two and to buy tickets for the outer zones as and when you need them. The *Navigo Découverte* pass is on sale at Métro stations and *tabacs*. Similar to the Oyster card used in London, it is validated simply by touching it against the electronic readers at the entrance to the Métro or the bus. It costs 5€ as it is designed to last for about ten years, and you will need a passport-size photo. You then top it up with the *forfait Carte Orange hebdo-madaire,* which runs from Monday morning to Sunday evening and can be bought from Friday for the following week. It currently costs 16.30€ for zones one and two.

Reductions are possible if you buy certain types of ticket. Within the Ile de France, there is the *Carte Mobilis*, a one-day travelcard allowing unlimited travel on all forms of public transport, although it is not valid for airport journeys. No photograph is needed and you can buy the ticket in advance. Remember to validate it by writing your name on the card and signing it and writing the card number and date when you travel on the ticket. The price varies according to the number of zones, from 5.60€ for zones one and two to 15.90€ for zones one to six, but it rarely represents a saving on one return journey unless you are travelling to zone six.

Reductions of 25 per cent apply to all SNCF journeys outside the Ile de France (*Grandes Lignes*) if you are under 26 or over 60 (take your passport as proof of age when buying a ticket). These reductions apply to the visits to **Chantilly**, **La Ferté-Milon**, and **Senlis**, which are outside the Ile de France.

Trains

Paris is not only the hub of the Ile de France train network, it is also the hub of the national train network and a major international destination. Main line stations such as the Gare du Nord are intersections for the Métro, the RER and for SNCF local, national and international trains. The following signs help you to navigate main line stations:

RER (Réseau Express Régionale, pronounced 'air-er-air'): Suburban express trains. The five RER lines, A, B, C, D and E, cross Paris, converging at or near Châtelet and intersect with Métro and SNCF stations. They are the most heavily-used commuter lines, especially line A. (Underground in most of Paris, over-ground outside).

SNCF Transilien ('across the Ile de France') or **Ile de France**: Suburban trains (over-ground).

SNCF Grandes Lignes: Main line trains to other parts of France and abroad.

TGV (Trains à Grande Vitesse): High speed trains to other parts of France and abroad.

The **frequency** of suburban trains depends on proximity to Paris. The RER and SNCF trains serving the inner suburbs generally run every 15 minutes, more often during the rush hour. Stations further away from Paris are served by trains every half hour, every hour or more on certain lines. At lunchtime, on Sunday afternoons and during August the gaps between trains may be longer. The RER runs up to 1 am and inner suburban SNCF trains run up to about midnight, but check return times carefully for remoter destinations.

SNCF platforms: The main suburban departures board (*Départs Transilien/Ile de France*) shows the departure time of the train, its ultimate destination (*direction*) and the platform number (*voie*). So if you were going to Ecouen, you would look for 'Persan–Beaumont' or 'Luzarches' on the departure board. If you arrive with less than 15 minutes to spare, your train may no longer be shown. Don't panic – scan the platform departure boards for a train leaving at the right time and run your eye down the list of stations at which the train stops until you find the right one.

RER platforms: The platform display board shows the train's code name (e.g. NORA, ROMI) which refers to its destination and which stations it stops at. All the stations on the line are listed underneath but not all of them will be lit up or indicated by a white square next to the name, meaning that this train doesn't stop there. Wait until your station is indicated before getting on the train. On the way to remoter destinations on the RER C line the train may divide at certain stations and this will be indicated in sneaky smaller letters underneath the station name. If you are in any doubt, ask fellow-passengers if you are in the right carriage for your destination ('Ce train va-t-il à...?').

Information on train times and ticket prices: The RATP and SNCF websites will plan your route for you, showing buses as well as a choice of trains with a local map, in English. They contain detailed information on train times, downloadable maps and much else besides. The RATP site is by far the more user-friendly. www.ratp.fr and www.transilien.com for Paris and the Ile de France, www.sncf.com for all other regions.

If you don't speak French, the simplest way to find out about ticket prices is to use the RATP **ticket machines** in Métro stations, labelled 'Carte Orange - Billets Ile de France'. You turn the roller and validate to select English and then the station you want in the Ile de France. The SNCF Transilien ticket machines labelled 'Billeterie automatique' in mainline and RER stations are operated by touching the screen and give information on train times as well as issuing tickets, in French only. Select 'Autres choix', then 'Billets Ile de France'. The SNCF Grandes Lignes ticket machines at mainline stations can display information on times and prices in English.

If you speak French (and even if you don't - some of the staff may speak English), you can ring the following numbers:

SNCF Transilien, tel 08 91 36 20 20, (0.23€ a minute). Daily, 7 am–10 pm. Timetables and ticket prices for the Ile de France.

SNCF Grandes Lignes, tel 36 35. Premium rate line (0.34€ a minute). Daily 7 am–10 pm. Information and reservations for main line trains but includes remoter parts of the Ile de France. Cut the automated options short by pressing 311 to be put through immediately to a human being.

RATP, tel 08 92 68 77 14, (0.23€ a minute). Weekdays 6 am–9 pm, weekends 9 am–5.15 pm, recorded information after 9 pm. Information on Paris and Ile de France trains and buses.

You could even just turn up at the station without bothering to check the times beforehand. This is not as risky as it sounds, as there will usually be a train within 15–20 minutes if you arrive at about 10 am, even on a Sunday. If you arrive close to midday, however, there may be a longer wait, especially if you are travelling to the outer suburbs.

Train timetables: Ideally, you want a *fiche horaire*, a free pocket timetable to take with you, so that you can change your mind if necessary about which train to take back. You get these from the relevant SNCF ticket office, either in Paris or at your destination and you have to ask, as local timetables are rarely on display. SNCF train times change slightly every summer and winter, so it is always worth having the latest one. You can download *fiches horaires* from the French version of the Transilien website.

Buying a ticket: The simplest way to avoid queues at busy main line stations is to **buy your ticket at a Métro station**. This also saves you a Métro ticket, as the Métro journey is always included in the price of tickets for the Ile de France. The more central Métro stations can issue tickets for most, although not all, destinations in the Ile de France. If necessary, write out the name of the station you want and show it at the ticket office window, or use the ticket machine.

It is no cheaper to buy a return ticket than a single, although it will save you time and trouble on the way back. On the other hand, there may be a more interesting way back, via a different station, by bus or even by boat, so you might want to leave your options open. Be warned that if you do return from another station, even one in the same zone, a return ticket will not go through the machine, and it is not refundable.

The only advantage of buying your ticket at the main line station is that you can pick up a *fiche horaire* at the same time, although you can usually do this at the other end. You can also buy your ticket from the SNCF *Transilien* ticket machines.

On the way back you may have no choice but to buy your ticket from a machine, as many of the smaller stations in the Ile de France are not staffed at the weekends. These machines, which both issue and validate tickets, are located on the platform and do not give change, or take credit cards.

Regulations and fines: There can be a certain arbitrariness in the way regulations are enforced in France, the good side of this being that your innocence or charm can sometimes melt an official. On the other hand, it is assumed that everyone knows the regulations and doesn't need to have them spelt out. For those of us who do, here they are:

If you have a *forfait Carte Orange* for Paris only, you must buy a separate ticket for journeys beyond zone two. All train tickets are valid for two months, so it is up to you to demonstrate that you have no intention of using them more than once. You do this by putting your ticket in one of the orange or yellow *composteurs* near the platform to be validated i.e. date-stamped before you get on the train.

If you have not had time to validate your ticket, be warned that this can mean an on-the-spot fine of 25€. Travelling without a ticket, for whatever reason, carries an on-the-spot fine of 35€, but smoking in a non-smoking area or putting your feet on the seats carries an even higher penalty of 45€. These lapses fall into the category of *infractions de comportement* (behavioural misdemeanours) which are viewed more seriously than merely travelling ticketless, although you will see people cheerfully infringing these 'rules' all the time.

If you have not had the time to buy or to validate your ticket, it is in your interest to show your *bonne foi* (good faith) by approaching the inspector or guard as soon as possible after getting on the train. You are then unlikely to be fined.

Buses

In general, trains are the main form of public transport outside Paris, buses being regarded as plugs to fill the gaps in the train service. For example, on Sundays the train service from Esbly to Crécy-la-Chapelle is replaced by a special local bus, which waits outside the station. The journey is included in the ticket price.

RATP buses linking the inner suburbs to Paris may offer a more adventurous, although slower, alternative to the train. The routes are clearly displayed on the *Grand Plan de l'Ile de France* and in the detailed *plans de secteur*. They are also on the RATP website.

Local bus services linking rural *communes* are geared to local needs, so they do not usually operate at weekends or during school holidays. Even if they do, the gaps in the service are so long that you would probably be better off walking or taking a taxi. The easiest way to find out about these bus services is to ring the local tourist office. Ask for the telephone number of the local bus company if you need more detailed information. Bus timetables are also shown on the websites www.transport-idf.com and www.transbus.org/ reseaux.

Taxis

You can always ring for a taxi from the station where you arrive. Make sure you have a *télécarte*, as public phones no longer accept coins. It might be a good idea to ring the local tourist office beforehand to find out which taxi services are operating in the area. Prices tend to be higher than in Paris, as you are also paying for the driver to come and pick you up.

Boats

There are some interesting local boat trips on the 724 km of canals and rivers in the Ile de France, such as the cruise along the Seine and the Marne mentioned in the visit to Créteil or the one along the Canal de l'Ourcq described in the visit to La Ferté-Milon. See the section 'Promenades et Croisières' in the brochure *Levez l'Ancre*, described on p. 242. Apart from a few well-established names like Canaux-rama, companies tend to be very small and local and publicity is not their strong point. Always ring to check the times and dates in any leaflet you are given before setting out.

It is always worth asking the local tourist office about boat trips in the area, as new ones may have started up. The clearest **map** of the 50 km-long canal network, *Le réseau fluvial de la Ville de Paris* can be sent to you by the Mairie de Paris, which also produces a beautifully illustrated booklet containing a map, *Les canaux de Paris*. These publications are all free. (See p. 241).

Bicycles

Information on Vélib', the Paris bicycle rental scheme (see p. 42) is available in French and English on the website www.velib.paris.fr and in the brochure *Vélib'* at Métro stations (in French). Useful information on cycling in Paris is included in the brochure *Le Guide* and on cycling in the Ile de France in *Prenez l'air*, both produced by the Ile de France tourist office. (See p. 241). You could also ask them for the excellent free **map** of cycling routes, *Carte des pistes cyclables en Ile de France*, or view it online at www.iaurif.org/fr/sig/pistecycle/vue1200.html.

Walking

There are several walking guides to the Ile de France for the serious rambler/hiker, available at the IGN bookshop (see p. 243). For the non-serious walker, at whom this guide is aimed, it is useful to know that the FFRP (Féderation Française de la Randonnée Péde-stre – the French version of the Ramblers' Association, www.ffrandonnee.fr) has a system of letters and coloured markings which help you to find your way across country and are shown in the IGN large-scale maps. Footpaths are classified as follows:

GR (Grande Randonnée): Major footpath crossing several regions. Red and white stripe at eye level along the route, red on IGN maps.

GRP (Grande Randonnée de

Pays): Major footpath circling an entire region. Red and yellow stripe along the route, red on IGN maps.

PR (Promenade Randonnée): Shorter circular routes taking one to eight hours. Yellow stripe along the route, red on IGN maps.

Two horizontal stripes mean you are on the right path, a horizontal stripe above a right or left turn means the path will fork soon and a horizontal St Andrew's cross means you will stray off the path if you take this route.

The red and white or yellow markings are rather discreet, usually painted on a tree or lamppost. However, once you start looking for them you will notice them everywhere, including central Paris. It is generally a good idea to follow the FFRP paths, which avoid busy roads as far as possible, sometimes leading to an unsuspected underpass or taking you through a pretty wood.

Maps

* = indispensable

Regional maps: The clearest overall map of the Paris region is the *Michelin no. 106, Environs de Paris* which covers 40–80 km around Paris, on a scale of 1 cm to 1 km. The Blay Foldex, *Ile de France,* covers a radius of 100 km around Paris on a scale of 1 cm to 1.5 km. Both these maps are available in very practical pocket-sized versions. Railway lines are shown,

but you need practice to identify the tiny white square which indicates a railway station, as their names are not given.

By far the most useful map for public transport users is the *RATP Grand Plan de l'Ile de France* (no. 3) which shows the routes of all trains, trams, Métro lines and buses against the physical background, within a radius of about 20 km from Paris. The reverse side shows the entire SNCF/RER train network for the Ile de France, a radius of around 80 km from Paris, reproduced on p. 6. You could pick up the *Grand Plan de Paris (no. 2)* at the same time, which shows bus, Métro and train routes against a background of main street names and green spaces. These maps are usually available from the ticket offices at Châtelet-les-Halles and at St Michel (RER B, Hôtel Dieu exit), and can be viewed on www.ratp. fr. The tourist office map *Escapades Paris Ile de France* is quite useful for a historical and geographical overview of the region and its administrative limits, more clearly shown than on other maps.

Local maps: The *IGN Cartes Topographiques* on a scale of 1 cm to 250 metres are the French equivalent of the Ordnance Survey maps. At around 8.50€ each, they are worth investing in if you want to do a lot of country walking, as they show the GR and PR footpaths very clearly. Station and street names are not shown, but the online versions at www.geoportail.fr will show this level of detail if you click on 'Routes'. The RATP website also shows local maps linked to bus and train routes.

The excellent and little-known *RATP plans de secteur (nos. 4–15)* of the inner suburbs are by far the best of the local maps available, on a scale of 1.5 cm to 250 metres. They cover 12 areas within a radius of about 20 km of Paris and clearly show all public transport routes against the physical background, including main street names. For example, no. 12 covers the Val-de-Marne area. It is well worth asking for these at the local Métro or RER station for the area which interests you. They may also be available from the RER stations at Châtelet-les-Halles and St Michel. However, be prepared for blank looks, as people rarely ask for them.

Local tourist office maps vary enormously in detail and usefulness, but they show street names as well as local phone numbers and they do give you an immediate impression of the spirit of the place you are visiting and its priorities.

The **canal map** *Le réseau fluvial de la Ville de Paris* and the booklet *Les canaux de Paris* can be ordered from the Mairie de Paris, Direction de la Voirie et des Déplacements, Section des Canaux, 6 quai de la Seine, 75019 Paris, tel 01 44 89 14 20, jean-pierre.dubreuil@paris.fr or downloaded from the City of Paris website, www.paris.fr/portail. Go to 'Thèmes' and then 'Déplacements' on the French version of the site and type in 'Carte du réseau fluvial'.

Other useful sources of information

Espace du Tourisme d'Ile de France, Carrousel du Louvre, 99 rue de Rivoli, 75001 Paris, tel 01 44 50 19 98 (best number) or 08 26 16 66 66 (0.15€ a minute). www.pidf.com. Métro: Palais Royal. Daily 10 am–7 pm. Has an RATP/SNCF ticket office and a selection of brochures on specific activities in the different *départements* of the Ile de France, such as horse-riding in Yvelines. The following general brochures are very useful, but you need to ask for them, as they are not on display and not all of them are mentioned on the website. You can order them by telephone or by emailing the tourist office direct on info@etif.net:

Escapades Paris Ile de France map

Le Guide (The French version is called *Ze Guide*). Contains a useful list of eclectic information and addresses for activities in Paris and the Ile de France, from roller-blading and clubbing in Paris to barefoot water-skiing in Villeneuve St Georges, with details of access by public transport.

Prenez l'air (in French only). Extremely useful list of addresses for outdoor pursuits in the Ile de France, including walking, cycling, boating, golfing, hang-gliding and *accrobranche* (tree-climbing for adults, a concept invented in France in 1989 according to the brochure).

Levez l'ancre (in French only). The official list of companies operating cruises or boats for hire in Paris and the Ile de France, with sketch maps of the navigable waterways around Paris

Mairie de Paris, Hotel de Ville, Bureau d'accueil, 29 rue de Rivoli, 75004 Paris, tel 01 42 76 43 43. www.paris.fr. Métro: Hotel de Ville. Monday–Saturday 10 am–6 pm. Mostly information on Paris but some publications on cycling or walking cover the Ile de France, such as the booklet *Les canaux de Paris*.

For the addresses of *guinguettes* near Paris, visit www.culture-guinguette.com.

For scholarly studies, maps and statistical information on the Ile de France, visit the government agency www.iaurif.org (Institut d'aménagement et d'urbanisme de la région Ile de France).

Books

In English

Ardagh, John, *France in the New Century*, Penguin 2000. Comprehensive and lively overview of post-war France, economic, social, cultural and political. Especially good on the relationship between Paris and the *banlieue* and on France's treatment of ethnic minorities. Out of print but available on Amazon and still the best overview I have read.

Michelin Green Guide series, *Northern France and the Paris Region*, 2006. Concise, attractive descriptions of the main places of interest en route for car drivers heading to Paris from England. It covers the better-known places in the Ile de France, very much from a driver's point of view.

Platt, Polly, *French or Foe?*, Culture Crossings 1994, third edition (UK) 2003. Aimed at Anglophones working for multinational companies in France, an accurate and highly readable guide to cultural differences. The same author's *Savoir Flair*, Culture Crossings, 2000, reprinted 2006, is aimed more at tourists visiting France for the first time.

In French

Michelin Guides Verts series, *Ile de France*, 2006. Concise and determinedly reader-friendly. Covers far more of the Ile de France than the English language *Northern France and the Paris Region*. Includes brief details of access by public transport for some of the visits.

Le Guide du Routard, 2001, *Ile de France*, Hachette, 2006. Lively, opinionated guide to the suburbs within a radius of approximately 30 km of Paris, aimed mainly at those who live there.

Debièvre, Antoine, *Un tour à la campagne*, Parigramme, 2005. Forty two well-chosen and presented hikes in the Ile de France, for serious walkers travelling by train. Very concise, aimed at French readers who know their way around.

Murat, Inès, *Colbert*, Fayard, 1980. A well-written and illuminating biography of Louis XIV's great minister, very useful to an understanding of modern France.

Bookshops

W. H. Smith, 248 Rue de Rivoli, 75001 Paris, tel 01 44 77 88 99. www.whsmith.fr. Métro: Concorde. Monday–Saturday 9 am– 7.30 pm, Sunday 1–7.30 pm. Good selection of maps, guides and books in English on Paris and France.

Gibert Jeune, ground floor, 5 Place St Michel, 75005 Paris, tel 01 56 81 22 22. Métro: St Michel. Monday–Saturday 9.30 am– 7.30 pm. University bookshop selling a comprehensive range of maps and guides, mostly in French. Some are recent secondhand copies, marked 'occasion'. Has a good history section on the second floor.

L'Espace IGN (Institut Géographique Nationale), 107 Rue La Boétie, 75008 Paris, tel 01 43 98 80 00. www.ign.fr. Métro: Franklin Roosevelt. Tuesday– Friday 11 am–7 pm, Saturday 11 am–6.30 pm. All IGN maps and a good selection of other maps and guides, mostly in French.

Virgin Megastore, Galerie du Carrousel du Louvre, tel 01 44 50 03 10. Monday–Tuesday 10 am– 8 pm, Wednesday–Sunday 10 am–9 pm. Conveniently located next to the Espace du Tourisme de l'Ile de France. Small selection of maps and guides in French and English.

General Glossary

abbaye abbey
aire de jeux playground
alimentation grocery store
arènes arena
arrondissement district of the
city
auberge inn

bac ferry
baignade bathing place
(river, lake)
bal-musette dance with
accordion music
banlieue suburb
barrage weir
bergerie sheep-farm
bois wood(s)
brasserie café/restaurant serving
meals or snacks throughout
the day
boulangerie baker's shop
boules bowls (game)
buvette drinks stall

café-tabac café licensed to sell
stamps and cigarettes
camping camp/caravan site
carte map; menu
cascades waterfall
centre equestre riding school
château castle, palace, stately
home, mansion, manor
château d'eau water tower
château-fort fortified castle
château de plaisance
stately home
chaumière (thatched) cottage
chemin path, lane
chemin de halage towpath
cimetière cemetery
collègiale collegiate church
commode non-flushing toilet

commune urban or rural
district, the smallest
administrative unit
Conseil Council
couvent convent, monastery
curé priest

département administrative
area, usually smaller than an
English county
donjon (castle) keep
douves moat

écluse lock
école school
école maternelle nursery school
église church
exposition exhibition

ferme farm
férié, jour férié public holiday
fête festival, celebration
forêt forest
formule (restaurant) starter and
main course or main course
and dessert
fosse pit (feminine)
fossé ditch (masculine)
France profonde deepest France
fromager cheesemonger

gendarmerie police station
goûter children's afternoon
snack
guinguette open air restaurant
with dance floor, usually by
a river
grand(e) great, important,
big, tall
grille gate

hôpital hospital

hôtel-Dieu general hospital
hôtel de ville town or city hall

île island
îlot islet
jardin public public garden, park
jardin à l'anglaise landscape garden
jardin à la française formal garden
jardin potager vegetable garden

kir aperitif made with wine and fruit liqueur

lac lake
laveuse washerwoman
lavoir former public washhouse next to stream or river
lycée secondary/high school

mairie town or city hall
maison de retraite retirement home
marché market
menu set menu, usually of three courses
merguez North African spicy mutton sausages, popular in couscous and at barbecues
moules-frites mussels and chips, a popular Belgian dish
moulin mill
musée museum

navette shuttle bus

office de tourisme tourist office

palais palace
parc park
passerelle foot-bridge
patron(ne) proprietor, boss
pavillon detached house, lodge
pays country, region, district (*spécialités de pays* – local specialities)
pétanque petanque (bowls)
pichet jug (of house wine)
piéton pedestrian

piscine swimming pool (*couverte/découverte*) (indoor/outdoor pool)
place square
plage beach
plat du jour dish of the day
plan map, plan
pont bridge
porte gate, door, porch
Poste Post Office
poterne postern (back or side entrance)
préfecture administrative head-quarters of a *département*
prieuré priory
P.T.T. Postes, Télécommunications et Télédiffusion, former name for the Post Office

radeau raft
randonnée pedestre walk, hike
région administrative area, larger than a county, consisting of several *départements*
remparts ramparts
réseau network
résidence secondaire 'second home', house in the country
ruelle alley, lane

salon de thé tea room
sanitaires wc
sente path, footpath
sentier path, footpath
siècle century
spectacle show, entertainment
stade stadium, sports ground
syndicat d'initiative small tourist office

tabac tobacconist's
table d'orientation viewing table
tennis tennis courts
tarif réduit concessions
terrain de sport sports ground
terrasse terrace (in a café, refers to the tables outside)
toilettes (les) wc
tour tower

Train Traveller's Glossary

Buying your ticket

ticket *billet*
ticket-office *billetterie/vente de billets*
suburban ticket-office *billets banlieue/Transilien/Ile de France*
ticket-office window *guichet*
single ticket *aller simple*
return ticket *aller retour*
A single ticket to...
  Un aller simple pour...
I would like to go to...
  Je voudrais aller à...
timetable/schedule *horaire*
pocket timetable *fiche horaire*
Have you got a timetable for...?
  Avez-vous une fiche horaire pour...?
fare *tarif*
half fare *demi-tarif*
travel pass (weekly, monthly)
  Un passe Navigo Découverte (hebdomadaire, mensuelle)
A travel pass for zones 1 and 2
  Un forfait Carte Orange pour Paris (zones une et deux)
What time does it leave/arrive?
  Il part/arrive à quelle heure?
Does this train go to...?
  Ce train va-t-il à...?/
  Ce train dessert-il...?
I want to get off at...
  Je veux descendre à...

In general

à l'approche (train) approaching
arrêt Stop/Halt (as opposed to a proper station)
arrivées arrivals
chef de train guard
compostez votre billet validate your ticket
composteur ticket validating machine
contrôleur ticket inspector
correspondance/changement change trains/intersection/ transfer
départs banlieue/Ile de France/ Transilien suburban departures
direction destination
gare railway station
gare routière bus/coach station
grève strike
perturbé disrupted
repère platform marker
retardé delayed
quai platform
queue du train back of the train/last carriage
sortie exit
tête du train front of the train/ first carriage
train court/long short/long train
Ce train dessert...
  This train stops at...
voie track/platform
voiture carriage/car
voyageur passenger *Que tous les voyageurs descendent du train* All change

Chronology of French rulers

*Names in **bold** are mentioned in the text*

Merovingians	(481-751)
Clovis	481-511

Carolingians	(751-987)
Pépin le Bref	751-768
Charlemagne	768-814

Capetians	
Hugues Capet	987-996
Robert II (le Pieux)	996-1031
Henri I	1031-1060
Philippe I	1060-1108
Louis VI	1108-1137
Louis VII	1137-1180
Philippe Auguste	1180-1223
Louis VIII	1223-1226
Louis IX (St Louis)	1226-1270
Philippe III	1270-1285
Philippe IV (le Bel)	1285-1314
Louis X	1314-1316
Philippe V	1316-1322
Charles IV	1322-1328

Valois	
Philippe VI	1328-1350
Jean II (le Bon)	1350-1364
Charles V	1364-1380
Charles VI	1380-1422
Charles VII	1422-1461
Louis XI	1461-1483
Charles VIII	1483-1498
Louis XII	1498-1515
François I	1515-1547
Henri II	1547-1559
François II	1559-1560
Charles IX	1560-1574
Henri III	1574-1589

Bourbons	
Henri IV	1589-1610
Louis XIII	1610-1643
Louis XIV	1643-1715
Louis XV	1715-1774
Louis XVI	1774-1792
Louis XVII	(never reigned)

First Republic	
National Convention	1792-1795
Directory	1795-1799
Consulate	1799-1804

First Empire	
Napoléon I	1804-1814

Restoration	
Louis XVIII	1814-1824
Charles X	1824-1830

Constitutional monarchy	
Louis Philippe	1830-1848

Second Republic	1848-1852

Second Empire	
Napoléon III	1852-1870

Third Republic	1870-1940

Vichy government	1940-1944

Provisional government	1944-1946

Fourth Republic	1946-1958

Fifth Republic	1958 to present

Acknowledgements

Special thanks to Elizabeth Leafy Feld, Joan Fleming Le Bras and Amanda Metcalfe-Menguelti for their unfailing support and encouragement; Charles Arnold, whose enthusiasm and constructive suggestions helped to turn the book into a reality; Alexander Fyjis-Walker, Ted Hammond and Ava Li at Pallas Athene and Michel Hénin of l'Institut d'Aménagement et d'Urbanisme de la Région d'Ile-de-France (IAURIF) for their practical support and help; and, of course, my mother, my sister and her husband for their encouragement, support and constructive criticism.

I am also indebted to the many organisations who generously supplied illustrations or otherwise offered practical help, and to countless friends and strangers for their encouragement and suggestions. I would particularly like to thank:

Dominique Bard (Musée National de la Renaissance); Galit Bernard; Adam Bevan, Sylvia Méchain, Bronwen Nicolas (France Télécom); Alexandre Bigle, Christian Vuaillet (RATP); Lorna Birch; Lewis Bolan; Stephanie Brann; Jean-Paul Cacheux; Marilyn and Lu Carpenter; Mitchell Cohen; Paul Coleshill; John Dawes; Agnès Delannoy (Musée Départemental Maurice Denis); Catherine Domain (Pays d'Ulysse bookshop); Carmelle Denning; Peter and Mary Dineen; Patrick Dugas; Rayanne Dupuis; Danielle Durkin; Marie-France Duburque; Jean-Paul Ferrand (S.A.N. Marne-la-Vallée); Jean-Paul Guerin (Nestlé, France); Nicole Garnier (Musée Condé); William Hannigan (Société d'Histoire et d'Archéologie de Senlis); David Hervé (JC Decaux); Lynn Hoggatt; Mathias Huber (Editions Olizane); Laure Joliet; Christian Le Bras, Philippe Louchart, Micette Hercelin (IAURIF); Susan Luraschi; Thierry Maillard (Mastercom); Josiane Marchaudon (OECD); Elaine McCarthy; Jean-Claude Menou (château de Champs); Alain Moreau, Laurence Frecher, Nathalie Golliet (Comité Régional du Tourisme d' Ile-de-France); Christiane Métreau (Office de Tourisme, Montfort-l'Amaury); Marie-Laure and Philip O'Shea; Katherine Revington; Alain Robillard, Lucie Decelle (SNCF); Alastair Sawday; Christiane Schaefer-Hernandez (Comité Départemental du Tourisme, Seine et Marne); Fabienne Si; John Spears; David and Hiroko Sweden; Vic Tapner; Grace Teshima; Pierre Tran; Gérard Uyttersprot (Direction Départementale de l'Equipement, Oise); Thirza Vallois; Camilla Webster.

Picture Credits

Index